OXFORD POLITICAL THEORY

Series Editors: David Miller and Alan Ryan

—————

# CREATING CITIZENS

# OXFORD POLITICAL THEORY

Oxford Political Theory presents the best new work in contemporary political theory. It is intended to be broad in scope, including original contributions to political philosophy, and also work in applied political theory. The series will contain works of outstanding quality with no restriction as to approach or subject matter.

# CREATING CITIZENS

## POLITICAL EDUCATION AND LIBERAL DEMOCRACY

EAMONN CALLAN

CLARENDON PRESS · OXFORD
1997

Oxford University Press, Great Clarendon Street, Oxford OX2 6DP

Oxford New York

Athens Auckland Bangkok Bogota Bombay
Buenos Aires Calcutta Cape Town Dar es Salaam
Delhi Florence Hong Kong Istanbul Karachi
Kuala Lumpur Madras Madrid Melbourne
Mexico City Nairobi Paris Singapore
Taipei Tokyo Toronto Warsaw
and associated companies in
Berlin Ibadan

Oxford is a trade mark of Oxford University Press

Published in the United States
by Oxford University Press Inc., New York

British Library Cataloguing in Publication Data
Data available

Library of Congress Cataloging in Publication Data
Callan, Eamonn.
Creating citizens : political education and liberal democracy /
Eamonn Callan.
(Oxford political theory)
Includes bibliographical references and index.
1. Citizenship—Study and teaching.   2. Democracy—Study and
teaching.   3. Political science—Study and teaching.   4. Moral
education.   I. Title.   II. Series.
LC1091.C24   1997   370.11'5—dc21   97–14447
ISBN 0–19–829258–9

1 3 5 7 9 10 8 6 4 2

Typeset by Hope Services (Abingdon) Ltd.
Printed in Great Britain
on acid-free paper by
Biddles Ltd.,
Guildford & King's Lynn

FOR THREE TEACHERS
John Nolan
Malcolm Latham
Gerry Gaden

# ACKNOWLEDGEMENTS

MANY people helped me to write this book. Will Kymlicka provided a long and trenchant critique of the paper from which Chapters 2 and 3 are descended, and he helped to clarify much that is basic to my argument as a whole. He also stiffened my resolve to write the book at a time when I was inclined to think it not worth the trouble. Ken Strike was the ideal philosophical interlocutor and friend thoughout the process of writing. He has been in equal measures sympathetic and sceptical, always ready to answer questions that troubled me, and if his answers sometimes diverged from the ones that I have (provisionally) given here, they helped me greatly in developing my own. Steve Macedo has been another valuable source of criticism and encouragement. His *Liberal Virtues* had a crucial influence on the overall conception of this book. Shelley Burtt gave me some very useful advice on a quasi-final draft of Chapter 2, as did Fran Schrag on a draft of Chapter 6. Bill Hare helped me interpret Mill more carefully than I had originally done. Two anonymous readers for Oxford University Press made perceptive comments. Dominic Byatt has been the efficient and unfailingly supportive editor that all authors hope to have.

I was very fortunate to participate in symposia on my work in progress in the *Canadian Journal of Education* and *The Review of Politics*. Michael Manley-Casimir and Walter Nicgorski were my indulgent editors on those occasions, and I am very grateful to my fellow symposiasts for all they taught me, even when disagreement became somewhat heated. These were Robin Barrow, A. E. Goerner, Mark Holmes, Tasos Kazepides, Steve Macedo, and Ken Strike.

The book reworks a good deal of material that I have published elsewhere. The relevant papers are: 'Finding a Common Voice', *Educational Theory*, 42 (1992): 429–41; 'Tradition and Integrity in Moral Education', *American Journal of Education*, 101 (1992): 1–28 [© University of Chicago. All right reserved.]; 'Beyond Sentimental Civic Education', *American Journal of Education*, 102 (1993): 190–221 [© University of Chicago. All rights reserved.]; 'Common Schools for Common Education', *Canadian Journal of Education*, 20 (1995): 251–71; 'Virtue, Dialogue and the Common School', *American Journal of Education*, 104 (1995): 1–33 [© University of Chicago Press. All rights reserved.]; 'Political Liberalism and Political Education', *Review of Politics*, 58 (1996): 5–33. A much abridged version of Chapter 7 will appear in the *Journal of Philosophy of Education* (June 1997).

My research was greatly assisted by funding from the Canadian Social Sciences and Humanities Research Council and the Spencer Foundation. But the views I express in the book are entirely my responsibility. Finally, I want to thank Corinne, Julia, and Garrett who made the writing of this book what I wanted it to be: no more than an interesting distraction within a life whose centre lies elsewhere.

# CONTENTS

# CHAPTER 1

―――

# Education and the Politics of Virtue

## 1. Introduction

Political debate in our liberal democracies is largely confined to questions about the pursuit of material prosperity and the maintenance of civil peace, respect for liberty, and the just distribution of wealth and privilege. Political debate about education follows the same pattern. We talk about how schools and other educational institutions could help to create a more productive workforce, mitigate the violence and lawlessness that afflict our cities, accommodate the freedom of people who want very different kinds of education for their children, and contribute to more just distributive patterns. These are certainly important questions, and what I have to say in this book bears on some of them. But most of the book is about what gets excluded from political debate about education when the questions I have just posed are thought to be the only really serious ones.

The importance of what gets excluded can be approached through a quick thought-experiment. Imagine an enviably wealthy and peaceful society that has descended, through a couple of generations, from the society to which you or I belong. Imagine also that the society exhibits whatever distribution of wealth you think best. The particular rights we require of any liberal democracy—rights to political participation, freedom of expression, religious practice, equality before the courts and the like—continue to have the force of law. But when elections are held, scarcely anyone bothers to vote. The mass media ignore politics because the consumers to whom they cater do not care. The parties who vie for power are sponsored by more or less the same political elites, and so virtually nothing separates one party from another. Freedom of speech has been reduced to a spectral existence because speech is no longer commonly used to defend a distinctive vision of the good and the right or to say anything that might initiate serious ethical dialogue with another.

That is so because citizens are either indifferent to questions of good and evil, seeing the point of their lives simply as the satisfaction of their desires, or else they commit themselves so rigidly to a particular doctrine that dialogue with those who are not like-minded is thought to be repellent or futile. This Brave New World, as I shall unimaginatively call it, still contains much of the religious, racial, and ethnic diversity of the society that preceded it. But although citizens respect each other's legal rights, they shun contact with those who are different so far as possible because they despise them. When transactions across cultural divisions are unavoidable, everyone tries to extract as much benefit from the other (or cause as much harm as possible) within the limits imposed by law.

The institutions of liberal democracy seem poised for collapse here because the shared public morality that once enlivened them has vanished, and therefore, they survive only as a pointless system of taboo or a modus vivendi among antagonistic groups who will support it only so long as support serves their interests. We might also feel that this society is appalling as it is, regardless of any worse fate that is imminent for its inhabitants. If its probable decline into a less orderly barbarism could be arrested, it would still be a place that many of us regard with sheer horror. The culture that has vanished was a great good, and the institutional framework it leaves behind is divested of much of its value because of that loss alone.

The point of my story can be brought out by reflecting on one of the commonplaces of democratic politics, a commonplace as familiar to ordinary citizens as to political theorists. To believe in liberal democracy is to believe in free and equal citizenship. Part of what that demands of us is the development of public institutions that function in ways we can justify on the basis of that ideal, and much of our politics is about how well we have succeeded or how badly we have failed in that project. The consensual core of liberal democracy resides in just those matters of institutional design where we can all agree that free and equal citizenship unambiguously requires certain social rules, such as legal protection for rights to free speech. But free and equal citizenship is also about the kind of people we become, and the kind of people we encourage or allow our children to become. The Brave New World I described is a world in which we have failed utterly in that second project, and that failure substantially undermines the point of the first project as well. Furthermore, the relevance of my Brave New World to our world cannot be dismissed by pretending that what is lost there is so secure for us that we can take its continuity for granted. That is wrong for the obvious reason that my thought-experiment strains the imagination far less than we might like. You are simply asked to consider a possible world in which certain illiberal cultural tendencies already abroad and powerful in our own have intensified and countervailing cultural resources have disappeared.

I said that what is lost in my Brave New World is a distinctive kind of political culture. More precisely, it is a shared way of public life constituted by a constellation of attitudes, habits, and abilities that people acquire as they grow up. These include a lively interest in the question of what life is truly and not just seemingly good, as well as a willingness both to share one's own answer with others and to heed the many opposing answers they might give; an active commitment to the good of the polity, as well as confidence and competence in judgement regarding how that good should be advanced; a respect for fellow citizens and a sense of common fate with them that goes beyond the tribalisms of ethnicity and religion and is yet alive to the significance these will have in many people's lives.

The constellation of psychological traits I just sketched amounts to a conception of public virtue. I do not pretend that the traits I have enumerated are all that distinguish the public culture of a liberal democracy.[1] And my account is controversial, even so far as it goes. But even if one objects to this or that item on my list, this or any similar list is enough to bring into relief a fact that is sometimes forgotten when we think of the proper ends of political activity. What we sometimes forget is that the vitality of the political order depends on an education that is dedicated to specific ideals of character. The Brave New World I described differs from the free societies we now inhabit in that those ideals continue to exert a substantial influence on our lives, even though their influence is powerfully opposed almost everywhere, and often defeated, by other cultural pressures. If the future in store for our children is not to be a Brave New World—or more likely, something far worse—that can only be because many learn to accept and internalize those same ideals of character. That being so, liberal politics is a politics of virtue in this sense: creating virtuous citizens is as necessary an undertaking in a liberal democracy as it is under any other constitution.

## 2. *Liberal Politics and Virtue*

The very idea that our basic political values require a distinctive education for virtue will seem wrong to some because liberal politics is often depicted as devoid of any distinctive ethical ideal, and in that respect, at odds with some versions of political conservatism, say, that prescribe

'soulcraft'- the moulding of citizens according to some traditional standard of human excellence (e.g. Will 1983). These brands of conservatism are
consistent with the essentials of liberal democracy. But many critics
regard them as a legacy of earlier, pre-liberal political thought that is
repugnant to the true moral sources of free government.

The antipathy between the demands of public virtue and basic liberal
values might seem even more obvious if we examine the radical incarnations of the politics of virtue. Robespierre is a prime example:

Robespierre's teachers at the Lycée Louis-le-Grand must have been important to
his political education since, in the end, he saw himself as a messianic schoolmas-
ter, wielding a very big stick to inculcate virtue. He came to conceive of the
Revolution itself as a school, but one in which knowledge would be augmented
by morality. Both, moreover, depended on discipline. Terror and virtue, he was
fond of saying, were part of the same exercise in self-improvement, 'virtue without which terror is harmful and terror without which virtue is impotent' (Schama
1989: 827–8).

Robespierre is an extreme case of a familiar pathology in thought about
citizenship on the left of the political spectrum. The pathology is what
Herman van Gunsteren calls the 'irresponsible wishful thinking' of those
who say 'if men were different they would not have the problems they
have—let us therefore make a new man' (van Gunsteren 1996: 78). If we
are repelled both by revolutionary human engineering and the busybody
moralism of some contemporary conservatism, we may infer that liberal
politics properly has nothing to do with the character of the people whose
lives it regulates. The government of a free people does without terror,
along with the pettier ways in which states can meddle in our lives,
because it does not rely on the inculcation of any particular set of virtues.
That is why liberal political theory is sometimes thought to embody a
necessary indifference to questions about education and character:
'Liberalism is a theory about the rightful limits of state power, not about
the content of education for children' (Feinberg 1990: 88).[2]

There is something to this. If we compare any liberal democracy with a
society that firmly sets itself on a different path—a theocratic state governed by clerics, for example—one big difference is sure to be the many
ways of life that thrive under the democratic regime in contrast to the
sparser range that must fit the requirements of moral orthodoxy under
theocracy. An obvious explanation of the difference is that the liberal state
takes no stand on opposing convictions about the virtuous life, allowing
its citizens to make of themselves whatever they choose within very loose
boundaries fixed by law, whereas the religious state moulds and discip-
lines character according to a fixed model of well-being.

But consider an alternative explanation of the difference between theocratic unformity and liberal pluralism. One powerful source of diversity in a free society is the particular kind of character education that its political institutions depend on. The cultivation of serious and independent ethical criticism, and the enlargement of the imagination that process entails, will naturally conduce to diversity in how people live; and although it may be an important political principle that the state be impartial in regulating the different ways of life its citizens legitimately choose, this may be better understood in many cases as expressing a respect for the open-ended and Protean character of the ideals of character that liberal democratic culture promotes, rather than a blanket repudiation of all soulcraft. Recall that the difference between my Brave New World and the democracies we are familiar with is that the latter, for all their glaring imperfections, are societies in which certain ideals of character continue to have currency; and unless we take the absurd view that all of that difference is of no political consequence, we cannot coherently reject the importance of liberal soulcraft.[3]

The idea that virtue and liberalism simply do not mix is a common theme in so-called communitarian political theory. I say much about communitarianism in subsequent chapters. What is worth noting here is the way in which communitarian argument tends to misrepresent disagreement about what virtues are properly the ends of a politics of virtue or how commonly endorsed civic virtues are to be interpreted with the more basic issue of whether a politics of virtue is possible or desirable at all under a liberal dispensation. A revealing example of this confusion can be found in Michael Sandel's recent book, *Democracy's Discontent* (1996).

Sandel offers a reading of two famous decisions by the US Supreme Court on saluting the national flag in public schools, a reading that purports to signal America's drift away from from a politics of republican virtue. In *Minersville School District* v. *Gobitis* (1940) Justice Felix Frankfurter, writing for the majority, dismissed the conscientious objections of Jehovah's Witnesses to the expulsion of their children from public schools for refusing to salute the flag. Frankfurter justified his decision on the grounds that the expulsion enforced a legitimate policy of promoting the historical continuity of a treasured civic life. But soon thereafter in *West Virginia State Board of Education* v. *Barnette* (1943), compulsory flag salutes were struck down for reasons expressed by Justice Robert Jackson: 'If there is any fixed star in our constitutional constellation, it is that no official, high or petty, can prescribe what shall be orthodox in politics, nationalism, religion, and other matters of opinion' (*West Virginia Board of Education* v. *Barnette*: 638). Sandel does not say that Frankfurter was right and Jackson wrong. But he portrays

Frankfurter as the voice of a waning republican patriotism in American jurisprudence and Jackson as the harbinger of a civically attenuated polity in which a proceduralist understanding of justice comes to dominate public life and civic virtue is but one option among others for citizens (Sandel 1996: 53–4).

But Jackson's appeal to a 'fixed star in our constitutional constellation' is patently no invocation of justice cut adrift from patriotic loyalty; as a claim about the moral core of the American political settlement, it is as much an affirmation of a treasured common life as Frankfurter's opinion. Moreover, Jackson's argument, like Frankfurter's, was essentially about the cultivation of political virtue: 'That they [i.e. public schools] are educating the young for citizenship is reason for scrupulous protection of Constitutional freedoms of the individual, if we are not to strangle the free mind at its source and teach youth to discount principles of our government as mere platitudes' (*West Virginia Board of Education* v. *Barnette*: 637). What Jackson stood for was not procedural fairness against patriotism but a patriotism that tolerated heterodoxy where Frankfurter's did not.[4] Similarly, a school in which children are not forced to participate in patriotic rituals is not necessarily a less patriotic school than the one that does; the difference may simply be that it teaches a patriotism that takes rights more seriously and is more hospitable to the diversity a free society will nourish. And the latter patriotism may be every bit as ardent as the former. What is at stake between Frankfurter and Jackson is not whether schools are rightly understood as an arena for the politics of virtue—the arguments of both judges correctly assume that they are—but how we should interpret the virtues, and hence the particular educational practices, to which the best of our political traditions commits us.

Sandel's misreading of Jackson's opinion is important for my purposes because it exemplifies the common error of confounding the characteristic openness to pluralism of liberal virtue with the supposed irrelevance of virtue to liberal politics. The error is not unique to communitarians: it even mars Stephen Holmes's brilliant defence of liberal constitutional design. Holmes argues that constitutional framers properly rely on devices such as checks and balances rather than the character of citizens to ensure justice and stability. It would be 'positively undesirable' to try to erect a liberal order on the foundation of virtue: 'This would overburden individual conscience, force a character standardization on citizens, and deprive society of an extra-political variety of selves. Discussion would be pointless in such a pre-harmonized society' (S. Holmes 1995: 175). But political discussion is also pointless in my Brave New World. And it is pointless there not because the state has forced a 'character standardization on citizens' but because the virtues that enable morally competent discussion have been extinguished. If public deliberation is sometimes undermined by a stifling homogeneity in soulcraft, it is also defeated by the failure to sustain the common dispositions that liberal dialogue presupposes. Virtue is no substitute for judicious institutional design. But neither is institutional design any substitute for virtue.

## 3. Political Virtue and Pluralism

To agree that liberal democracy requires a distinctive education for virtue leaves much room for disagreement about what that education rightly includes. The sources of disagreement are many and various.

Terence McLaughlin has suggested that notions of civic virtue can be 'roughly mapped in terms of a continuum of minimal and maximal interpretations' (McLaughlin 1992*a*: 245). Toward the 'minimal' end of the continuum are interpretations that ask little of citizens in the way of public responsibility or participation. The interest in citizenship that arose during the 1980s on the right of the political spectrum in Britain and elsewhere, for example, was notably minimalist in scope. The interest was confined to increasing law-abidingness and encouraging a spirit of public service to offset some of the suffering and social dislocation that followed in the wake of a shrinking welfare state. Near the maximal end of the spectrum are readings that impose much more extensive demands, and at the limit swallow virtually all of life, as Robespierre would have wished, in some exorbitant vision of self-sacrifice. Other disagreements are not adequately mapped in terms of any continuum because they are about the content rather than the extent of the responsibilities that political virtue would require. What divides Frankfurter and Jackson in their understanding of patriotism is a case in point.

The fact that we might accept that liberal democracy entails a politics of virtue and yet disagree strongly about both the range and substance of the relevant virtues gives shape to the argument of Chapters 2 through 5. There I outline and defend a conception of political virtue grounded in the ideal of free and equal citizenship, a conception adumbrated in my version of a Brave New World. The conception I defend draws heavily on the work of John Rawls, although I make use of his ideas in ways he does not anticipate and in many instances would not commend.

Rawls's theory of justice has had an overwhelming influence on political philosophy in the English-speaking world (and beyond) since the publication of *A Theory of Justice* in 1971. The enormous secondary literature the theory has spawned is largely devoted to Rawls's argument for 'justice as fairness'. That argument supports two strongly egalitarian principles designed to regulate the distribution of liberties and other goods within the basic structure of society. Rawls selects these principles through an ingenious imaginative construction. He asks us to consider what distributive principles would be rationally chosen if choice were constrained by ignorance regarding the particular position one would occupy in the society to which the principles would apply. That context of choice is what Rawls calls 'the original position'. But the ideas I borrow from Rawls are prior to his construction of the original position and the particular principles of justice he defends on that basis. Since the beginning of the 1980s, Rawls has represented justice as fairness as rooted in a more fundamental notion of democratic citizenship, the so-called 'political conception of the person'. The particular constraints on knowledge imposed in the original position, for example, are said to depend on the idea of the reasonable that inheres in the conception of citizenship (Rawls 1993: 305). But the values of citizenship at the base of Rawls's theory might be accepted without endorsing either the original position or the particular distributive principles he champions. Indeed, the critical moral ingredient in Rawls's conception of citizenship—the idea of the reasonable—has been developed by other philosophers in arguments that are strongly Rawlsian in spirit but depart significantly from justice as fairness (e.g. Scanlon 1982; Barry 1995).

My own use of the idea of the reasonable is to develop an informal account of the cardinal personal virtue of liberal democratic politics. I call this 'justice as reasonableness'. But the virtue of justice as I conceive it is not the application of a tidy moral calculus as some have thought it to be (cf. Kohlberg 1981). Justice as reasonableness devolves into a cluster of mutually supportive habits, desires, emotional propensities, and intellectual capacities whose coordinated activity requires contextually sensitive judgement. Future citizens need to develop some imaginative sympathy for compatriots whose experience and identity incline them to see political questions in ways that differ systematically from their own. A respect for reasonable differences and a concomitant spirit of moderation and compromise has to be nurtured. A vivid awareness of the responsibilities that the rights of others impose on the self, as well as a sense of the dignity that one's own rights secure for the self, must be engendered. All these accomplishments may be subsumed under the idea of justice only so long as we bear in mind that the idea captures no simple master-rule rule for moral choice.

An important criticism of Rawls's views on citizenship is that they are unrealistically cerebral (e.g. Miller 1995*a*: 435–9; 1995*b*: 93). Reasoned agreement on principles of justice and their interpretation is the end of public deliberation as Rawls conceives it. He often seems insufficiently sensitive to the role of particularistic civic ties in making such agreement possible and stable. Yet here again we may learn more by developing Rawlsian ideas than by confining our attention to the details of his own stated position. An interpretation of liberal patriotism is part of the conception of virtue I defend, an interpretation that connects our understanding of justice with the values of trust, community, and generosity. The interpretation draws heavily on Rawls's suggestive account of the 'morality of association' in *A Theory of Justice*.

The account of political virtue I defend is explicitly designed to cohere with the many differences in creed and identity that a liberal society will properly welcome. Yet another source of pluralism in any extant or feasible liberal democracy is not to be explained by the open-endedness of its distinctive public virtues. I have in mind diversity that is in part a consequence of our tolerance of ways of life that are flatly opposed to liberal democratic ideals of character and a persistent threat to the institutions they inform. The rights that free institutions confer are not granted on the condition that they will be used in virtuous ways. Rights are sometimes permissibly exercised in behalf of convictions and practices that are deplorable according to liberal democratic norms. Furthermore, so far as forbearance is morally justified in such cases, it will inevitably extend to educational processes intended to promote conformity to convictions and practices we rightly condemn. The family is a potent educational institution. But no one proposes that we make liberal virtue a necessary qualification for parenthood.

This presents us with a dilemma. A necessary feature of free societies is the extension of a particular set of rights to all citizens, including rights to liberty, association, and political participation. But so far as citizens use their rights to protect or advance the different ways of life they cherish, any such society is also pluralistic in ways that may pose a threat to liberal democracy. If the role of the state in education is to keep faith with its constitutive morality, a path must be found between the horns of a dilemma. The need to perpetuate fidelity to liberal democratic institutions and values from one generation to another suggests that there are some inescapably shared educational aims, even if the pursuit of these conflicts with the convictions of some citizens. Yet if repression is to be avoided, the state must give parents substantial latitude to instil in their children whatever religious faith or conception of the good they espouse. Similarly, the state must permit communities of like-minded citizens to create educational institutions that reflect their distinctive way of life, even if that entails some alienation from the political culture of the larger society. How can we honour both the commitment to a shared political morality and the accommodation of pluralism that is commonly in tension with that morality? In Chapter 6 I address the educational rights of parents and children as they bear on that question. Chapters 7 and 8 examine common and separate schooling and the ways in which policy regarding them might be duly responsive to rights and the task of creating citizens.

## 4. Liberal Democracy and Autonomy

This book is about political education under liberal democracy. I have used and will use 'liberal', 'democratic', and 'free' interchangeably to distinguish the kind of regime I have in mind, and at one level, my usage will seem innocent enough. No liberal wants a constitution that does not honour rights to political participation, and no morally credible exponent of democracy is indifferent to the liberties that people will justly claim outside their civic roles. But even if there is a morally indissoluble marriage between liberalism and democracy, the terms of the marital agreement are a matter of some dispute, as Amy Gutmann has noted, and the dispute is educationally significant (Gutmann 1993: 139).

The core of the dispute lies in competing understandings of the sense in which equal citizens are free. For those inclined to stress the primacy of liberalism in liberal democracy, the liberty of free citizens is the necessary social space for individuals to create meaningful lives for themselves in ways that are often idiosyncratic and sometimes even anti-social. The moral discipline of civic participation, with its acceptance of shared burdens and deference to collective purposes, is not fulfilling for all, even if the perpetuation of liberal politics depends in no small measure on the willingness of many to submit to it. The individuality extolled by John Stuart Mill and other liberals might be evinced in the setting of politics. But then again its unfettered development might also lead many towards ways of life that dismiss citizenship as an irksome or corrupting distraction from what really matters, given the many opposing perspectives on what matters that a liberal society will protect (e.g. Flathman 1996).[5]

On the other hand, if we think of democracy as the basic concept, the liberty of equal citizens is first and foremost free participation in collective self-rule. This republican liberty is under siege so far as the allure of collective self-rule is eroded by the many charms of private life under pluralism. For example, democratic anxiety about the centrifugal tendencies of liberal freedom is an important current in John Dewey's philosophy of education. Dewey's insistent emphasis on democracy as a shared way of life rather than a mere mode of government, and his impatience with all that was insufficiently 'social' in education , attest to priorities in which what is democratic in liberal democracy overshadows what is liberal (e.g. Dewey 1916: 81–99). A Millian education for liberal individuality and a Deweyan education for democratic competence and fidelity are not the same thing.

Like Gutmann, I think the value of autonomy or reasoned self-rule is the key to understanding what rightly holds together liberal and democratic principles (Gutmann 1993). In what follows I argue for a conception of political virtue that presupposes autonomy. The autonomy that is presupposed cannot be confined to the sphere of politics but will pervasively affect our lives outside politics as well. Nevertheless, autonomy cannot give us as closely integrated a political theory as we might like. That is so not only for the important reason that Gutmann stresses— namely, that equally reasonable autonomous agents will still often disagree profoundly on political questions (Gutmann 1993: 155–6). What she aptly calls the 'disharmony' of democracy is greatly intensified by two additional factors. First, even if a wide-ranging ethical autonomy is intrinsic to political virtue, its free development may often pull against the civic responsibility those same virtues entail. Autonomous reflection does not necessarily lead everyone to a way of life in which civic engagement has an impressively prominent place. Political education in a liberal democracy will discourage civic alienation. But it cannot foreclose the outcome without repudiating its necessary commitment to individual as well as collective self-rule. Second, the liberal democracy worth having will also respect the right to live in some ways that renounce the stringent ideal of autonomy intrinsic to political virtue. The claims of democratic virtue and liberal pluralism can in general be reconciled. But it is a much more tense and precarious reconciliation than we might like it to be. The marriage of liberalism and democracy is a turbulent one, and its turbulence is inevitably manifest in our educational thought and practice.

# CHAPTER 2

## Pluralism and Political Liberalism

### 5. Introduction

What are the proper ends of civic education in a liberal democracy? At the level of our political commonsense we can say something sensible in answer to that question. We can talk of encouraging a sense of justice, tolerance, or mutual respect, and within the political culture of any secure democracy, what we say will be widely acceptable so long as our talk remains loose and vague. But once we try to be precise about what constitutes such ends, how they relate to one another, and how they might be encouraged in our children's lives, agreement is likely to disappear. When commonsense fails us, we must look to the theory of liberal democracy to shed light on the kind of political education that would create the citizens we should want. The ascent to theory is prompted by the hope that the more commanding perspective on political controversy to which theory aspires might help to resolve disputes that remain at a standstill within the confining limits of our commonsense.

But if a theoretically-informed view of civic education is to be morally defensible, it must do more than tell it what our children should learn in order to become good citizens; it must also affirm the importance of respecting the many different ways of life that individuals permissibly choose within the framework of free institutions, even when those differences divide them at the deepest levels of identity. Indeed, it is the enduring social presence of such differences in our midst that makes agreement on the nature of political education such an elusive goal. The challenge of pluralism is, in part, the problem of conceiving the ends and means of civic education in a way that does not wrongly impair diversity.

An interpretation of the virtues and responsibilities of citizens that is notably sensitive to that challenge is offered in Rawls's important recent book, *Political Liberalism*. The title is intended to mark a contrast with the so-called comprehensive liberalisms of the great liberal political theorists such as Kant, Mill, and their recent philosophical heirs, including the earlier Rawls who wrote *A Theory of Justice*. The supposed contrast lies in the different scope of political and comprehensive liberalism and in the different arguments they offer for the enforcement of political values. According to Rawls, we can see some of the importance of the contrast by tracing the divergent educational implications of the two varieties of liberalism. Political liberalism supposedly generates an ideal of the just society, and companion conceptions of citizenship and political education, that meet the challenge of pluralism. Rawls says that comprehensive liberalism is inherently repugnant to pluralism. I claim that Rawls is mistaken. The distinction between political and comprehensive liberalism is far more porous than its devotees suppose, and Rawls's political liberalism in particular is really a disguised instance of comprehensive liberalism.

What divides political and comprehensive liberals might appear tediously academic, especially if I am right in saying that the contrast between the two is overblown in current political theory and that the more cogent versions of each have substantially the same educational implications. But the theoretical dispute plays out a very familiar and important political controversy in a more intellectually rigorous manner than it is usually discussed, and that is why the dispute is so revealing. The familiar controversy is conflict between those who see education primarily as a matter for individual choice, with the state rightly intervening only to secure modest goals that virtually everyone would approve, and others who say that the moral imperatives of liberal politics warrant an education that shapes the self in profound and often disturbing ways. Rawls can be understood as attempting to offer a rationale for something fairly close to the first of these two views, but he fails in that attempt. His argument pushes him much closer to the second view than he is ready to admit. The central thesis of this chapter is that political education at its best will be far less banal, and much more corrosive of some powerful and long-entrenched sources of diversity, than many would like. That is not something we should be apologetic about: liberal democracy at its best, in education as in other social endeavours, will not leave everything as it is.

## 6. From Comprehensive to Political Liberalism

Comprehensive liberalism has a wide scope because it affirms some general and comprehensive or partially comprehensive moral doctrine

(Rawls 1993: 13). An example is Mill's ideal of individuality, which entails that the best human lives are characterized by eccentricity and a daring spirit of experimentation (Mill 1976 edn.). The doctrine is general because it applies to many subjects including, say, individual conduct in personal relationships and the political organization of society. Thus Mill's ideal tells us something about how to pursue our own good in concert with friends and associates, as well as how public institutions might be designed so as to encourage good lives.

By virtue of their generality, moral doctrines that ground the many versions of comprehensive liberalism must be at least 'partially comprehensive' in identifying and connecting virtues and principles that have some application across our lives, beyond the sphere of politics. A moral doctrine becomes fully comprehensive if it claims to organize all relevant values into a systematic whole. (Following Rawls, my use of 'comprehensive doctrine' includes those that are only partially as well as those that are fully comprehensive.) Whatever doctrine is favoured must also support the cardinal values of liberal politics, such as the principle of free citizenship and the political rights that principle entails, and the same doctrine may be used to discern solutions to more contentious public issues (Rawls 1993: 13, 175).

Rawls says that comprehensive liberalism must fail once the doctrine it hinges on is advanced as the source of political legitimacy under the conditions of pluralism. No doctrine can win the assent of all reasonable citizens in a diverse society, even if it were true and powerful arguments available in its defence. Therefore, once the public justification of state action appeals to Millian individuality, for example, those who have moral convictions at odds with Mill's are required to submit to political authority on grounds they reasonably reject (Rawls 1993: 37). That outcome defeats liberal politics as a project in which legitimacy is achieved by appealing to reasons that citizens can share, rather than reasons that divide some against others and authorize the oppression of those who dissent.

This objection to comprehensive liberalism presupposes a connection between moral dissent and oppression that requires explanation. Many citizens are likely to be morally critical of policies under even the best feasible regime, given the persistence of pluralism on any substantial scale. Yet everyone supposedly has at least a defeasible obligation to comply with the offending policies, if only by dutifully paying taxes that go to fund them. This is now very commonly the case in policies regarding the environment, the arts, and the redistribution of wealth, and it could not be otherwise so long as moral attitudes continue to be as irreconcilably diverse as they are in most contemporary Western societies. But we do not automatically infer, and Rawls is not asking us to infer, that the state must be oppressive in such circumstances. The inference would be a mistake because policies that are morally objectionable to some citizens might still be interpreted by all within a larger political framework that satisfies defensible conditions of legitimacy. Controversial policies may be enacted by a regime in which questions of constitutional essentials and basic justice have been settled in a manner that is morally acceptable to all. Shared answers to these questions will fix the general structure of government and the political process, determine the basic rights and liberties of citizens, and mark the limits of tolerable social and economic inequalities (Rawls 1993: 227–30). Where answers to these questions are shared among the citizenry, the potential for destabilizing moral disagreement in politics is foreclosed by consensus about conditions in which political decisions we regard as wrong should nonetheless be recognized as legitimate. Rawls would say the dissent we should expect in a regime grounded in comprehensive liberalism cuts much deeper than this. Since the right answer to questions of constitutional essentials and basic justice is thought to depend on the truth of some comprehensive doctrine that many conscientious citizens will reject, the background of reasonable consensus is precluded that might make the enforcement of morally controversial policies into something other than sheer oppression.

This highlights a further inadequacy. Political authority exercised in the name of a comprehensive moral doctrine is not merely an affront to the dignity of citizens who reasonably think otherwise; it also threatens the unity and stability of the polity. The danger of disintegration in societies that can no longer be forced into unity around a shared religious faith has haunted the liberal tradition since its inception, and comprehensive liberalism may be thought to exacerbate the danger by attempting to ground legitimacy in a divisive secular analogue to religious faith (Rawls 1993: 37–8).

Political liberalism is intended to circumvent the perceived liabilities of its disreputable comprehensive cousin, though the general theoretical strategy is like comprehensive liberalism in a couple of ways. A framework for political deliberation is devised that supports the established verities of liberal politics and also enables the creation of reasoned agreement on new and contentious political problems. That framework is given by the theory of public reason. By 'public reason' Rawls means the canons of argument appropriate to political reflection on constitutional essentials and basic justice among a democratic people. These canons are defined by principles of justice constructed from the idea of free and equal citizenship, as well as accompanying 'guidelines of inquiry that specify ways of reasoning and criteria for the kinds of information relevant to political questions'. The object of public reason is to secure a consensus on political questions that is acceptable to all who participate (Rawls 1993: 218, 223).

A conception of public reason devised within political liberalism does not express any single comprehensive doctrine because it is designed to be compatible with the full range of values that citizens might reasonably endorse. That is to say, its perspective is free-standing in that it can be presented and defended apart from the rival doctrines citizens embrace as moral agents outside their civic roles, though their beliefs must nonetheless cohere with the demands of liberal citizenship. So Rawls is delineating a moral conception of narrow scope that applies only to one subject—the basic structure of society—and eschews any appeal to divisive convictions. This suggests an attractive solution to the problem of legitimacy. Since the political conception is crafted so as to fit the full range of citizens' reasonable convictions, when political authority is exercised in its behalf no one must acquiesce to a creed she might responsibly reject; instead, authority is legitimated and rendered stable by appeal to a family of political values located within an overlapping consensus among all extant ethical views that deserve our respect. The range of these views marks the boundaries of reasonable pluralism (Rawls 1993: 11–22, 63–4).

Rawls's contrast between comprehensive and political liberalism is said to yield opposing conceptions of political education. Indeed, education is the only substantial example he gives of how political might differ from comprehensive liberalism in shaping answers to questions of practical politics (Rawls 1993: 199–200). The basis of the supposed contrast is obvious in the light of what I have said so far. An education derived from any instance of comprehensive liberalism would have to inculcate whatever distinctive doctrine it affirms. That education must itself be wide in scope, transforming the selves of future citizens in ways that push beyond the sphere of political obligation as they learn to live according to the prescribed comprehensive values, and this requires a pedagogy pitted against all sources of diversity at odds with those values. Alternatively, political liberalism sets the aims of political education in a way that avoids any oppressive assault on diversity. Its aims are circumscribed to accord with the ethical heterogeneity that abounds under free government. Nevertheless, these aims are supposed to secure the shared political benefits an education grounded in comprehensive liberalism seemed to offer: a common allegiance among citizens to the central ideals of liberal politics and the basic rights these entail, as well as collective deliberative resources to move towards mutually acceptable answers to other questions of public moment.

So far I have followed Rawls's distinction between comprehensive and political liberalism, using the broad brush-strokes that he uses. The sharpness of the distinction he makes depends on stressing what he takes to be the oppressive common ground between comprehensive liberal and illiberal doctrines. But closer attention to the contrast between political and comprehensive liberalism exposes a much more blurred and complex picture than the one Rawls paints.

## 7. Varieties of Comprehensive and Political Liberalism

The starkness of Rawls's contrast between political and comprehensive liberalism has a certain superficial persuasiveness. That is so because the philosophical defence of liberal politics has typically been undertaken as part of more ambitious and more dubious theoretical undertakings. The political principles of the great liberal philosophers are connected with general ethical or metaphysical theses at variance with the deepest convictions of many liberal citizens. Mill's argument for liberty is connected to his utilitarianism. Dewey's (putative) liberalism is enmeshed with his pragmatism. Most religious creeds fit very badly with both utilitarianism and pragmatism. So a liberalism that required everyone to be a utilitarian or a pragmatist would be at war with pluralism (Strike 1994: 12). The appeal of political liberalism is that it seems to call a permanent truce.

Yet nothing in the concept of comprehensive liberalism entails a commitment to an all-purpose criterion of right and wrong such as utilitarianism or a grand epistemological theory such as pragmatism. A liberal political theory is an instance of comprehensive liberalism once it has some ethical or metaphysical content beyond the minimal scope and generality of political liberalism. That is entailed by the inclusion of partially comprehensive doctrines in the category of comprehensive liberalism. No doubt the theoretical exponents of liberal politics have often joined philosophical battles that are no more than a damaging distraction from the real task of constructing an adequate political theory. But their hubris is no reason to suppose an adequate theory could have no more than the minimal scope and generality of political liberalism. If the genre of comprehensive liberalism is to be discarded altogether, we need a better reason than the fact that its practitioners have often wrongly thought that the justification of free institutions depended crucially on many partisan philosophical theses that real liberal citizens can and should agree to disagree about.

But according to Rawls, oppression is latent in the very idea of comprehensive liberalism. Once liberal politics is understood as uniquely warranted by any comprehensive ideal, it must become 'but another sectarian doctrine' (Rawls 1985: 246). For if the maintenance of free institutions depended on enduring, collective assent to any particular comprehensive doctrine, massive coercion would be needed. Coercion would be the only way of opposing the inevitable emergence of large-scale dissent from any doctrine in a free society. This is the so-called 'fact of oppression' that unites the religious politics of the Inquisition with the many kinds of comprehensive liberalism (Rawls 1993: 37).

An affinity between the liberalism Rawls now abjures and overtly illiberal, sectarian politics is imputed through the very label 'comprehensive liberalism'. As the name for a family of political theories, the phrase naturally suggests that whoever commends what it names would advocate pervasive interference in citizens's lives to secure the comprehensive implementation of liberal values. But although it might make sense to talk of a comprehensive Islamic or Christian politics, on some but not all interpretations of Islam or Christianity, the centrality of individual freedom to any recognizably liberal polity is incompatible with a comprehensively enforced ordering of values. An authentically liberal moral doctrine could not dictate the content of the good life in all its fine detail. What liberal doctrines characteristically indicate is something of the style or manner with which we should conduct our lives, without insisting on the priority of any particular ends. Millian individuality can thrive in devotion to political activism as well as in lives that accord civic obligations a marginal place; it may be cultivated by those who sacrifice familial intimacy for art or professional success and by others who invert those priorities; it is compossible with fervent piety as well as steadfast unbelief. Mill does not tell us what the good life consists in; he merely argues for the necessity of one particular virtue to the processes of finding out and enacting whatever it consists in for this or that individual. Since Rawls admits that comprehensive doctrines may be only partially so, he can also acknowledge a difference between the Protean character of the ethical values traditionally enunciated by liberals and the more full-blooded comprehensive doctrines of their avowedly illiberal rivals. But the little word 'partially' does not do justice to the moral chasm that separates garden-variety sectarian politics from the views of Mill or Kant. Whatever else it may be, Mill's *On Liberty* is not but another example of the political genre in which John Calvin wrote.

Comprehensive liberalism is also internally diverse in ways that make some varieties more responsive to pluralism than others, and hence, less clearly vulnerable to the charge that Rawls thinks damns the category as a whole. Liberal doctrines vary in what I call their expansiveness—that is, the extent to which their ethical requirements limit choice beyond the primary sphere of application in politics. Millian individuality entails the overall superiority of lives that exhibit eccentricity, dissent, and innovation over others; and to that extent, a liberalism based on individuality becomes a more expansive doctrine than liberalisms which take their bearings from a general ideal of autonomy that is neutral on the choice between individualistic and more conventional ways of life (cf. Mill 1976 edn.: 67–90; Kymlicka 1990: 203). Similarly, autonomy may be understood as precluding all reliance on moral or religious authority or, less expansively, as permitting certain kinds of obedience in the case of even the fully virtuous agent (cf. Kant 1970 edn.: 54–60; Adams 1987: 123–7). Comprehensive liberalisms differ in their responsiveness to pluralism in other ways as well. The reasons they offer for restraint in the political enforcement of ethical norms may vary in strength and field of application. Mill and some of his contemporary disciples argue for an absolute or quasi-absolute embargo on paternalism; other liberals are less unyielding on that point (cf. Mill 1976 edn.: 13; Feinberg 1986; Raz 1986: 422–33; Barry 1995: 87).

If comprehensive liberalisms are variable in the degree to which they can be reconciled with pluralism, so too are the possible varieties of political liberalism. Political liberalism is defined in part by a respect for reasonable pluralism, not pluralism pure and simple. 'The basic motive behind political liberalism . . . is the desire to respect reasonable people' (Macedo 1995*a*: 474). Versions of political liberalism differ according to how lax or stringent are the criteria of reasonableness they employ. We cannot assume in advance that the more lax the criteria of reasonableness, and hence the more ethically inclusive the particular conception, the more morally defensible that conception must be.

Yet so far as meeting the challenge of pluralism goes, political liberalism might still seem to have a necessary advantage because it is constructed with an exclusive eye to the political domain. Its minimal scope means that it does not tell us what to believe or choose within the lives we lead beyond politics. In that respect, it seems more congenial to diversity than even the most modestly expansive version of comprehensive liberalism, regardless of the different interpretations to which the core idea of reasonable pluralism might be subject. But a critical issue is overlooked in this train of thought. When we have developed a conception of public reason adjusted to the fact of reasonable pluralism, there can be no guarantee that whatever ends of political education our conception supports will not deeply constrain the development of ethical identity outside politics. The aim of devising a political conception that coheres with the many different ways of life that people happen to affirm in a given society and the aim of accommodating within that conception reasonable and only reasonable pluralism are not necessarily compatible. Reconciling those dual aims turns out to be the Achilles' heel of political liberalism, as we shall subsequently see.

Be that as it may, what I have shown so far should at least make us wary of Rawls's sweeping claims regarding 'the fact of oppression' that supposedly unites comprehensive liberalism with other forms of political sectarianism. Of course, Rawls does not mean that Mill or Kant would have recommended the suppression of heretical deviations from their doctrines. Nor does he mean that they could have endorsed doctrinally inspired oppression without ceasing to be liberals in any sense (Rawls 1993: 37 n. 39). So far as I understand it, Rawls's point is that the 'fact of oppression' traps comprehensive liberals within a paradox. To ensure the perpetuation of liberal politics, conformity to the true liberal doctrine must be politically enforced. However, the necessary political enforcement would render the polity illiberal. So comprehensive liberalism is inherently self-defeating.

But this is much too quick. Once the internal diversity of both comprehensive and political liberalism is clear, so too is the rashness of the claim that any instance of the former must come to grief on the same 'fact of oppression' which the latter can avoid. For if the power of the state is used to advance some modestly expansive comprehensive ideal it does not immediately follow that we have oppression that destroys the liberal character of that state. Before the charge of oppression can even be understood, we need to know much more about the content of the ideal that is at stake, the manner in which political power is used in its support, and the particular moral reasons that might tell for and against that use of power. Indeed, if the chosen standard of reasonable pluralism is oppressively stringent in a given version of political liberalism, public antipathy to what is wrongly derogated as unreasonable pluralism might well undermine the liberal character of the state. Here again, so much seems to depend on the particularities of the version of political or comprehensive liberalism that we are considering.

The moral superiority of political over comprehensive liberalism is not established by juxtaposing coarse-grained stereotypes of each and then comparing their general assets and liabilities. The relevant categories are too heterogeneous for that strategy to work. If the challenge of pluralism suffices to establish the superiority of political liberalism, two things must be shown: some version of political liberalism respects the ethical diversity worth having (and *only* the diversity worth having); any version of comprehensive liberalism falls short of such respect, or at least, the best available versions fall short.

I argue that if we take Rawls's political liberalism as our prime candidate for establishing these two conclusions, it fails to do so. It fails because the conception of reasonable pluralism that Rawls needs to establish the first conclusion makes his political liberalism into a version of comprehensive liberalism. Therefore, the contrast between the two liberalisms which the second conclusion presupposes is undermined. But to see how this occurs, we need to look much more closely at the concept of reasonable pluralism.

## 8. *Reasonable Pluralism*

Why say the accommodation of reasonable pluralism rather than simple, unqualified pluralism is the appropriate moral basis for political liberalism? If pluralism is so wonderful, why not opt for the latter, more capacious category?

Imagine two societies that are alike in all morally relevant respects except one: some practice that systematically oppresses a particular social group continues in one of the societies, and those who engage in the practice are subject to no public criticism; the same practice died out in the other as a consequence of widespread public condemnation. The society that contains the oppressive practice instantiates a more inclusive political accommodation of pluralism than the society that does not. So if the reason for taking the challenge of pluralism seriously is our interest in avoiding oppression, as it certainly is in Rawls's case, then our accommodation must be morally discriminating. That is why reasonable pluralism has to be our starting-point rather than pluralism pure and simple. The word 'reasonable' registers, at the very least, the need for a morally selective deference to diversity. No doubt the constraint of reasonableness may be misunderstood in ways that conduce to oppression, and it is an open question whether Rawls's understanding is the best one. But we only avoid the consequences of an oppressive interpretation of reasonableness by finding a morally better one, not by denying the need for moral discrimination in the first place.

The challenge of pluralism requires us to distinguish two issues that are easily confused here. The boundaries of reasonable pluralism fix the range of values and perspectives that properly enter into political deliberation in a just society. Thus a political culture that systematically slighted the views of women whenever these tended to diverge from hegemonic male beliefs would circumscribe reasonable pluralism too narrowly. But notice that the operative (mis)conception of reasonable pluralism need not issue in coercion towards those whose views are wrongly deemed unreasonable. Women with dissident views might still be listened to, perhaps with a patronizing courtesy. But they are still not heeded because the establised criteria of relevance within public reason say that their judgements do not count. This brings the first issue into view. An interpretation of reasonable pluralism will address the problem of *inclusion*. How do we conceive the standards that govern public reason in a liberal democracy so as to include all sources of diversity (and only those sources of diversity) that deserve our respect?

Notice that the problem of inclusion is in part a problem of appropriate exclusion. For public reason is as susceptible to moral defeat through the failure to exclude the distracting and corrupting as it is through the failure to include the full range of what is morally relevant. Not regarding a perspective as worthy of accommodation because it is a woman's is not the same as dismissing it because it is racist. Of course, the standards that regulate participation in public reason must be such that what we discount as racist is indeed so or is at least very likely to be so. But this does not touch the basic point at issue: the problem of inclusion is as much about filtering out various moral toxins that threaten to contaminate public reason as it is about honouring the differences that we ought to honour.

Now suppose we solve the problem of inclusion and have a broad consensus on that solution so that public reason is generally conducted in a manner attuned to the correct distinction between reasonable and unreasonable pluralism. That would not mean unreasonable pluralism had died out. Within any feasibly just society, unreasonable pluralism will continue to exist (Rawls 1993: 39, 65). The second issue now comes into relief. How should we respond politically to the continued social presence of unreasonable pluralism? This is the problem of *toleration*. In my example of a polity corrupted by sexism, women with dissident views are effectively excluded from public reason by virtue of established standards regarding what counts in democratic deliberation. But they are also tolerated to the extent that their views do not meet with a coercive political response.

Even in a society where the problem of inclusion has been resolved in a morally satisfactory way, a combination of exclusion plus political toleration is likely to be prominent in the way we cope with unreasonable pluralism. Homeowners sometimes choose to sell their houses when those who are racially different move in next door. That conduct is politically tolerated in our very imperfect liberal democracies. But so far as racism persists within the unreasonable pluralism of a more completely just society, such conduct might be tolerated there as well (Johnston 1994: 2, 13–14). After all, considerations of privacy are a large moral obstacle to any attempts coercively to block decisions to buy or sell a home whenever the decision has some racist motivation. That will be as true in some better world than ours as it is in ours. But what is not possible is that the problem of inclusion might be reasonably resolved in such a way that racists would be heeded when they made a case for tax incentives to help create racially homogeneous neighbourhoods.

The boundaries of reasonable and unreasonable pluralism do not automatically reveal the borders of tolerable and intolerable pluralism. The first distinction has to do with the range of values and voices we should embrace in a suitably inclusive public reason, where citizens adjudicate among different views each of which properly elicits a robust respect; the second is about a particular problem we must confront within a suitably constructed public reason because of the inevitable persistence of some measure of unreasonable pluralism in our midst. A good solution to the problem of inclusion does not guarantee a good solution to the problem of toleration (and vice versa).

I return to the question of toleration at greater length later in the book. I stress its distance from the question of inclusion now because by conflating the two we invite worries about the political relevance of reasonable pluralism that are dissipated once the distinction is held clearly in view. Consider William Galston's argument for a political response to diversity that honours 'simple' rather than reasonable pluralism: 'All too often the alternative to finding a way of living together—a modus vivendi—is cruel and bloody strife. Liberalism arises in large measure from the conviction that, regardless of the contending parties' truth claims, religious faith cannot justify such strife' (Galston 1995: 519).

As an objection to the political relevance of reasonable pluralism, I assume this has to be understood along the following lines. To classify something as an instance of unreasonable pluralism is to declare it to be intolerable. Therefore, the standard of reasonable pluralism, however it is understood, will support state intervention against those who are deemed unreasonable. But that will trigger cruel and bloody strife. To avoid the evils of strife, we should seek a basis for cooperation that is neutral on the reasonableness of our culturally established patterns of diversity. At least that is what Galston would seem to want us to believe in the passage I have quoted.[1]

The germ of truth in Galston's view is that it would be morally catastrophic to use reasonable pluralism as a criterion of toleration. Then we would have a kind of Jacobin liberalism, at permanent war with all who deviate, however slightly, from the righteous community of reasonable citizens. The rights of the heretical to privacy or freedom of conscience would count as nothing. Their children would have to be educated in ways that protected them from their parents' baneful influence, and that could hardly be done without depriving their parents of all rights as parents. All this would no doubt plunge us into the 'cruel and bloody strife' against which Galston warns.

But the avoidability of Jacobin liberalism is obvious once we keep a grip on the difference between the problems of inclusion and toleration. The bare idea of reasonable pluralism does not license an aggressive moralism on the part of the liberal state; it merely signals the need for thoughtful moral discrimination in the way we respond politically to the fact of diversity. If Jacobin liberalism is one of the hazards to be avoided in exercising the necessary discrimination, so too is the failure to distinguish adequately between liberal virtue and vice within the sphere of conduct we rightly tolerate. Failure in that regard might lead us to conceive the ends of political education too unambitiously, as if the tolerable could be identified with the virtuous. But liberal democracies are hardly likely to endure, much less thrive once we cease to care about the difference between laudable political virtue and tolerable political vice.[2]

## 9. *The Political Conception of the Person*

If reasonable pluralism is the key moral concept in political liberalism, how do we interpret that concept in developing a theory of justice and public reason?

Rawls's answer is implicit in his so-called 'political conception' of the person. The conception is offered as a gloss on the democratic truism that society is properly a scheme of fair cooperation between free and equal citizens: 'The basic idea is that in virtue of their two moral powers (a capacity for a sense of justice and a conception of the good) and the powers of reason (of judgement, thought and inference connected with these powers), persons are free. Their having these powers to the requisite minimum degree makes them equal' (Rawls 1993: 19). As citizens, we supposedly have highest order interests in the realization of these powers, and our conception of political justice must be constructed accordingly. The political conception of the person has two related functions. First, possession of the two moral powers and the powers of reason 'to the requisite minimum degree' is the normative qualification for the status of citizenship. Second, the conception is the moral source from which the political morality is to be constructed that all who share that status should endorse together. I am interested in what the conception says about the virtue of justice that citizens are enjoined to cultivate.

The development of the sense of justice unfolds within that basic facet of human reason which Rawls subsumes under the concept of the reasonable. The application of the concept to persons has two aspects. First, a commitment to moral reciprocity is necessary. Reasonable persons are predisposed sincerely to propose principles intended to fix the rules of fair cooperation with others; they are ready to discuss proposals made with the same intention by others; and they are prepared to comply with such proposals should others be willing to do likewise. The other aspect is 'the willingness to recognize the burdens of judgment and to accept their consequences for the use of public reason in directing the legitimate exercise of political power in a constitutional regime' (Rawls 1993: 54).

The idea of 'the burdens of judgment' is basic to much of the enusing argument throughout this book. Rawls introduces the idea both to explain the possibility of irreconcilable ethical disagreement among reasonable people and to justify the mutual accommodation that public reason will promote when disagreement threatens to become destructive social conflict. The 'burdens' are those particular sources of divergent judgement that persist among us when all factors that signify a remediable failure to reason competently and to exhibit reciprocity are inoperative, such as logical bungling or inordinate self-interest. They are the contingent but inescapable imperfections of our capacity to reason together towards agreement (Rawls 1993: 55).

To suppose that a shared reasonableness guarantees consensus overlooks the general liabilities to error and disagreement that afflict even the most accomplished exercise of reason, as well as the special difficulties we face when reason is harnessed to reciprocity in public deliberation. In that setting, we face difficulties not only in weighing our own interests against those of others, but also in balancing the interests of different others, and these combine with the general frailties of reason to suggest that many residual sources of discordant judgement would survive the disappearance of the vices of unreason. Rawls offers an unsystematic and non-exhaustive list of these sources: all our ideas are to some degree subject to hard cases, but this is an especially striking feature of our ethical and political concepts; judgement is likely to be affected by contingencies of experience and perspective that we cannot altogether surmount, however reasonable we might be; the values we live by are chosen from a wide range of possibilities, those we choose have to be arranged in some order of priority, and both tasks may be discharged in many reasonable but incompatible ways.

Rawls presents reciprocity and acceptance of the burdens of judgement as two 'basic aspects' of the idea of the reasonable (Rawls 1993: 54–8). I shall outline what I take to be the correct interpretation of the relationship between them, an interpretation that is not to my knowledge explicitly endorsed by Rawls but is consistent with what he says.

Reciprocity is a virtue designed to help us find and implement mutually acceptable terms of cooperation in circumstances where we initially disagree about what fairness requires. In exhibiting reciprocity, I begin by putting before you what I take to be fair. But I must also be ready seriously to discuss the opposing proposals that you make in the hope of moving, through the discipline of dialogue, towards a common perspective that each of us could adhere to in good conscience. Your viewpoint is as important as mine to the fulfilment of that hope, and only through empathic identification with your viewpoint can I appreciate what reason might commend in what you say. For if I am to weigh your claims as a matter of fairness rather than a rhetorically camouflaged expression of sheer selfishness, I must provisionally suspend the thought that you are simply wrong and enter imaginatively into the moral perspective you occupy. But since you and I are reasoning about fairness, I cannot be uncritical about your view (or my own) and simply split the difference between us as if we were just haggling about how best to satisfy divergent preferences. Empathic identification must be combined with a willingness to bring the shared resources of reason to bear on the conflict at hand by assessing, for example, the comparative strength of the assumptions behind our prereflective judgements or by exploring together the plausibility of the implications that flow from the rival moral principles we invoke in defence of our opposing views.

Notice that reciprocity might sometimes operate effectively in a social setting where many of the burdens of judgement that Rawls mentions are not accepted by anyone. Suppose members of an ethnically homogeneous society are agreed in affirming a common religious conception of the good and the right, and are agreed also in regarding all alternatives to what they believe as intolerable abominations. Their ethnic homogeneity precludes many familiar kinds of social conflict, and they regard the practices of other cultures, even when they share the same religious beliefs, with sheer disdain. Nevertheless, conflicts about what is fair still occur because the application of moral concepts is coloured by different experiences and interests that people tend to have as occupants of different social roles or because occupants of the same roles may yet have conflicting but equally rational factual beliefs about the world that affect their moral judgement. Other less innocent conflicts about what is fair might be due to careless reasoning, culpable ignorance, and the psychological pressures of overweening self-interest. So notwithstanding moral unanimity at the level of general principles and ends, as well as the additional cohesion that ethnic homogeneity supplies, citizens disagree about what is fair because they interpret the relevance of their shared morality to questions of social cooperation in different ways. Some but not all of their disagreement is correctly explained by some of the burdens of judgement.

The point I want to underscore is this. If reciprocity is to function adequately in the circumstances I have described, citizens must be capable of distinguishing, with a fair degree of reliability, those sources of conflict in their moral practices that are due to the burdens of judgement from those that are not. To the extent that they fail to make the distinction appropriately, the difference is muddied between collective, reasoned moral reflection on what fairness demands and non-moral bargaining among rival and sometimes irrational interests. The very point of reciprocity—reasonable agreement on fair terms of cooperation—cannot be achieved without acceptance of some of the burdens of judgement, even in the idealized circumstances of an ethnically and religiously monistic society.

Now suppose the cultural unity of my hypothetical society begins to unravel; many different factors conspire to make it increasingly pluralistic. Some changes result from social pressures that countervail the ideal of the reasonable. New economic arrangements, for example, are defended or criticized in ways that use the language of justice to disguise a desire for domination, and an increasingly complex social world leaves ever greater scope for disagreement that arises from ignorance or other remediable failures of reason. Yet many instances of the emerging diversity are a consequence of particular burdens of judgement that reciprocity did not require members to accept under the conditions of monism. The competent exercise of reason within increasingly free institutions now generates conflicting comprehensive doctrines so that the old moral concord is now irrevocably lost, even if the lust for domination could somehow be contained and everyone reasoned as well as any human being feasibly could. Other novel sources of diversity might be ethnic rather than doctrinal, as immigrants enter the society whose creed might be the same as the indigenous population but whose folk-ways become a source of social friction, or as already established groups—women perhaps—develop an explicit sense of solidarity that pits them against the regnant political orthodoxy.

Reciprocity can no longer function adequately as it did under the old dispensation. Only part of the reason for that has to do with new sources of unreason and domination within the culture, and so members do not solve the problem simply by developing a discerning eye for these. For within the old dispensation, no heretics to the received orthodoxy made claims to fair treatment that required anyone to acknowledge the reasonableness of heresy. The cultural development of the society now requires a fuller recognition of the burdens of judgement if reciprocity is to operate as it should. The reach of that virtue must now be enlarged beyond the limits of reasonable orthodoxy to include reasonable heresy as well.

Failure to extend reciprocity in this way will thwart the social realization of its distinctive end because ethically heretical citizens, if they continue to be regarded by most people as living beyond the moral pale, will be denied the terms of social cooperation that a reasonable understanding of their claims would warrant. I use 'reasonable heresy' broadly here not just to cover those who accept comprehensive doctrines in explicit conflict with the old orthodoxy but also those whose ethnic or gender identity, say, puts them in conflict with tradition without making them unreasonable. Rawls concentrates on the former case, but the idea of the burdens of judgement is properly applied to the latter phenomena as well.[3]

If my reading of the relationship between reciprocity and acceptance of the burdens of judgement is correct, then it is wrong to think of the idea of the burdens, as some have suggested, as an unfortunate and disposable residue from Rawls's earlier comprehensive liberalism (Wenar 1995; Strike 1996). Acceptance of the burdens is rather a necessary manifestation of reciprocity. Once the free exercise of human thought has shown that no one conception of the good and the right is uniquely defensible, and that the reasonable interpretation of such conceptions is deeply affected by ethnic and similar differences, reciprocity will have to be attuned to these burdensome truths as well.

The idea of the burdens of judgement stands or falls with Rawls's notion of reciprocity, and together these give a powerful answer to the question I posed at the beginning of this section. How should we understand the condition of reasonable pluralism on which political liberalism is to be constructed? Rawls's political conception of the person indicates the following answer. The limits of reasonable pluralism are coterminus with the diversity of beliefs and practices that are a consequence of the burdens of judgement. This in turn yields a Rawlsian answer to the question I asked at the beginning of the chapter about the ends of political education and the challenge of pluralism. A political education that meets the challenge will teach the young the virtues and abilities they need in order to participate competently in reciprocity-governed political dialogue and to abide by the deliverances of such dialogue in their conduct as citizens.

## 10. The Burdens of Judgement and the Limits of Diversity

The Rawlsian account of political education I have just sketched is inferred from his political conception of the person. How is that conception to be reconciled with the claim that political liberalism offers a 'freestanding' view of public reason? The question is important because the answer will expose deep tensions in Rawls's thought between the radical educational implications of the political conception of the person and Rawls's apparent desire to construct a liberalism that is maximally hospitable to established patterns of diversity.

The notion of a free-standing political conception is introduced early in *Political Liberalism*. This is what Rawls says:

> a political conception of justice . . . is neither presented as, nor as derived from . . . a [reasonable comprehensive] doctrine applied to the basic structure of society, as if the structure were simply another subject to which that doctrine applied . . . To use a current phrase, the political conception is a module, an essential constituent part, that fits into and can be supported by various reasonable comprehensive doctrines that endure in the society regulated by it. This means that it can be presented without saying, or knowing, or hazarding a conjecture about, what such doctrines it may belong to, or be supported by. (Rawls 1993: 12–13)

A free-standing political conception presupposes an ethically pluralistic audience to whom an argument for principles of justice and other norms of public reason can be persuasively presented. But the persuasion has to take a particular shape. To make the argument and its conclusions free-standing, the 'mode of presentation' must achieve two things: each member of the intended audience must be convinced that the political conception can form a 'module' within the larger context of her doctrine or worldview; each must also see that the conception is no mere application of her general ethical or philosophical creed because the same conception may also be a module within the many rival doctrines that divide members of the intended audience from each other. Presumably, given the range of the burdens of judgement, it must also be free-standing in that it can be endorsed from the perspective of any ethnic identity or the like that might be reasonably embraced.

Notice that a political conception cannot be free-standing in some absolute sense; it is free-standing relative to an audience that is characterized in a particular way. The characterization matters because the more inclusive the audience is, the wider is the reach of the argument Rawls offers for his political conception. The members of the intended audience are divided in the doctrines they accept, but all are alike in accepting only 'reasonable' doctrines. Rawls says that such doctrines have three main features. They engage theoretical reason in offering a 'more or less consistent and coherent' reading of the main aspects of human life; they involve practical reason in singling out the values that should guide our conduct; and they normally belong to a tradition of thought and conduct. This account is 'deliberately loose' in order to avoid the risk of it being 'arbitrary or exclusive' (Rawls 1993: 59) There is no suggestion here that the relevant exercise of theoretical or practical reason has to be even moderately competent. Rawls even says that many doctrines we regard as 'plainly unreasonable and untrue' outside public reason are nonetheless reasonable in the sense relevant to his political liberalism (Rawls 1993: 60, 14 n.).

The laxity of Rawls's account of reasonable comprehensive doctrines suggests that the conception of public reason might succeed in being free-standing relative to an audience in which crazy dogmatism of many kinds abounds.[4] Yet at the very core of the political conception to be presented in this generously accommodating way, we find the powerful and exact-ing Rawlsian ideal of reasonableness as it applies to persons, the ideal I outlined in Section 9. That ideal embodies an onerous standard of public virtue rather than some negligible threshold of reason that virtually everyone exceeds. The ideal entails that *any* doctrine held in a way that repudiates the burdens of judgement, for example, pushes the believer beyond the borders of reasonable pluralism. Exponents of Millian indi-viduality are beyond the borders, along with the more familiar enemies of freedom and equality, if they believe that basic political institutions should be designed to promote individuality and that those who think otherwise are simply unreasonable.

How do we make sense of the discrepancy between Rawls's paltry explicit criteria of reasonable doctrines and his ideal of the reasonable cit-izen? Rawls could say that those to whom the political conception is addressed might agree to comply with the demands of reciprocity and the burdens of judgement within the special context of public reason and then discount those demands once they turn their attention elsewhere. You can be a crazy dogmatist in private life so long as you sober up when it comes to voting. That view is supported by his willingness to think of the polit-ical conception of the person as an artificial and specialized viewpoint that we might step into and outside of at will (Rawls 1980: 545; 1985, 245; 1993: 30–1). But this does not help here because acceptance of the burdens of judgement cannot have the moral consequences Rawls wants to infer unless they are understood as applying broadly to the understanding of our own extra-political beliefs, as well as the wider convictions of our fel-low citizens within the background culture of a democratic polity. This is clear in the following passage:

The evident consequence of the burdens of judgment is that reasonable persons do not all affirm the same comprehensive doctrine. Moreover, they also recognize that all persons alike, including themselves, are subject to those burdens, and so many reasonable comprehensive doctrines are affirmed, not all of which can be true (indeed none of them may be true). The doctrine any reasonable person affirms is but one reasonable doctrine among others. (Rawls 1993: 60)

The fact that we must interpret our own comprehensive doctrines as well as those of our fellow citizens in a manner that acknowledges the burdens of judgement wreaks havoc on Rawls's distinction between the public and non-public spheres. That is so because how we understand such doctrines is of paramount consequence in the lives we lead outside politics. After all, it would be absurd to teach citizens to adopt the required interpretation of their general ethical or religious convictions when they address fundamental political questions while insisting that they are at liberty to reject it whenever they are thinking or acting in a non-civic capacity. That would be to invite them to oscillate between contradictory beliefs about the rational status of their deepest beliefs, and that is hardly an alluring fate for anyone.

I do not say people cannot learn to shift reliably between contradictory beliefs about such matters. That is an empirical question on which it would be rash to pronounce without hard, empirical evidence. But my point here is ethical rather than empirical. To retain a lively understanding of the burdens of judgement in political contexts while suppressing it everywhere else would require a spectacular feat of self-deception that cannot be squared with personal integrity. Liberal politics on its best interpretation will no doubt demand some compartmentalization of our reasons for action. A politics of mutual respect may require us to prescind from our religious differences when it comes to political argument and choice. But however the idea of compartmentalization is understood, we will need to worry about the difference between integrity-preserving and integrity-destroying ways of dividing compartments.

Indeed, Rawls has shown some sensitivity to the need for the perspective of citizenship to be integrated within a coherent picture of the self: 'Within different contexts we can assume diverse points of view toward our person without contradiction so long as these points of view cohere together when circumstances require' (Rawls 1980: 545). But the necessity for coherence among the different points of view is precisely what is threatened here. A strategy for distinguishing between the political and other aspects of the self that depends on juggling contradictory beliefs about the rational basis of our most central ethical convictions plainly yields the wrong kind of compartmentalization.

The application of the burdens of judgement to the background culture is not a point that Rawls could retreat on because he needs it to make his case for limiting the appeal to general moral or religious doctrines inside public reason. If the doctrine that any reasonable person affirms is but one reasonable possibility among others, as the burdens of judgement implies, then to argue for state action because some such doctrine is true and all reasonable alternatives irrelevant is to violate the conditions of reasonableness. We could not in these circumstances keep faith with reciprocity because our argument relies on grounds that others must reject by virtue of opposing doctrines they reasonably hold. Suppose I am deeply convinced of the truth of atheism and think that human life is wasted by the illusion of religious belief. You believe with a passion that matches my own that life can have no meaning without belief in God. We want to engage in reciprocity-governed dialogue about the role of the state in regulating our children's education. But we get nowhere so long as either of us insists that the religious or irreligious beliefs of the other deserve no respect in the making of policy.

The idea of the burdens of judgement is necessary to Rawls's political liberalism because it alone supports reasonable accommodation among contending views both in selecting which principles of justice best satisfy the ambitions of political liberalism and in deliberation about how such principles are to be applied once they are selected. Without that idea, Rawls has no grounds for arguing that principles of justice be constructed in a way that allows for the great variety of beliefs and practices that reasonable citizens might embrace and no grounds for claiming that their application be based only on considerations that are widely acceptable to reasonable citizens. Furthermore, the idea is necessary not merely in that sense that the principles of justice enforced in a liberal society must be defensible from a perspective that acknowledges the burdens of judgement and their political consequences. Acceptance must be an end of political education because to the extent that citizens fail in this regard the society will not achieve the goal of publicity in whatever principles of justice regulate its basic structure, and publicity is essential to the kind of stability to which a just society might aspire.

Rawls distinguishes three levels to the publicity of liberal justice, but only the shallowest level needs to be looked at to see the necessary supporting role of the burdens of judgement. At that level, the basic institutions of society are effectively regulated by a conception of justice that citizens accept and know their fellow citizens to accept. The fact that basic institutions instantiate the relevant principles is also public knowledge (Rawls 1993: 66–71). But to share in this collective knowledge about justice and its institutional embodiment I must accept the burdens of judgement. Otherwise, liberal principles of justice whose defence and interpretation within public reason require me to forgo or at least moderate the appeal to my religious convictions, say, will seem an arbitrary restriction on appeals to the truth on matters of the highest moral significance. In that event, I am morally alienated from the polity and denied the benefit that the condition of publicity secures:

When a political conception of justice satisfies this condition [of publicity]... citizens can give reasons for their beliefs and conduct before one another confident that this avowed reckoning itself will strengthen and not weaken public understanding. The political order does not, it seems, depend on historically accidental or established delusions, or other mistaken beliefs resting on the deceptive appearance of institutions that mislead us as to how they work. (Rawls 1993: 68)

Yet for a citizen who has not learned to accept the burdens of judgement, a political order which presupposes acceptance must seem to depend on unfortunate historical accident, established delusions or other mistaken beliefs, and its claim to legitimacy will seem a preposterous hoax. Publicity thus presupposes the recognition of legitimacy, and so publicity also presupposes a civic education which instils acceptance of the burdens of judgement.

Rawls's conception of public reason cannot be free-standing relative to an audience as inclusive as the one to which his argument is explicitly tied. That is so because the ideal of civic virtue latent in that conception cannot fit appropriately as a 'module' within all comprehensive doctrines that are reasonable in the minimal sense. Rawlsian public reason is only free-standing relative to a much more restricted range of persons—namely, those who adhere to the strenuous ideal of the reasonable contained in his political conception of the person.[5]

The motivation behind Rawls's oddly lax account of reasonable comprehensive doctrines seems to be the hope that his political liberalism might extend its welcoming embrace to the bulk of established cultural and credal patterns in the societies we actually live in. If that hope were realized, reasonable pluralism and our existing pluralisms might coalesce without any great friction. A conception of public reason that is free-standing relative to an audience that includes just about everyone would place the justice and stability that political liberalism promises within easy reach. Rawls's argument would then clarify what is best in the practice of free government, and essential to its educational transmission, without posing any profound moral challenge to the established cultural background of civic life.

This is Rawls's hope when he says that his conception of justice 'wants no part' of any philosophical controversy: 'it aims to leave these [comprehensive] doctrines as they are and criticize them only so far as they are unreasonable, politically speaking' (Rawls 1993: 179).[6] But he cannot have it both ways. Leaving everything as it is cannot be squared with the wide-ranging ethical criticism that commitment to the political conception of the person would require. So far as that conception is a morally appealing basis for addressing the problem of inclusion, a complacent accommodation of extant beliefs and practices is untenable.

## 11. How Burdensome are the Burdens of Judgement?

I have argued that Rawls's political conception of the person severely erodes the distinction between public and non-public spheres and that the values embodied in that conception are necessary to the political education that Rawlsian political liberalism supports. To the extent that there is erosion, political education must mould and constrain the identity of citizens beyond the public sphere.

But how substantial should we expect the moulding and constraining to be? The idea we need to focus on here is the burdens of judgement. The burdens are a more subversive idea than Rawls's anodyne discussion of them would suggest. But to see this clearly, we need to keep a grip on the sense in which people must accept them in order to be reasonable. Presented as an abstract catalogue of causes of error and disagreement, the burdens of judgement are platitudinous, and their implications for the background culture of liberal politics appear slight. But nominal assent to a list of abstractions is not enough; the relevant acceptance must rather be an active and taxing psychological disposition, pervasively colouring the beliefs we form and the choices we make. A merely nominal assent, however widely shared, could not create the kind of mutual forbearance and respect in social cooperation that Rawls sees as the necessary manifestations of a shared reasonableness. After all, it is one thing to grant the truism that the concepts employed in framing our comprehensive doctrines are subject to hard cases or that we always select from an array of values that admit reasonable alternatives; it is quite another, when the doctrine I ardently uphold entails a particular resolution of a hard case or a certain choice from the range of available values, to acknowledge that opposing views are equally reasonable, and that the political significance of the doctrine I cherish must be curtailed by deference to the reasonableness of beliefs I vehemently reject.

If an active rather than a merely nominal acceptance of the burdens of judgement is a necessary end of the political education that Rawlsian political liberalism supports, how might such an acceptance be encouraged in children and adolescents among whom it has yet to develop? Imagine a child growing up in a home where a particular comprehensive doctrine is affirmed that entails strong views on matters of both ethical and political controversy, such as homosexuality, economic inequality, abortion, and the like. These views might or might not be taught with respect for the child's growing powers of reason, but even if they were, active acceptance of the burdens of judgement is hardly the inevitable outcome. For the most part, parents will naturally reason with the child inside the framework of the comprehensive doctrines they favour. The desire to perpetuate their own deepest values in the lives of their children is fundamental to the project of parenthood as most people understand it, and so we should expect some tendency to soften the hardness of hard cases and to overlook the selectivity among values that any doctrine will embody. The family is no doubt the first and most important school of justice. Rawls knows that as well as anyone else (Rawls 1971: 462–7). But there may yet be some aspects of justice for which the family is generally an unsuitable educational vehicle. The argument of Chapters 6 through 8 will give a clearer picture of why that is so. But even in advance of that argument, it is surely obvious that acceptance of those particular burdens of judgement that stem from pluralism in conceptions of the good and the right is an end of political education for which many families will be ill-suited.

The natural partiality of the family as an instrument of moral education may make it a powerful ally for political liberalism by securing the survival across generations of strongly held convictions that compose an overlapping consensus of doctrines in support of a liberal constitution. Yet the same partiality is also a threat to political liberalism so far as doctrines learned in the family press outside the boundaries of a reasonable pluralism. That outcome is avoided only so far as future citizens learn at some stage to accept the burdens of judgement in other institutional settings, and the school is an obvious candidate for that role. If acceptance has to be the complex and onerous psychological disposition I have specified, the hardness of hard cases must be brought out by investigating specific ethical questions from multiple perspectives once the child or adolescent can learn to understand something of the variety of reasonable views from the inside; the effects of contingencies of social position and experience on disparities among such views must be imaginatively explored; and the various ways in which reasonable ethical doctrines select and order values must also be appreciated as these give shape to conflicting ways of life.

Now the educational task I have just described, although it is intended to address only the development of the sense of justice in tandem with the powers of reason, will profoundly affect the development of a conception of the good as well. That is inevitable once the burdens of judgement are applied to comprehensive and partially comprehensive doctrines. Indeed, Rawls explicitly notes that these burdens apply to the rational—that aspect of reason which corresponds to our capacity for a conception of the good—as well as to the reasonable (Rawls 1993: 56); and from the standpoint of education, the cultivation of the two moral powers cannot be parcelled out into separate, mutually insulated processes of learning. The attempt to understand the reasonableness of convictions that may be in deep conflict with doctrines learned in the family cannot be carried through without inviting the disturbing question that these convictions might be the framework of a better way of life, or at least one that is just as good. That question is unavoidable because to understand the reasonableness of beliefs that initially seem wrong or even repellent I must imaginatively entertain the perspective those very beliefs furnish, and from that perspective my own way of life will look worse, or at least no better, than what that perspective affirms. Although many who undergo this kind of education might eventually answer the question in a way that reaffirms commitments instilled within the family, these have a new psychological context that makes it implausible to say that the 'same' conception of the good is affirmed before and after we have come to accept the burdens of judgement.[7] One obvious difference is that the original commitments are now ratified on the basis of independent reflection rather than sheer deference to the dictates of the family or community into which one is born. Stephen Macedo has observed that the public virtues of liberalism 'have a private life' (Macedo 1990: 265). That is obviously true of comprehensive liberalism, and it looks as if political liberalism is no exception to the rule.

## 12. Political Liberalism and the Fate of Religion

A powerful constraint on the background culture of liberal politics is an inevitable consequence of the education that Rawlsian political liberalism entails. But Rawls is anxious to mitigate that constraint. He insists that though reasonableness teaches us to place allegiance to comprehensive doctrines outside public reason, this does not oblige us to be 'hesitant and uncertain, much less skeptical, about our own beliefs' (Rawls 1993: 63). That may be true, but even if it were, its truth cannot allay all the concerns of those who feel their way of life is threatened by an education in schools or elsewhere that conduces to reasonableness.

The scale of the threat to established patterns of moral or religious conviction can be brought out by considering more closely how the ends of a Rawlsian civic education are to be reconciled with assured belief outside politics. Suppose we learn to see that reasonable agreement has the limits Rawls stresses and we (actively) accept the practical consequences he infers from those limits. We might still coherently claim that other truth-disclosing resources are accessible to us, such as the divine grace that can be sought through prayer or the study of sacred texts. We could believe these resources support confidence in our own comprehensive doctrine, despite the fact that others are entirely reasonable in rejecting it. Therefore, acceptance of the burdens of judgement would not make us hesitant and uncertain, much less skeptical, about our own beliefs. So even if all citizens accepted the burdens of judgement, that would still leave room for many faith-based comprehensive doctrines in the background culture. But the faith-based doctrines that are accommodated belong to a restricted subset—call it sophisticated belief—that harbours internal tensions.

The tensions are easily exposed. Sophisticated believers think that certain things are true with an assurance that self-consciously goes beyond the limits of the reasonable. But they also think it would be wrong to draw on these convictions in political argument, at least about constitutional essentials and basic justice, because doing so would transgress the same limits. That is a high-wire act. One falls off if adherence to a comprehensive doctrine influences (perhaps unconsciously) political judgement, and precisely because one is sure of its truth, the influence may be hard to resist (Nagel 1991: 168). One also falls if acceptance of the burdens of judgement eats away at the creed that public reason pushes outside its boundaries. This would be an acute worry for many religious families regarding the kind of education political liberalism implies.

Rawls's account of the burdens of judgement emphasizes the insecurities of reason in a way that is akin to some conservative religious views. The claim that human reason is a pitifully flawed and unreliable thing is common in some religious traditions: 'God knows the cogitations of the wise, that they are vain' (Psalms 93). But that claim is utterly incompatible with sophisticated belief because it denies the status of reasonableness as a cardinal social virtue. To stay on the wire, respect for the limits of the reasonable in our dealings with fellow citizens must be regarded not only as an authentic virtue; it must be prized as the paramount virtue there because to relax in our respect is to open the door to contempt towards those who reasonably disagree with us. Sophisticated believers must agree that reasonable pluralism 'is not an unfortunate condition of human life' while regarding themselves as especially fortunate in affirming important truths which many who live within the borders of reasonable pluralism would emphatically deny (Rawls 1993: 37).

Perhaps the chief intellectual question for sophisticated believers will be to find a suitable explanation of why, within public deliberation on fundamental questions, the failure to be reasonable should be regarded so differently than the failure to make good use of whatever other truth-disclosing resources underwrite their own non-public ethical convictions. A suitable explanation must establish the political irrelevance of those convictions without implying that the supposed truth-disclosing resources they rely on outside our shared reason are less trustworthy than reason itself.

The high-wire act of sophisticated belief is a matter of learning to combine a vigorous faith with an intelligent humility about the possibility of its reasoned vindication. That being so, we should be sceptical when we are told that political liberalism is irrelevant to the conduct of religious education. 'The political liberal avoids saying anything about how religion is to be studied: that is left to churches and other private groups. The political liberal can live with the notion that fundamentalism may be the truth in the religious sphere—so long as it does not claim political authority' (Macedo 1995*a*: 479–80) But acceptance of the burdens of judgement makes a big difference to how we understand the significance of religious truth in our own lives and the lives of others. If acceptance is compatible with some kinds of fundamentalism, these will have to be very different from many that are currently familiar, and the religious education intended to sustain them would have to depart drastically from the insular and dogmatic education that characterizes garden-variety fundamentalism (e.g. Peshkin 1988; Rose 1993). Political liberals may indeed avoid saying anything about how religion is to be studied. But the avoidance is evasion because if, as Macedo himself suggests, respect for reasonable people is the nerve of political liberalism, it cannot coherently deny that religious education should honour the limits of the reasonable (Macedo 1995*a*: 474).

Even though the internal tensions of sophisticated belief should be candidly acknowledged, religion will not inevitably succumb to them. It would be foolish to suppose that outcome was even likely if Rawlsian civic education were widely diffused. To learn to accept the burdens of judgement is not to endorse secular humanism, blanket moral scepticism or any other anti-religious posture one cares to imagine. For Christians, the particular tensions I have identified are but another variation on the conflict between Athens and Jerusalem that was powerfully evident near the very beginnings of their tradition and has shaped its development ever since (Shestov 1966 edn.; Kolakowski 1982). We also know that the political face of a religion can change dramatically in new social and intellectual conditions without losing its grip on the faithful. Many of the descendants of fierce Scottish Calvinists became sedate American Presbyterians who vote for the Democrats and yet remain loyal to the religion of their ancestors. The phenomenon is not unique to Christianity. Some argue for developments within Islam that would liberalize its civic aspects without forfeiting its distinctiveness as a potent source for individual and group identity (e.g. Bilgrami 1992). For all we know, their voice may be the future of Islam. Liberals will certainly hope so.

The adaptability of religion in changing environments is easy to underestimate if we attend only to the forms it takes at a particular moment in history; it is easier still to underestimate if we equate religion with official church teachings. Some of Rawls's account of the burdens of judgement is repugnant to the current teachings of the Roman Catholic Church (Wenar 1995: 44–5; Haldane 1996*a*: 66–7). But that does not mean Rawls's political conception of the person is repugnant to all Catholics, even at our brief moment in history. In contemporary liberal democracies, a great many Catholics have combined their faith with a steadfast disregard of official church teachings on issues such as birth control. No doubt many are also capable of a similar accomplishment in reconciling their faith with acceptance of the burdens of judgement.

If the education that political liberalism supports would penetrate the background culture in the manner I have indicated, a genuine pluralism would thrive under its aegis. Those who are doubtful of all comprehensive doctrines would be at home. Established religious and other cultural practices would probably endure, though often perhaps in new and unexpected forms. A common acceptance of the burdens of judgement might also nourish much new ethical diversity, while weakening the sway of ancient dogmatisms. Yet even if I am right about all this, the likely cultural consequences of Rawlsian civic education will still seem like a catastrophe to many people. The education they want for their children is one that perpetuates a way of life in the particular form they cherish. The fact that reasonableness might cohere with some altered form will not placate them. Scottish Calvinists of the seventeenth century would be horrified at what many of their American descendants take to be a Protestant faith. Contemporary religious conservatives might feel a comparable horror at the prospect of a faith their children could one day have that was as thoroughly liberalized as Rawls's political conception of the person would require.

## 13. Back to Comprehensive Liberalism

But what is left now of the contrast between political and comprehensive liberalism in their relation to pluralism? Rawls wants to say there is a large difference, and that the difference is brought into relief in the practice of civic education:

The liberalisms of Kant and Mill may lead to requirements designed to foster the values of autonomy and individuality as ideals to govern much if not all of life. But political liberalism has a different aim and requires far less. It will ask that children's education include such things as knowledge of their constitutional and civic rights. . . . Moreover, their education should also prepare them to be fully cooperating members of society and enable them to be self-supporting; it should also encourage the political virtues so that they want to honor the fair terms of cooperation with the rest of society. (Rawls 1993: 199)

But the contrast Rawls draws is bogus because the political virtues that implement the fair terms of cooperation bring autonomy through the back door of political liberalism. That becomes obvious once we reflect on the educational task of securing active acceptance of the burdens of judgement. Future citizens must be taught to think in particular ways about doctrines that properly lie outside the scope of public reason: they must become critically attuned to the wide range of reasonable political disagreement within the society they inhabit and to the troubling gap between reasonable agreement and the whole moral truth. This will require serious imaginative engagement with rival views about good and evil, right and wrong, and this in turn means that these views must be confronted in their own terms, without the peremptory dismissal they might receive according to whatever doctrine a child learns in the family. The moral authority of the family and the various associations in which the child grows up must be questioned to the extent that the society contains reasonable alternatives to whatever that authority prescribes. All this looks like a pretty familiar depiction of central elements in an education for autonomy because the psychological attributes that constitute an active acceptance of the burdens of reason, such as the ability and inclination to subject received ethical ideas to critical scrutiny, also constitute a recognizable ideal of ethical autonomy.[8]

Rawls is ready to concede that the accidental effect, though not the intention, of the education that political liberalism demands might sometimes be acceptance of a comprehensive ideal such as autonomy by children whose families adhere to other moral doctrines: 'The unavoidable consequences of reasonable requirements for children's education may have to be accepted, often with regret' (Rawls 1993: 200). But the distinction between educational intentions and unintended effects marks no distance between comprehensive and Rawls's political liberalism. Learning to accept the burdens of judgement in the sense necessary to political liberalism is conceptually inseparable from what we ordinarily understand as the process of learning to be ethically (and not just politically) autonomous. Rawls cannot coherently say that coming to accept the burdens of judgement is an unintended effect of the education his theory implies. And since coming to accept the burdens means attaining a substantial ethical autonomy, he cannot regard the achievement of autonomy as a merely accidental consequence of the pursuit of humbler educational goals.

The upshot of all this is that Rawlsian political liberalism is really a kind of closet comprehensive liberalism. My argument has been an attempt to pull it out of the closet. To agree with Rawls is to accept a pervasive and powerful constraint (the burdens of judgement) on how we should think about the various convictions and practices that proliferate in the background culture of liberal politics and how we should form our own convictions and make our own choices in that setting. That constraint enjoins us to be ethically autonomous to a substantial degree and, given the requirement of reciprocity, to respect the autonomy of others when we cooperate politically with them.

The Rawlsian doctrine of autonomy is certainly less expansive than its major precursors within the liberal tradition. The style of thought and conduct the doctrine requires does not preclude assent to any of the major philosophical or moral positions that have divided liberal theorists among themselves. Utilitarians and Kantians can accept the ideal of the reasonable citizen without ceasing to to be utilitarians and Kantians. But although a reduced expansiveness is part of the appeal of Rawls's liberalism for those of us who care about pluralism and share his distaste for hubristic political rationalism, that does not suffice to take it outside the category of comprehensive liberalism.

For the partition Rawls labours to erect between comprehensive and political liberalism has now collapsed. Acceptance of the burdens of judgement ramifies widely across our thought and conduct outside the public sphere, and in so doing, undermines Rawls's sharp distinction in scope between comprehensive and political liberalism. The distinction in generality is gone because the burdens of judgement are relevant to all subjects—personal relationships as well as the basic structure of society—to which our comprehensive doctrines have possible application. This means the contrast in answers to the question of legitimacy is also erased. Comprehensive liberalism is supposed to claim that political coercion is legitimate only when it is justified by a true doctrine, like the idea that autonomous are better than heteronomous lives, whereas legitimacy is established according to political liberalism by values inside an overlapping consensus among the many ethical views that prosper under reasonable pluralism. The problem is that 'reasonable' pluralism is freighted with a significance that makes this bold distinction vaporous. A partially comprehensive doctrine of the sort that comprehensive liberals have traditionally advanced is embedded in Rawls's idea of the reasonable.

The journey from comprehensive to political liberalism turns out to be a matter of running very hard to find oneself in more or less the same place. That does not mean the journey was wasted. For Rawls offers a distinctive and powerful argument for a partially comprehensive doctrine of ethical autonomy that derives not from speculative metaphysics or contestable intuitions about value but from a principle of reciprocity and a shared recognition of the limits of the reason we must employ with each other when we try to live by that principle. The distinctiveness of Rawls's new position depends not on its restricted generality and scope; it hinges instead on the particular case he makes for a partially comprehensive ethical doctrine with broad political implications.

Rawls's argument for his doctrine of autonomy is strictly political because it focuses exclusively on the public benefits that accrue to us by conceiving citizenship and public reason in a particular way. I say more in defence of Rawls's political argument in Sections 14 to 16. But regardless of what else might be said in its defence, the argument is incomplete so long as its focus remains exclusively political. Because the Rawlsian doctrine must shape our lives beyond politics in ways that Rawls does not explicitly acknowledge, we need to ask whether the autonomy we should cultivate in ourselves and our children makes our lives better or worse all things—not just the political things—considered. If the deepest sources of human good had little connection to politics, and if personal autonomy estranged us from these sources, then perhaps we should go back to the drawing-board and revise our theories of politics and civic virtue so that they did not require the cultivation of so unfortunate a disposition as autonomy. The development of a broadly ethical rather than a specifically political defence of autonomy is not Rawls's concern. But I want briefly to note one important way in which Rawls's work bears on that larger project.

Suppose for the moment that the political argument for autonomy is sound so far as it goes. That would leave us with a more manageable ethical question about the overall value of autonomy than we would otherwise have. The success of the political argument would mean that the justification of educational practices that encourage autonomy in future citizens does not require us to show that it is necessary to the good life, even under the general social conditions of modern liberal democracies. All that needs to be shown is that autonomy does not make our lives bad. For only if it had that consequence would we have grounds to think that the general liabilities of autonomy might outweigh its substantial political benefits as a necessary ingredient of the virtue of justice.

The claim that autonomy makes our lives bad might be pressed from many different perspectives. The most interesting general objections will identify some widely prized goods and try to show that the growth of autonomy is at odds with their realization. Recent communitarian objections to liberal conceptions of autonomy have taken this form, and these certainly deserve a careful response. But this takes me to the business of the next chapter.

# CHAPTER 3

## Autonomy, Justice, and the Good

### 14. Introduction

Good citizens have the virtue of justice. That is a truism. But the argument of Chapter 2 gave the truism a controversial twist. The justice we need under pluralism requires us to think for ourselves in a much more radical way than we must when all can take for granted the same conception of the good and the right. To give the respect due to ethical viewpoints in deep conflict with our own, we must learn to enter them imaginatively and to understand that much of the pluralism that permeates our social world is a consequence not of evil or folly but of the inherent limits of human reason. That is a pivotal idea in Rawls's political conception of the person, even though he is reticent about its full civic and educational significance. Since that conception amounts to a (partially) comprehensive doctrine of personal autonomy, the distinction between political and comprehensive liberalism has been undermined.

Rawls's abortive attempt to move beyond comprehensive liberalism is spurred by anxiety about the seemingly oppressive and divisive character of a liberalism that insists on the superiority of some wide-ranging ethical ideal that many people will conscientiously reject. But if political liberalism is merely a novel species of comprehensive liberalism, it may be renounced for the same reasons that motivated Rawls's blanket rejection of comprehensive liberalism in the first place, and again, education may seem to be a telling example of why rejection is justified. The state-sponsored pursuit of educational ends that conflict with many traditional religious and moral understandings will strike many people as oppressive and divisive, regardless of whatever political theory might be used in defence of the policy.

If we insist that political education be conceived so as to pose no such threat, we need a reading of the liberal democratic tradition to be transmitted through education that is far more circumspect than what we find in Rawls. But the retreat to a circumspect reading arouses the worry that in so doing we betray principles fundamental to free government in order to placate interests that are essentially hostile to it. This issue has deeply divided philosophers and political scientists who have recently written about political education. In their respective theories of democratic education, Patricia White and Amy Guttmann argue for an education strongly committed to securing the autonomy of future citizens (P. White 1983; Gutmann 1986: 48–70). Alternatively, William Galston, Loren Lomasky, and Shelley Burtt have claimed that the public interest in education is modest, and that policies that defer to parental values are morally necessary (Galston 1991*a*: 241–56; Lomasky 1987: 171–87; Burtt 1994, 1996). Rawls writes about education as if he wanted to commend a position akin to Galston's, Lomasky's, or Burtt's, although the logic of his political liberalism pushes him in the direction of White and Gutmann. I want to press some further considerations, drawn from the resources of Rawls's own theory, to suggest that that is broadly the right direction to take.

But here again, the distinction must be underlined between the ends that properly inform political education and the extent to which we should tolerate deviations from those ends in a world where reasonable and unreasonable pluralism are entangled and the moral costs of coercion against the unreasonable variety are often prohibitive. Our theoretical as well as our commonsense discourse do not always respect the distinction. But the distinction matters a lot. If some of the official teachings of the Roman Catholic Church conflict with our best theory of the ends of civic education, it does not follow that we have any reason to revise our theory; but neither does it mean we have any reason to impose those ends on Catholic schools and the families they serve.[1] My interest here is still confined to the ends of civic education on its best interpretation, and nothing can be directly inferred from that about the propriety of marshalling the power of the state against those who would reject the interpretation.

## 15. *Political Education and Constitutional Consensus*

A stable overlapping consensus on principles of justice and a companion agreement on methods of inquiry and reasoning that should govern their application is the aim of Rawlsian political liberalism. Rawls wants to offer us a conception of public reason that we could share together, despite the pluralism that divides us. But Rawls's project is defeated if its aim is utopian. The aim would be utopian for any society that lacked 'sufficient political, social or psychological forces either to bring about an overlapping consensus (when one does not exist), or to render one stable (should one exist)' (Rawls 1993: 158). Rawls tries to meet the objection by sketching a plausible two-stage historical process through which an overlapping consensus might evolve and become stable. The stages mark political conceptions that mould the character and conduct of citizens in increasingly powerful ways. So if we want a liberalism that lies more lightly, so to speak, on traditional sources of diversity than Rawls's political liberalism, we might try to find it within the earlier stage.[2]

The beginning of the first stage is what Rawls calls a modus vivendi on principles of justice; its terminus is a constitutional consensus. A modus vivendi obtains in a diverse society when reasons of mutual advantage persuade rival groups to agree on terms of cooperation sufficient to restrain open conflict, at least for the moment. A modus vivendi is lacking in genuine moral content, and the concord it establishes is easily broken because any shift in the distribution of power among groups is liable to make it rational for some to abandon the agreement in favour of renewed strife. If provisionally accepted principles of cooperation are to evolve into a genuine political morality, citizens must cease to affirm them merely on the basis of mutual benefit; instead, the principles must come to have an independent standing in deliberation, to be weighed against, and characteristically to outweigh, considerations of self- and group interest (Rawls 1993: 159). What might bring that transition about?

Rawls's answer is that over time the benefits that principles of cooperation make available may lead citizens to endorse them as a stable constitutional consensus, rather than a contingent strategy to advance factional aims. First, so long as cooperation is maintained merely for the sake of group interest, the insecurity and potential hostility of public life remain perilously high. But once a basic catalogue of rights and liberties is taken irrevocably outside the arena of political contest, the risks of the contest for everyone are dramatically lowered. The precarious benefits a modus vivendi offered are now guaranteed against the unpredictable contingencies of power among groups. Second, in the ongoing application of principles of cooperation, a limited public reason must take shape that relies on arguments and evidence acceptable to citizens generally. So far as the practice of public reason takes hold, partisan conflict will become more muted in public life (Rawls 1993: 161–2). Third, both these developments will tend to nurture the distinctive virtues of liberal coexistence: 'the virtue of reasonableness and a sense of fairness, a spirit of compromise and a readiness to meet others halfway, all of which are connected with the willingness to cooperate with others on political terms that everyone can publicly accept' (Rawls 1993: 163).

The persuasiveness of these three claims depends in part on a distinctive moral psychology which emphasizes reciprocal goodwill as a motive that is strengthened the more it is exercised. Rawls also assumes that many unreasonable doctrines that initially enter into a modus vivendi might gradually become reasonable because of the benefits to all that principles of justice make possible. Given these assumptions, Rawls says it is plausible to think that a modus vivendi will eventually give way to a constitution that would 'guarantee basic political rights and liberties and establish democratic procedures for moderating political rivalry, and for determining issues of social policy' (Rawls 1993: 163–4).

A constitutional consensus falls short of the aspirations of political liberalism because it is less deep and broad than a full-blown overlapping consensus: less deep because the parties to the consensus do not agree on underlying conceptions of person and society; less broad because its narrowly political range leaves many urgent questions about the basic structure completely untouched, such as the provision of economic necessities, the protection of intellectual liberty, as well as rights to speech and association where these have no clear political function (Rawls 1993: 164–5). All such matters are to be settled through the operation of majoritarian procedures. Yet precisely because it is shallow and narrow, a constitutional consensus will not require a political education whose ends directly challenge traditional moral and religious values. Because it asks so much less of us politically than an overlapping consensus, it seems to leave intact so much more of the cultural background of politics.

The limited aim of educating the young so as to protect a constitutional consensus would doubtless be accepted by the great majority of citizens in most contemporary liberal democracies. Once we argue for a political education that extends beyond that in either breadth or depth, the argument becomes controversial and the level of support we might expect dwindles rapidly. But does it follow that a political education limited to the maintenance of a constitutional consensus must be regarded as the less oppressive alternative to what Rawls's political liberalism would suggest? To answer the question we need to look closely at the possible drawbacks of that more limited education.

The protection of a constitutional consensus requires the development of some sense of justice in citizens' lives, although the justice it requires is a far less taxing ideal than the virtue discussed in Chapter 2 because it does not engage the complex family of dispositions and capabilities implicit in Rawls's political conception of the person. The issue is whether the less taxing version would be morally adequate. David Johnston has an argument that suggests it might be. He claims that the virtue of justice is independent of autonomy.[3] Johnston is not interested in defending the idea of a constitutional consensus; in fact, the reconstruction of liberal theory he recommends goes far beyond the confining boundaries of any such consensus. Johnston also writes perceptively on the connection between autonomy and wider questions about human well-being. I return to these later in this chapter and again in Chapter 5. My focus now is the relationship between autonomy and the virtue of justice. If Johnston were right in thinking that these are independent of each other, then political education under a constitutional consensus might well issue in a fully just citizenry without pushing us onto the morally controversial terrain of Rawlsian civic education. Johnston's argument does not succeed. But it is an instructive failure.

## 16. *Justice Without Autonomy*

According to Johnston, to see others as justice demands I must regard them as agents with projects and values of their own that are of moral consequence. To act justly I must regulate my conduct according to the moral importance of these projects and values. But having some sense of justice and being just in the manner and to a degree that suffice for the moral purposes of citizenship are not the same thing. Johnston acknowledges this. He says that universal possession of a sense of justice is not enough because in many cases it might be too weak or too narrow: it is too weak when the sense of justice is easily defeated by opposing desires and too narrow when only a restricted set of people are thought to fall within its purview (Johnston 1994: 72–4, 86). Another requirement has to be added. Some agreement is necessary on the substantive rights and duties we must honour in dealings with each other. A constitutional consensus accomplishes this. A shared, minimal list of political rights and acceptance of democratic procedures for resolving conflict give a core of common content to the sense of justice that citizens can endorse together.

Now consider Johnston's example of someone who has the virtue of justice without autonomy. Michael is born, raised, and lives his entire life in the same town. The career he chooses is the same as his father's, and when he marries and has children, he and his wife 'raise them in much the same way as other people from their town with backgrounds similar to theirs'. What makes Michael's life less than autonomous, however, is not its unrelenting conventionality but the shallowness of his thought about how he should live: 'He never seriously questions his fundamental values. . . . He is intelligent and he makes choices, but the choices he makes are mainly about the particulars of his life, rather than about his fundamental values or about his way of life as a whole' (Johnston 1994: 76). Johnston rightly insists that Michael could still have a sense of justice. In fact, he may have an impeccably strong and broad sense of justice. Nothing in his indifference or antipathy to the deeper ethical questions rules that out. If we also assume that the society in which he is born, lives, and dies is held together over time by a constitutional consensus, the sense of justice he develops will derive its primary political content from that consensus, and he will be a virtuous citizen according to the standard it provides.

The educational aims of a constitutional consensus might be fully accomplished in Michael's life. Are they morally adequate? Consider again the role of public reason in a constitutional consensus. The role is weak because public reason applies only to a small subset of fundamental political questions and requires no agreement on ideals of the person and society. Therefore, arguments that are acceptable to all will settle only a few features of the society's basic structure, with the rest to be determined by the free play of other social forces as these operate within the procedural framework of majoritarian politics. The large residue of matters left unresolved by public reason means there is ample room for ethnic or religious majorities or coalitions of minorities to rule in ways that systematically dominate others. Similarly, economic and other elites are at liberty to abuse public opinion to their liking within lax constitutional constraints. These possibilities might not come about under a constitutional consensus, but if they do not, that outcome will be a fortunate accident rather than a matter of political and educational design. Furthermore, what admits the possibilities of domination and manipulation is precisely the persistence in the background culture of values and practices at odds with the requirements of reasonableness. For domination is a denial of reciprocity, and a citizenry is primed for manipulation whenever it lacks the virtues of critical reason to resist fear-mongering and other manipulative political tactics.[4]

The openness of a constitutional consensus to domination and manipulation requires us to revise our initial thought that such a consensus, and the educational requirements it entails, would extend a more inclusive respect to established patterns of diversity than would the Rawlsian alternative. Whether or not a more inclusive respect is forthcoming will depend on the will of the majority. Minorities whose traditional educational aspirations are viewed with contempt or indifference by most people are unlikely to fare well in these circumstances.

Precisely because Michael falls unreflectively into received cultural patterns, and lacks the ability or inclination to do otherwise, he is blind to the oppression that might persist under a constitutional consensus. To that extent, his sense of justice is fundamentally defective as a virtue. The flaw is disguised in Johnston's description of the case because the description is so thin. Michael seems admirable if we imagine his life unfolding in some idyllic small town painted by Norman Rockwell, where the pieties of family, church, and neighbourhood are unthinkingly replicated from one generation to another, and everyone is perfectly happy and decent. But nothing in the given facts of Michael's life is incompatible with the complacent bigotry of a man who thinks that women count for much less than he does or that systematic discrimination against those who differ from him in race or religion is just fine. For his sense of justice need not affirm the full moral equality of all citizens so long as he lacks a full commitment to reciprocity, and a constitutional consensus does not require him to make that commitment.

I do not say that the sense of justice possible for those who lack autonomy is necessarily implicated in the maintenance of oppression. Autonomy is not the high road to all that is good nor is its absence a guarantee of evil. We can easily imagine a version of Michael's story in which the moral fabric of the culture that engulfs him is not corrupt. But then the adequacy of his sense of justice would be a matter of moral luck that he could not even know he had without a degree of autonomous reflection that would carry him far beyond his current moral innocence.

Johnston himself is not entirely comfortable with the breach between justice and autonomy that his depiction of Michael seems to exhibit. A bit later he suggests that there is an 'indirect' connection between the two. But the connection he affirms is still too weak:

Moreover, a person who is wholly unable to reappraise his projects and values would probably be incapable of having an effective sense of justice. . . . For in order to restrain his actions and claims in recognition of the fact that other human beings are agents with their own projects, values and claims, a person must be able to appraise his projects and values in a critical way. (Johnston 1994: 97)

So Michael's unreflective cast of mind cannot be quite so thorough as it initially seemed: he will 'probably' need to think occasionally about his fundamental values when they need to be adjusted because of the receptiveness to the claims of others that justice requires of him. But this seriously understates the pressure towards autonomy that justice exerts within the circumstances of pluralism. Those circumstances mean that the 'projects, values and claims' of the others to whom one owes justice are often very different from one's own; and that being so, a reliable understanding of what justice demands will require us to engage critically with the pluralism of our moral environment. The necessary autonomy is certainly compatible with a life that leaves much room for spontaneity and habitual engrossment in pursuits of many different kinds; it is consistent too with a thoughtful attachment to custom and a strong partiality for the familiar over the exotic. But it is still a more onerous autonomy than the capacity for occasional adjustments to basic values that Johnston seems to have in mind.

The ideals of person and society in which an overlapping consensus is grounded would militate against the domination of the relatively power-less by the relatively powerful. The more strenuous public reason it entails would also undermine, or at least greatly reduce, the political effi-cacy of manipulative persuasion. So institutions, like schools perhaps, that acquiesce in a constitutional consensus, forswearing any active role in the development of political morality towards an overlapping consensus, thereby leave a liberal political order acutely vulnerable to distortion in ways that are oppressive or conducive to social conflict.

The problems of oppression and social conflict under a constitutional consensus are worth distinguishing at this point because obvious strat-egies are available to address the second problem that merely disguise the first. A sentimental patriotism may be instilled that obscures relations of dominance while entrenching a tolerably stable constitutional regime, and schools have often played an important role in implementing that strat-egy. Indeed, the familiarity of the strategy reveals an important difficulty that Rawls ignores: How is the development of a deep and broad concep-tion of liberal politics to prevail against opposing cultural currents in an imperfectly liberal social setting? The taint of utopianism clings to Rawls's account of the evolution of an overlapping consensus because he imagines that process occurring in an environment without powerful forces that would arrest or reverse the process.

That oversight may explain why Rawls thinks political liberalism can be reconciled with an agenda for political education that is modest to the point of banality. If the virtues of liberal politics can be confidently expected to flourish as a constitutional consensus develops over time, the deliberate pursuit of controversial educational aims in schools or else-where is simply unnecessary. The gradual emergence of a common alle-giance to the political conception of the person can be safely left to the historical evolution of political morality. Yet once we acknowledge the power of countervailing cultural and economic pressures in any given society, we are also compelled to see its public institutions as sites of acute ethico-political conflict in which the triumph of liberal democratic values is by no means assured (Doppelt 1989: 842–51; Exdell 1994). No doubt some arenas of conflict will be far more important than the school, the economy being only the most obvious of these. But given its traditional role in the shaping of intellect and character, it would be absurd to infer that schools might somehow be insulated from friction between liberal ideals and opposing values in the larger social environment.

The compatibility of a constitutional consensus with massive domination and political manipulation exposes the moral limits of an education that simply acquiesces in these failings by aspiring no further than the perpetuation of the elementary political rights and democratic procedures. Of course, efforts in schools or elsewhere to encourage the virtue of reasonableness under a constitutional regime in which domination and manipulation abound will predictably lead to conflict with those whose convictions or interests are thereby imperilled. The decline of their convictions across generations or the defeat of their interests may be accurately described as a loss of diversity. But it does not follow that educational policies with these consequences are socially divisive in any sense that counts morally, much less oppressive. They are divisive only in that any attempt to curtail domination and manipulation will divide people who want to curtail them against people who would prefer that they not be curtailed. And there can be no oppression in the moulding of a character that would refuse to resort to domination or manipulation in dealing with fellow citizens and would resist these measures when others use them. In fact, a more promising corrective to oppression is hard to imagine.

Stuart Hampshire has astutely observed that *Political Liberalism* is too temperate and gentle a defence of the liberalism it champions (Hampshire 1993: 47). The gentle and temperate tone is in one respect appropriate to the book: in the well-ordered society on which Rawls serenely fixes his gaze, the pluralism within the background culture of public reason has been gently tempered by citizens' identification with the moral conception that occupies the foreground. But the conspicuous disparity between this reasonable pluralism and the historically established pluralisms we are familiar with is virtually ignored. In the imperfectly liberal societies we live in, an amicable reconciliation with existing sources of diversity is often not possible for those who prize liberal values. I think Hampshire's point is (or should be) that this cannot be overlooked if we want to construct a liberalism adjusted to the moral ambiguities of real diversity.

So far in this chapter I have tried to shore up the political argument for the conception of civic education implicit in Rawls's political liberalism. But as I noted in Section 13, the political argument is necessarily incomplete. If the education we should want for our children would transform the character of the self in ways that have large consequences for how they will live beyond the realm of civic responsibility, we need to ask about the overall value of the life that such a self could enjoy and not only about the political benefits that would flow from the desired transformation. Some familiar worries about autonomy have to be confronted once we ask about its broad ethical significance. I now turn to these.

## 17.  Autonomy and the Exaltation of Choice

The ideal of autonomy at the moral centre of liberal politics is said to give us an inflated picture of the significance of choice in good lives and to alienate us from some of the deepest aspects of human well-being. These are now common claims in the communitarian critique of liberalism. That critique embraces a range of disparate issues that are commonly confused, with the consequence that liberals and their communitarian adversaries end up talking past each other. My focus is narrow. I address only some moral arguments that communitarians have levelled against the values of autonomy and justice in liberal politics.[5]

Notice that the communitarian claims I just rehearsed might be true even if the political argument in defence of the doctrine of autonomy were faultless so far as it goes. The political argument purports to show that justice as a virtue under pluralism requires autonomy. But the autonomy that is required might come at a prohibitive ethical cost: the irrevocable loss of much that makes our lives good. Some communitarians would add that justice is really unattainable under a liberal regime or that liberalism assigns too large a role to justice in political morality. Yet even if communitarians were wrong about these additional matters, they might still be right about the inherent antipathy between autonomy and well-being. And if they were right about that, we would have strong reason to turn away from the pluralism of contemporary liberal societies, as Alasdair MacIntyre has recommended (MacIntyre 1981: 244–5; MacIntyre 1988: 157), in the hope of constructing more morally integrated communities in which a justice that consorts with our own good becomes once again a feasible achievement.

Consider a revised version of Michael's story. Instead of living his entire life in a state of heteronomous equanimity, as Johnston's tale suggests, this Michael learns during middle age seriously to examine the basic commitments of his life. These are no longer taken for granted as the virtual fate of someone born and reared in particular circumstances; he now sees them as revisable elements within one way of life among others, to be embraced or set aside according to the verdict of his own reason. Even if deliberation convinces him that the life he has lived is worthy of continued fidelity, fidelity will now cohere with a more explicit awareness of the many worthwhile possibilities he forfeits through fidelity. He now chooses his way of life in a sense that he did not when he lacked autonomy.

Whether this is good or bad for Michael, all things considered, will obviously depend in large part on how good or bad are the consequences that follow from his choices when he exercises his new-found autonomy. But the communitarian argument must do more than point to the sheer possibility that his choices might turn out badly in the long run. We also know that unreflective identification with tradition can be bad, even disastrous, for many people, and so we cannot adjudicate between autonomy and its alternatives merely on the basis of these abstract and variable possibilities. The target of communitarian criticism must rather be the change that necessarily takes place in people when they come to think of received cultural ties and responsibilities as objects of choice.

This takes us to Sandel's famous argument about the notion of the autonomous self that has supposedly exerted a corrupting influence on American political thought and practice in recent decades. What is essential to that idea, according to Sandel, is the assumption that the self is unencumbered by any ends prior to choice (Sandel 1982: 54–9, 1996: 2–5); and that assumption might seem to fit well with the accession of autonomy in my revised version of Michael's story. Autonomy appears to enable him to choose ends (or forgo them) that he had previously taken for granted as ineluctable constituents of his identity. But Sandel would have us believe that the enlarged scope for choice comes at a certain cost. The ideal of the unencumbered self rules out 'any view that regards us as obligated to fulfill ends we have not chosen—ends given by nature or God, for example, or by our identities as members of families, people, cultures, or traditions' (Sandel 1996: 12). Indeed, Sandel would say that the ideal does not merely block some worthwhile ends; it generates an alienated sense of our relation to all ends. The ideal declares that all are contingent possessions of the self, to be retained or disowned according to its sovereign choosing (Sandel 1982: 54–9).

Sandel says that the ideal of the unencumbered self has debilitating effects in many areas of our political and legal thought. But prominent among these is the eclipse of the principle of freedom of conscience by the more light-minded notion of free choice. The need to safeguard religious liberty was understood by America's Founders as a matter of respect for the religious character of 'encumbered selves'—individuals whose very identities are constituted by religious affiliation. If citizens understand themselves as 'claimed' by religious duties that differ according to the content of rival creeds, the dictates of conscience and law will collide unless the scope of political obligation is limited by respect for the wide range of conscientious judgement that different credal identities might motivate (Sandel 1990, 1996: 55–71). To suppose that respect for conscientious judgement can be translated without residue into regard for free choice is sheer confusion: 'But freedom of conscience and freedom of choice are not the same; where conscience dictates, choice decides. Where freedom of conscience is at stake, the relevant right is to exercise a duty, not make a choice' (Sandel 1996: 66).

Sandel says the difference between choice and conscience matters because once it is blurred the claims of those for whom religion is not an expression of autonomy are depreciated. The exercise of duty is construed as the mere pursuit of preference, with the consequence that duty is debased. He traces the alleged debasement in a series of US Supreme Court decisions in which the ideal of autonomy has loomed ever larger. Among the few exceptions to the trend, he cites the Court's decision in *Wisconsin* v. *Yoder* (1972) to permit the Old Order Amish not to send their children to school after the eighth grade. But even at that rare moment of judicial wisdom, Sandel detects the distracting voice of autonomy in the dissenting opinion of Justice Stevens, who insisted that the Amish adolescents should themselves be free to choose whether to continue their schooling or comply with their parents' wishes (Sandel 1990: 90–1).

Much of the criticism this has provoked is directed towards Sandel's thesis that liberal autonomy hinges on the bizarre metaphysics of the unencumbered self. The truth is surely that whatever reflection autonomy requires does not demand that we can detach ourselves from all our ends. The requirement is only that we be capable of asking about the value of any particular end with which we currently identify and able to give a thoughtful answer to what we ask (Kymlicka 1989*b*: 51–8; R. Dworkin 1989: 488–9; Macedo 1990: 105–31). Liberal theory invites us to conceive the self as revocably encumbered in the sense that we can reject ends currently constitutive of identity should we come to see them as worthless. Yet although this is importantly true, much of Sandel's argument can be recast as a case against the revocably encumbered self that liberal politics sponsors, and that is how I shall interpret it.

A curious feature of the argument is its highly contrived opposition between choice and conscience. Sandel writes as if each were an independent mental faculty, with mutually exclusive spheres of operation. The characteristic sin of the unencumbered (or revocably encumbered) self is allegedly to substitute the frivolity of choice for the gravity of conscience. But imagine how choice and conscience might be implicated in the emergence of autonomy in Michael's life. Suppose he comes to reject as immoral some established cultural norm he had never questioned before. In other words, his conscience tells him that he should act in defiance of that norm. That means he faces the choice of either enacting the dictates of his conscience or succumbing to the temptations of conformity. The accession of autonomy thus embodies a new exercise of conscience as well as a larger sense of the alternatives among which Michael must choose.

But these are twin aspects of a single transformation, rather than the discrete and opposing psychological phenomena that Sandel's argument would indicate.

The interdependence of choice and conscience in autonomy also suggests a different reading of Justice Stevens's opinion in *Wisconsin* v. *Yoder* than the one Sandel gives. If conscience and choice are tightly interwoven in the development and exercise of autonomy, Steven's insistence on the Amish adolescents' right to educational choice entailed no arbitrary elevation of the claims of choice over conscience. What distinguished Stevens's opinion was mainly his sensitivity to the importance of what the adolescents themselves conscientiously believed. His concern with the restriction of choice that an abbreviated schooling might impose can and should be understood in terms of the value of respect for individual conscience: we rightly suspect the genuineness of conscientious endorsement of a particular way of life when the endorsement is accompanied by overwhelming ignorance of alternatives. Stevens's opinion might have been misguided, but that cannot be because he wrongly thought conscience less important than choice.

At the root of Sandel's bifurcation of choice and conscience is the assumption that choice reigns when the will is unconstrained by a given order of value beyond the sheer contingency of individual desire. The authority of conscience seems senseless in the absence of such an order,[6] and therefore, the enlarged scope for choice that autonomy brings in its train pushes back the borders of conscience, depriving practical reason of its seriousness and making the value of all liberties depend on the vagaries of mere preference. But this is wrong. If the autonomous Michael finds himself torn between the comforts of conformity and the dictates of conscience, it is not because a wider range of choice gives greater room for the indulgence of brute desire. What autonomy has really compelled him to confront is a conflict between his socialized desires and his sense of a moral order whose authority can no longer be easily reconciled with those desires.

The conception of autonomy that Sandel's argument addresses is not the one that inheres in Rawlsian or any other morally credible liberalism. But neither is it a mere figment of his hostility to an autonomy-centred liberalism. The idea that all values are no more than objects of desire is a familiar piece of foolishness in contemporary Western cultures, and we shall encounter some of its educational manifestations in Chapter 8. Sandel is right to deplore the currency of this debased notion of autonomy. But an autonomy-centred liberalism is not debunked by discrediting its least credible conceptions.

## 18.  Choosing and Willing

The communitarian repudiation of autonomy (or liberal conceptions of autonomy) is directed at the process by which attachments properly construed as unchosen come to be seen as objects of choice. Sandel cannot justify the repudiation on the basis of a spurious contrast between choice and conscience. But 'object of choice' is ambiguous, and uncovering that ambiguity yields a different, and also a more substantial version of the communitarian argument than we have considered so far.

Meir Dan-Cohen has usefully distinguished two models of choice, and he shows how assigning an ethically privileged status to one over the other generates rival interpretations of autonomy (Dan-Cohen 1992). In what he calls 'choice as choosing', the agent confronts a choice-set—a given array of more or less eligible options—and must select one on the basis of her preferences. That means ranking the options according to their relative desirability, and then taking the one that gets the highest ranking. Not all choice is like this; many express categorical rather than competitive valuation. This is 'choice as willing': 'I find in it [the object of willing] a perfection or an incontestable suitability which, because of its uniqueness, is not threatened by its competition with other contestants' (Dan-Cohen 1992: 230).

Rescuers of Jews in Nazi-occupied Europe typically claim they had 'no choice' but to help the people they saved (Monroe, Barton, and Klingemann 1990). The point surely is not that they did not choose at all, as one might if insane or sleep-walking; their words are more naturally understood as saying that their conduct was an instance of willing, not choosing. They did not survey items in a choice-set, rank their options, and then decide to help the Jews because that course of action was the most desirable member of the set. Their conduct expressed a categorical rather than a comparative valuation, and so the alternatives to their altruistic conduct never counted as eligible options at all. No doubt the rescuers were exceptional people, but that is not because their willing was exceptional. For willing is a commonplace phenomenon in even our unsaintly lives. The choices we typically make in cultivating friendships or other forms of intimate relationship, in creative endeavour, or even at less high-minded moments when the aptness of what we choose does not depend on rational comparison of the members of a choice-set, all show that willing is as ordinary an aspect of our experience as choosing. I do not choose my friends by making fine comparative judgements about the attractiveness of possible candidates for friendship, dropping some and selecting others as my choice-set expands or contracts when new contenders come along and old ones disappear. I would have no real friends if that were my attitude because real friendship entails a loyalty that is inconsistent with the mind-set of choice as choosing.

The distinction between willing and choosing does not mesh closely with the contrast between conscience and choice on which Sandel attempts to erect his argument against liberal autonomy. Conscience often operates through choosing rather than willing, as when we agonize about which is the lesser of two evils; and willing may apply to many decisions of the kind that Sandel associates with choice—namely, those in which sheer desire or taste permissibly determines conduct. But the difference between choosing and willing discloses an argument that does bear a resemblance to Sandel's and may express more perspicuously the anxieties about autonomy that motivate his. If willing is necessary to the enjoyment of some fundamental human goods, and coming to think about our lives as autonomous agents would tend to substitute choosing for willing, then the process that would replace willing is to that extent an evil.

The development of autonomy in my revised story of Michael might seem to be a case in point. Perhaps Michael thought that what made his life good was categorically so. He did not entertain the possibility of enjoying a more fulfilling career, a better marriage than the one he had drifted into, or a religion closer to the truth than the one his parents had taught him. But now he does. Therefore, even if he decides to stay in his job, remain with his wife, and keep the faith, his life might appear to have become a theatre of choosing rather than willing. The fear of some such transformation is doubtless familiar to many who resist educational practices that would expose their children to alternatives to a prescribed way of life. After all, it is one thing to be taught to identify with a particular religion categorically as the locus of meaning and fulfilment for human beings always and everywhere; it is another to learn to see it as the most attractive item on a menu of spiritual possibilities, to be chosen only so long as it maintains its edge over the competition.

Dan-Cohen claims that conceptions of autonomy that stress choosing at the expense of willing are inimical to the depth of commitment that is proper to a truly self-directed life. Real commitment to a way of life entails the foreclosure of options at odds with commitment. But conceptions of autonomy that exalt choosing make all commitment a constraint on the agent's autonomy, even when the commitment is voluntary. This does not mean choosing agents must remain forever disengaged; they might decide the benefits of engagement are worth the costs of constraint. The trouble is that engagement must always contend with a psychological enmity between choosing and deep commitment (Dan-Cohen 1992: 235–6, 240–1). If autonomous control of my life is simply a sustained process of rational choosing, I must always be ready to seize the opportunity of some expansion of my choice-set that would justify discarding current choices in favour of new and more desirable options, and that will naturally encourage a certain hesitation and fickleness in my current choices. The apparent triumph of choosing at the expense of willing in the liberal conception of autonomy might then compel us to agree with Stephen Macedo: 'Liberalism holds out the promise, or the threat, of making all the world like California' (Macedo 1990: 278). But maybe Hollywood rather than California would be a more precise cultural paradigm, and perhaps the threat is rather more lowering than the promise is inspiring.

A good life seems scarcely possible if choosing were to dominate deliberation because categorical valuation is not conceptually separable from love, friendship, or more expansive human loyalties. But autonomy in the sense relevant to my argument bears no simple relation to the process by which willing might be relegated to the periphery of our lives. That becomes clear once we see that the growth of autonomy in Michael's case might well induce him to adopt some forms of conduct as a matter of willing that he had previously assigned to the realm of choosing. If the customs of his society said that a man could beat his wife and children at his own discretion, and Michael gave up unreflective acceptance of that norm in favour of categorical condemnation of the conduct it licensed, then to that extent autonomy issues in willing at the cost of choosing. Autonomy in the sense that counts here is about the capability and inclination to reason for oneself, and to shape one's life on the basis of the deliverances of reason. Nothing in the process by which autonomy might take hold in our lives entails an alienating contraction within the sphere of choice as willing. On the contrary, so far as we have reason to want a life in which our deepest choices are instances of willing, those reasons will properly weigh heavily with us in autonomous reflection on how we should live.

Furthermore, although Dan-Cohen is right to say that willing does not strictly require a choice-set (Dan-Cohen 1992: 231), our interest in responsible choice, especially under the conditions of pluralism, will rightly incline us to episodic reflection on real or imagined alternatives to the objects of our willing. By 'responsible choice' I mean choosing and willing that picks out objects of volition that warrant the commitment we make to them. The interest we might have in enjoying a life in which many of our most crucial choices take the form of willing rather than choosing is surely conditional; we want the objects of our categorical valuations to be worthy of choice. That is why we can admire and envy the single-minded altruism of the rescuers, and yet be appalled by the equally tenacious commitment of many Nazis. To will responsibly is to choose with the knowledge that just because we have been taught to cherish something does not necessarily make it worthy of choice. Therefore, we cannot responsibly avoid the challenge to the correctness of our choices that obtains whenever many irreconcilable values engage the wills of different people who may be every bit as reasonable as we are. Michael's autonomous reflections on alternatives to his own way of life will be a matter of confronting that challenge, given that his willing is truly responsible.[7]

The conditional character of responsible choice does mean that in a sense our commitments must be 'detachable'; we choose on the condition that what we embrace merits choice, and that means we must be ready to reconsider should we come to see that we were mistaken (Kymlicka 1990: 201). But as Jeremy Waldron has noted, the detachability of commitment is not the same as superficiality: 'Having the capacity to reflect means *being able to make an effort* when one needs to, to wrench away and construct the necessary psychological distance. It does not require a continuous reserve of commitment and energy that could have been associated with one's attachment but is not' (Waldron 1990: 646–7, original italics; cf. Sandel 1982: 62). Responsible choice is not holding something back emotionally; it is simply the effective recognition that what is categorically valued might not be categorically valuable, and that if our lives are to be good we might need sometimes to think for ourselves about the possible gap between the two.[8]

Suppose we agree that autonomy need not inflate the sphere of choosing at the cost of willing; that responsible choice, given pluralism, will pull us towards autonomy anyway; and that the detachability of autonomous commitment implies no emotional parsimony in our relation to what we choose. These conclusions do not carry us beyond all that should disturb us in the communitarian critique of liberal autonomy. The conditions under which autonomy develops and is exercised might yet tend to induce a kind of fragmentation of the self, depriving our lives of an ethical coherence and rootedness we might otherwise achieve. These lost goods constitute a certain ideal of integrity that is available to us only when we see received roles and responsibilities rather differently than autonomy allows. MacIntyre gestures towards some such ideal in his charge that liberal individualism divests our lives of the kind of narrative unity we need in order to live meaningfully (MacIntyre 1981: 205–9). I think there is some truth to this. Autonomy might conflict with one alluring kind of integrity—call it simple integrity—but it is not the only kind, and it is unnecessary to our well-being.

## 19. Simple Integrity

Someone has simple integrity when three conditions hold. First, the roles with which the individual identifies circumscribe her pursuit of the good closely and locate that good within the shared practices of her community. Second, the responsibilities her roles entail are harmonized, so that there is ordinarily no or at most modest friction between them. Third, the individual identifies wholeheartedly with the role or configuration of roles that structures her life, and she lives in close fidelity to its requirements. That is not just to say that her commitment is characterized by a high degree of assurance; truly wholehearted commitment is also untainted by hypocrisy, self-deception, or evasion.

Membership of a particular religion is a role that commonly entails acceptance of the ideal of simple integrity, even if the ideal is only roughly approximated in the lives of most ordinary believers. The role gives a steady focus to one's pursuit of the good inside a community of like-minded people. Faith imposes the necessary harmony on the domain of responsibilities because its demands are accorded a paramount status in deliberation, and a coherent interpretation is provided of the significance of other attachments. The condition of wholeheartedness is affirmed in that the individual must be genuinely devoted to God or her gods if the demands of faith are to be met. So when a distinguished philosopher of religion, who also happens to be a Presbyterian minister, suggests that Christians must bring Jesus along on their honeymoon, especially on their honeymoon, he is not joking (Adams 1986: 188–9). Those of us who do not share his faith may smile, but that is only because we share the liberal assumption that all roles, whether it be as lover of this person or worshipper of that god, are discrete spheres of engagement among which the autonomous agent freely moves—or aimlessly flits. But some will say that our assumption merely betrays the prejudice of those who have forgotten the value of simple integrity.

Consider how the value of simple integrity might be used to argue against an education that would conduce to autonomy. The child who is born into a conservative religious family need not have made any independent choice to be a member of her particular religion for membership to be the supreme commitment that determines her good. By the time she is capable of choice, her religion already constitutes what MacIntyre calls 'the given starting-point' for pursuit of the good (MacIntyre 1981: 204–5). And if part of the value membership provides is simple integrity, there is reason to argue that induction into her role as one of the faithful should not have to pull against the appeal of rival values. To subject her faith to that crisis would be to endanger the wholehearted commitment upon which simple integrity depends. Notice that to accept this conclusion one need not take a favourable view of whatever metaphysical pretensions the child's faith might entail. The argument only asks of us to accept the centrality of simple integrity to the good life and that virtue's dependence on a particular kind of social and educational setting.

## 20. *Integrity and Pluralism*

I approach the question of the value of simple integrity indirectly by looking at an example of a life in which it is instantiated; then I compare it with a life in which is has been lost.

My example of simple integrity is Jacob of Josefov, the protagonist of Isaac Bashevis Singer's novel, *The Slave* (Singer 1980*a*). Jacob's story takes place in seventeenth-century Poland in the years immediately after a Cossack invasion. Jacob's family was slaughtered, and he has been sold into slavery far from his native village. There he tries to maintain his faith despite total isolation from his fellow Jews, recurring doubt about the goodness of God, and his love for Wanda, a gentile who shows him great kindness during his enslavement. Although Jacob is ransomed by the Jews of Josefov, he secretly returns to the village of his captivity after a dream that Wanda is pregnant. The Torah requires this, since he cannot allow his child to grow up among idolators. Jacob and Wanda flee together and begin a new life in a remote village. Wanda has converted and is now Sarah, Jacob's pious wife. But her original identity must be kept secret, since the penalty for conversion under Polish law is death. Sarah dies in childbirth, although not before the fact of her conversion is disclosed. So Jacob must run away with his newborn child, isolated once again from his people. But at another level, Jacob continues to belong to his people, and his sense of belonging is powerful even as he flees. Recalling the words of his biblical namesake upon his deathbed, Jacob sees his own tragedy as but another enactment of a story that is part of the history of God's inscrutable dealings with his chosen people:

His name was Jacob also; he too had lost a beloved wife, the daughter of an idolator, among strangers; Sarah too was buried by the way and had left him a son. Like the Biblical Jacob, he was crossing the river, bearing only a staff, pursued by another Esau. Everything remained the same: the ancient love, the ancient grief. Perhaps four thousand years would again pass; somewhere, at another river, another Jacob would walk mourning another Rachel. (Singer 1980*a*: 258–9)

The emotional resonance of this passage, and indeed the novel as a whole, depends on its evocation of a mode of life in which individual experience is invested with the significance of an immemorial narrative, and thereby rescued from the pointlessness of brute suffering. Jacob is the very antithesis to the ethically disinherited children described by MacIntyre, cast adrift by an upbringing that leaves them 'unscripted, anxious stutterers in their actions as in their words' because they have not been initiated into a world of narratively structured roles (MacIntyre 1981: 201). In Jacob's case, his role as one of the chosen people is the supreme commitment of his life, and all his experience is enmeshed with the story of Jews who accepted the burdens of that role before him and those who will accept them after he dies—his biblical namesake as well as the Jacob who will mourn another Rachel four thousand years hence. Despite his status as an outcast, his love and grief are not the emotions of a solitary man but 'the ancient love, the ancient grief' of all who have contended with suffering and evil while submitting to the authority of God.

So Jacob very obviously meets the first two conditions of simple integrity. His understanding of the good is fixed by the shared understandings of his community, and the roles in terms of which he defines his good entail no conflicting responsibilities because one role is absolutely sovereign. Jacob also evinces the wholeheartedness that simple integrity demands. One might be inclined to deny or at least qualify that claim because of the religious doubts which beset him throughout much of the novel. But there are different ways in which engagement with a particular role may be subject to doubt, and not all of these can be aptly viewed as a dilution of simple integrity. Although Jacob is sometimes racked with doubt, his honest and considered view is that this is merely the work of Satan. Thus he never identifies with his own doubts, never allows them to become part of the fabric of his commitments and beliefs. Doubt is a potent force in his life, but it is understood as an utterly alien thing, at odds with that true self who will follow wherever God leads. This purely episodic doubt is very different from misgivings that come to qualify a belief in the propriety of a particular role commitment. The man who arrives at the considered view that his doubts about the existence of God are well-grounded can no longer find his true self unambivalently in religious practice, unlike Jacob who 'can forget the fool within, with his fruitless questions' (Singer 1980*a*: 104).

If we insisted that immunity to even episodic doubt were necessary to the wholeheartedness of simple integrity, we would have an absurdly demanding condition of that virtue. But it does seem reasonable to say that simple integrity is destroyed when doubt about our commitments becomes a settled qualification to them. When that happens in the case of religious conviction, for example, one can no longer be confident that the self who worships (or tries to) rather than the self who doubts is not 'the fool within'. There is no longer a sharply delineated true self, pitted against the menacing forces of doubt; instead the self is simply a site for inconclusive warfare between faith and its enemies. There may be room for integrity here, but it could not be simple integrity.

My foil for Jacob of Josefov is his creator. The story of Isaac Bashevis Singer exhibits a very different pattern to the life of Jacob, despite obvious common ground. Singer was born into a devout Jewish family in Poland, and the doubts that assailed Jacob afflicted Singer at a very early age. But for Singer there could be no final victory over doubt. His brother introduced him to secular literature and modern science, and although these did not give him a creed he could live with, they further alienated him from the faith of his parents. That faith remained a thing to be admired, but from a distance that Singer himself could not traverse. The young man whom he describes in his autobiographical *Love and Exile* lives a life so chaotic that it borders on comedy. He is a philanderer with ascetic leanings, whose reading ranges from the Cabala to contemporary novels, and whose restless imagination seems the only fixed point in his identity. By the time the book ends, Singer's career as a writer in America is under way; but as an exile from his homeland and the traditions of his forbears, there can be none of the moral poise of Jacob of Josephov as he flees his community. *Love and Exile* closes with Singer's poignant declaration that he is 'lost in America, lost forever' (Singer 1984: 352).

The vocation of the artist does give shape to the story of this avowedly lost soul. But this is not a role with established conventions that closely circumscribe one's pursuit of the good and place one in a community with shared moral understandings. So even if Singer's commitment to his art were passionate and unambivalent, this would provide only a faint parallel to Jacob's integrity. The twentieth-century novel is a place where voices talk about everything in every possible way, as Salman Rushdie has said (Rushdie 1991: 428). That is certainly true of Singer's fiction and the mercurial self to whom it gives expression. For although he can sympathetically portray the virtues of Jacob of Josefov, he can also celebrate the implacable scepticism and contempt for tradition of a man who is Jacob's spiritual opposite (Singer 1980*b*). The world of Singer's imagination is shot through with moral ambiguity, and although good and evil are his abiding preoccupation he does not pretend to see them with the precision and certainty of Jacob.

Perhaps the deepest contrast between Jacob and Singer is revealed when we think of their lives in terms of MacIntyre's metaphor of the good life as a quest (MacIntyre 1981: 203). That metaphor has been taken by some to indicate a creeping liberalism in MacIntyre's thought (J. White and P. White 1986: 157–8; Macedo 1990: 327), as if what he had in mind were an open-ended search for life's meaning on the model that Singer's memoir might illustrate. But the quest MacIntyre envisages is informed from its beginning by some partly determinate sense of the ultimate end of human life, and progress in the quest is measured by the gradual real-ization of that end, as well as an unfolding understanding of its personal significance. Jacob's story is just such a quest. His task is to follow wher-ever God leads because he is God's 'slave'. His death as a man who main-tained simple integrity against the temptations of the world is the consummation of his long journey. On the other hand, when Singer con-fronts his future as a man who is 'lost forever' I take him to mean that insofar as his life can be construed as an ethical quest it is an irrevocable failure. People who cannot understand their lives in relation to a para-mount good higher than whatever else the world has to offer—the *telos* of human life, as MacIntyre would have it—can have no clear and constant sense of when they are moving towards or away from the good; and when that loss of direction is felt with grief or regret it will be natural to describe one's predicament, as Singer does, through images of disorientation or abandonment.

A life of integrity must exhibit some inner consistency or unity. We might compare such a life to a work of art that dissolves into absurdity in the absence of some overarching unity that makes it more than the sum of its parts. A musical composition cannot be just an assemblage of notes or phrases, a poem is not merely a rubble of words and images; and a life of integrity must be more than a random series of actions and experiences. Simple integrity may be seen as ensuring the necessary unity of a good or meaningful life. One might say that good lives express who we are, and then it might be tempting to add that without simple integrity there is nothing sufficiently determinate to express. Comparing lives with respect to unity, like comparing works of art along that dimension, may often be idle. But we are on very safe ground in saying that there is a lot more cohe-sion in Jacob's life than in Singer's, and that Singer's life seems perilously close to disintegration. And even if our own lives are rather more like Singer's than Jacob's, we may be inclined to contemplate the gap between us and Jacob with some of Singer's feeling at the end of *Love and Exile*: we too are lost in America, so to speak.

But these thoughts cannot amount to a credible argument for saying that simple integrity is the only integrity. A life can certainly descend into absurdity when riven by conflict between radically disparate roles or the kind of anomie which threatens to overwhelm Singer in his youth. Yet the sheer singleness of purpose of those with simple integrity is not the only alternative to absurdity. The analogy between the unity of a good life and the unity of a work of art is indeed a revealing one. But the trouble with equating integrity with simple integrity is that the equation does not take that analogy seriously enough.

Suppose a critic compares one of the great, sprawling novels of the nineteenth-century, *War and Peace* perhaps, with some clever little novella that belabours a single theme, and she deprecates Tolstoy's masterpiece for its comparative lack of unity. That would be a gross mistake. One might be tempted to object that there are other criteria of aesthetic excellence than unity—complexity or the like—and that *War and Peace* is peerless by these other standards. But that would be to concede too much to the critic because it would suggest that so far as unity goes she is right when surely she is wrong. What she does not understand is that the spacious structure of an epic novel can accommodate many diverse themes, weave together different and contrasting stories, without lapsing into absurdity, and at its best may achieve a depth which is itself a precious kind of unity. 'Depth involves discerning an underlying unity among apparently complex and unrelated phenomena' (Kekes 1990: 440). Of course, the unity of aesthetic depth can also be achieved by a narrow focusing of purpose. There is Kafka as well as Tolstoy, Racine as well as Shakespeare. But if the unity of a work of art is to be our model for that unity of a life to which we might rationally aspire, there seems no reason to suppose that a richly variegated life such as Singer's, which combines many diverse ideals and affinities into an intricate whole, might not achieve the kind of unity worth having.

Moreover, comparing Jacob and Singer with respect to the integration of their lives is only indirectly relevant to the real possibilities of integrity that each life affords. In an important recent article, Cheshire Calhoun proposes that standing for one's own best judgement about how to live, rather than the integration of the self, is the core of integrity (Calhoun 1995). This seems right. The religious doubts that torment Jacob in the wake of the Cossack massacres are part of the evidence for his integrity. His doubts are part of his struggle to form his best judgement about how to live in a particular deliberative setting. Singer contrasts Jacob's spiritual travails with the complacency and self-deception of those Jews who resumed their lives as if nothing important had happened. The faith that survives Jacob's ordeal of doubt is truly wholehearted, in the sense I stipulated above, not only by virtue of its ultimate assurance but also because it does not depend on the evasion of disturbing possibilities that others lacked the courage to face (Singer 1980*a*: 101–6). If the integration of a life were the key to integrity, then Jacob's self-satisfied fellow Jews would be the paragons of that virtue, and his wrenching doubts would be a stain on his integrity rather than its exemplary expression. A life of integrity requires an inner consistency or unity *only* to whatever extent standing for one's best judgement does.

But the human world that Singer so artfully creates in *The Slave* is not our world of pluralism. It is a world of sharp moral polarities of the kind we might find in an ancient folk tale, devoid of all gradation and ambiguity. Beyond the borders of Jacob's faith and the quest it enjoins, Singer depicts a nightmare of unremitting evil and ugliness, populated by bestial peasants and dissolute nobles. The moral contrasts that frame Singer's narrative are part of what persuades us to see Jacob as a man of simple integrity: someone struggling to form his best judgement about how to live in *this* world could not but choose as Jacob did, or so we are invited to think. But then the charm of simple integrity begins to seem like so much idle nostalgia. For our moral world is replete with gradations and complexities, a world in which reasonable people reach very different conclusions about the good and the right, and yet all must find some basis for a decent society in which they might live together. Reading a novel set in premodern Poland relieves us of worries about the voting habits that Jacob of Josefov might have if he lived among us. But someone who regards all gentiles as little more than benighted idolaters is perhaps unlikely to exhibit civility we would want.

The process of forming one's best judgement about how to live depends on careful assessment of the reasons available in a given social setting for living one way rather than another. That is why I cannot form my own best judgement without a keen, albeit critical regard for the best judgement of those who share the milieu within which I must choose (Calhoun 1995: 259–60). But reasonable pluralism means that the best judgement of many will be both very different from mine and yet defensible, and to pretend otherwise where reasonable pluralism holds is sheer bad faith.

This is the truth in Bernard Williams's much quoted observation that for us there is no route back from reflectiveness (Williams 1985: 163–4). As an empirical generalization, Williams's claim is false. Many if not most of us are still sufficiently unreflective that the question of whether to go back or not does not even arise, and we often raise our children so as to pre-empt the question for them too. Powerful forces in contemporary societies—from the revival of ancient tribalisms to the atomizing tendencies of a global economy—may further erode the social space for individual and collective thoughtfulness in our lives (Barber 1995). But Williams's observation can be read as expressing an important ethical truth: so long as reasonable pluralism obtains, the attempt to formulate one's best judgement about how to live must proceed in light of due reflection on the conflicting judgements of reasonable others, who may understand something important we ourselves have yet failed to grasp. We cannot change that predicament simply by silencing them or pretending that their thoughts are irrelevant to our integrity. Therefore, an education that seeks to arrest the development of autonomy so as to protect the growth of simple integrity runs the risk of being self-defeating. Such an education might well succeed in instilling the moral assurance that simple integrity entails, but only at the cost of entrenching a complacency or close-mindedness that is destructive of real integrity, simple or otherwise.

Unlike Jacob, Singer came to occupy a milieu of reasonable pluralism, initially through reading secular literature, and the result was that a life of simple integrity was no longer possible for him. To be sure, even the individual who fits the pattern of Singer must impose some order upon his life, sorting through the ambivalences and hesitations that respect for the best judgement of others will tend to elicit, and this cannot be done by harmonizing all possible values into some optimum composite. Yet if one lives in consciousness of the variety of good lives, it is natural to want to encompass many values in one's life, and so instead of the tight cohesion of a life of simple integrity one ends up with a pattern rather more messy and unsteady, but perhaps richly fulfilling for all that, and just as expressive in its own way of respect for an ethical order that is not reducible to the projections of individual desire.[9]

Paradoxically, those who live with an openness to the diversity of good lives will also be conscious of the losses which their openness exacts. If simple integrity is itself within the category of such lives, its loss may be felt with the pathos of Singer at the end of *Love and Exile*. But on reflection one may decide that the gains offset the loss or that what is lost is not a real option anyhow. Giving up on the good life as a linear quest may occasion a painful feeling of disorientation. But it may also yield a powerful sense of liberation.

## 21. Autonomy and the Good: A Modest Convergence

I have argued that autonomy is an ideal unscathed by a battery of communitarian objections that suggest its realization would alienate us from the good. But my modest thesis is only that the autonomy required by the development of justice need not make our lives bad; I do not say the autonomy intrinsic to justice is needed to make our lives good. The relation between autonomy and integrity that I sketched in Section 20 might appear to support the more ambitious thesis that autonomy is essential to our good under pluralism. If forming my own best judgement about how to live requires me to reflect autonomously on the judgements that others make and on the criticisms they might level against mine, then how can a good life be possible at all if I shirk the requirement?

The range of things that make our lives good are many and various. Plausible monistic theories of the good, such as the subtler forms of utilitarianism, cannot deny this. They only acquire some credibility by accepting the diversity of goods, and then telling a story about how the diversity disguises a unity that is revealed by the right theory (Becker 1992). Now the quality of anyone's judgement about how to live could hardly be more than one important element in the goodness of her life. If we could trade-off some autonomy to ensure that our children turned out well and did not die before us, I suspect that almost all of us would do so without thinking that might be a poor bargain. To say this is not to go back on my claim that under pluralism autonomy is deeply implicated in the virtue of integrity. But the value of maximal integrity may sometimes be an unreliable guide to what would make our lives good or better, all things considered, given the great variety of things that affect our well-being.

There is a difference between forming my best judgement about how to live and arriving at the judgement that is merely good enough, so to speak. The fact that some of the more philosophically inclined among us may say that only the best judgement will suffice does not mean that our cerebral idiosyncracies reveal the final truth about the good life for anyone, much less everyone. Some significant degree of autonomous development might be necessary to our well-being, even if it is not quite the radical and wide-ranging autonomy associated with the virtue of justice. That is likely for a couple of reasons that have already been touched on. A good life could not be devoid of integrity, although it might fall well short of maximal integrity, and a good life could hardly be lived in utter disregard of the conditions of responsible choice. Given the connection between integrity and responsible choice on the one hand and autonomy on the other, a life that spurns autonomy altogether and is yet good seems scarcely imaginable. This is an important idea that I set aside for the moment. I return to it in Chaper 6, where it is central to my discussion of parents' and children's rights in education.

The point to be emphasized here is that the ambitious thesis about the convergence between autonomy and the good is simply irrelevant to what I want to say about the proper ends of political education. The core of my argument is the thesis that the development of the virtue of justice under pluralism implies the growth of autonomy to a notably sophisticated level. We would have strong reason to reject an education that encourages that process if the autonomy at issue made our lives bad as a rule. Some communitarian arguments suggest that autonomy does make our lives bad, but these have turned out to be entirely unconvincing. Therefore, we have no grounds to revise the conception of civic education that Rawls's political conception of the person would warrant. The proposal that the very substantial degree of autonomy justice demands of us is also essential to our well-being is beside the point and probably false.

# CHAPTER 4

## Justice, Care, and Community

### 22. Introduction

The voice of justice is the loudest and most insistent in the public morality of liberal democracies, and rights are what it talks about. The principles of justice we strive to construct and apply in public reason specify the rights and duties that belong to citizens. But much feminist scholarship in recent years has suggested that the voice of justice, with its often querulous demands about who is entitled to what, is at the very least not the only one that merits our attention. Many have advocated an 'ethic of care' as an alternative moral voice to justice, and one whose neglect in theories of moral development and the practice of education may be profoundly damaging. Carol Gilligan's iconoclastic book, *In a Different Voice*, remains the most influential expression of these ideas (Gilligan 1982). Gilligan says that our very survival in the perilous world of the late twentieth century may depend far less on the realization of justice than on the cultivation of caring connections (Gilligan 1987: 32).

In Chapter 8 I examine some aspects of the education now advocated by those who argue for the priority of caring over justice. Here I address the more basic issue of the relation between caring and justice in public virtue, and hence, how they they might be conceived as ends of political education. My allusions to 'public' virtue and 'political' education will strike a discordant note for some because among the cardinal themes of recent feminist theory and activism has been scepticism about the customary distinctions in liberalism between public and private, the political and the personal. Kate Millet is a representative example: 'the term "politics" shall refer to power-structured social relationships, arrangements whereby one group of persons is controlled by another' (Millett 1970: 23). The point of the stipulation is well taken so far as it is intended to raise traditionally ignored questions about oppression in families and other supposedly private associations. No credible conception of justice could now deny that questions about violence in families, say, are politically relevant. All inequalities of power and control are of political interest once they create significant vulnerability to abuse and domination that a just society would seek to control. But a polity responsive to the value of pluralism will still need to distinguish between aspects of personal and social life that are properly subject to the power we hold and use together as citizens and aspects that are not. Millet's own strictures on the legal prohibition of homosexuality is an instance of that necessary distinction (Millett 1970: 337). A feminism that honours pluralism cannot annihilate the distinction between the political and the personal, the public and the private, and it will not assume that questions about civic virtue implicitly appeal to entrenched patriarchal dichotomies.

I claim that the bifurcation of morality into separate perspectives of care and justice, whether in civic or in other settings, is a mistake. The justice we need is itself grounded in a certain kind of care, and the care we should want, even in our most emotionally intense relationships, is properly shaped by the virtue of justice. This is not to deny the important possibility that our established patterns of moral thought and expression might engage different voices, some of which proclaim a crudely legalistic justice divorced from care and others a care that discounts rights. My point is only that neither the care nor the justice worth having can be adequately characterized in abstraction from the other; therefore, in the world we should want for ourselves and our children, justice and care blend into a common voice. Finally, I ask about the relation between the care internal to the virtue of justice and the care that inheres in attachment to particular political communities. That is the large and difficult question of patriotism, and its complexities will carry us forward into Chapter 5.

## 23. Towards a Common Voice

What does it mean for care to be a distinctive 'voice' or 'orientation' in morality that rivals the traditional authority of justice as the master-virtue of social cooperation? Calhoun's answer is helpful: moral orientations are 'loosely defined sets of concepts, themes, and theoretical priorities—which we understand sufficiently well to pick out who is speaking from which orientation, but which are not so rigid as to preclude a great deal of disagreement within each orientation' (Calhoun 1988: 451 n.). The possibility of 'a great deal of disagreement' within an agreed orientation is important because it means that some interpretations of the orientation will be better than others once they have the stronger case in whatever disputes arise within its agreed structure. Therefore, we can learn little simply by comparing 'the ethic of care' and 'the ethic of justice' in a way that abstracts from the disagreements internal to each since that comparison would inevitably blur the best that each putative orientation might offer. The question that really counts is about what might distinguish the best conceptions of each. But if we were in a position to identify a plausible conception of either, we might also find that we could no longer see the distinction between the so-called ethics of care and justice well enough 'to pick out who is speaking from which orientation'. I claim that this is in fact what will happen because care is basic to justice and morally commendable care cannot be divorced from the justice we need.

We do not care for others in some uniform, context-free manner; we care for them under different descriptions—as lovers, friends, compatriots, and the like (Callan 1988: 7–12). And any list of possible descriptions itself disguises an abundant diversity of attachment, since there are so many different loves, friendships, patriotic attachments, and so on. Some of these will be admirable while others are deservedly regarded with contempt. If I care for my wife merely as a source of domestic service, emotional solace, and sexual gratification, my care is morally infantile. The common denominator of the many affective connections that qualify as caring could only be the thinnest of abstractions, and that could not be a serviceable criterion of good character or right conduct. The bare concept of care tells us nothing morally interesting; the resources of the orientation must rather be found in the distinctive cluster of less abstract concepts, themes, and priorities for which 'care' is no more than an uninformative label. This is how Gilligan delineates the relevant cluster, contrasting it with the salient features of a justice orientation:

In this conception [of morality as care], the moral problem arises from conflicting responsibilities rather than competing rights and requires for its resolution a mode of thinking that is contextual and narrative rather than formal and abstract. This conception of morality as concerned with the activity of care centres moral development around the understanding of morality and relationship, just as the conception of morality as fairness ties moral development to the understanding of rights and rules. (Gilligan 1982: 19)

The appearance of clarity in these sentences is dissipated once we ask questions about what they actually mean. Two moral vocabularies are differentiated, with nothing that seems to join one to the other. The trouble is that as we reflect on the concepts that compose each, we find ourselves drawing heavily on those that constitute the other. Gilligan gives us a triple contrast: between rights and responsibilities; between contextual and abstract moral thought; between a morality that favours relationship over rules and one that prefers rules to relationships. None of these can create the requisite distance between a plausible conception of justice and the voice of care.[1]

Taking rights seriously means accepting appropriate responsibility for the rights of others, not just making a fuss about our own. Human rights activists are not notable for their indifference to moral responsibility. The problem is not only that rights and responsibilities are conceptually related; it is rather that no real moral difference separates those who would emphasize one or the other. People who champion the right to subsistence are talking about the same thing as people who insist on the responsibility of those who are not destitute to meet the needs of those who are.

The distinction between a way of thinking that is formal, abstract, and rule-bound and one that is contextual and narrative is more complicated. Gilligan's notion of different moral orientations was forged in the shadow of Lawrence Kohlberg's theory of moral development, a theory which claims to show that the summit of moral development is a conception of justice that is strikingly abstract and remote from the variable settings of deliberation. Kohlberg wrote about moral growth as if it were a progressive purification of judgement that prescinded in ever more drastic ways from the contingencies of our lives until the universal moral law alone determined judgement (e.g. Kohlberg 1981: 157–73). The fatal drawback of any such view is precisely described by Susan Wolf: 'even if one could agree that certain considerations were of universal significance, they would vastly underdetermine the kinds of institutions, practices and concepts a flourishing society might have. The more one detaches oneself from the contingent features of one's own society, therefore, the vaguer and less certain will be the normative conclusions one is able to reach' (Wolf 1987: 831). But given Calhoun's point about the possibility of many disagreements within a given moral orientation, we need to ask whether all who think and act within the orientation of justice would necessarily share Kohlberg's extravagant propensity for abstraction, and if they would not, whether he has the best conception within the parameters of the orientation he shares with them.

Kohlberg assumed that at the highest stage of moral development a specific intellectual procedure for identifying and establishing priorities among rights would settle moral conflicts. The procedure would reveal that the right to life trumps other considerations: 'With each stage, the obligation to preserve human life becomes more categorical [*sic*], more independent of the aims of the actor, of the commands and opinions of others' (Kohlberg 1981: 171). That might seem right so long as we confine our attention to cases such as Kohlberg's Heinz dilemma, in which a man must steal a drug from a venal pharmacist to save his dying wife. But many situations are very different from this. Suppose we drained resources from education and welfare policies so as to bolster funding for research and practices that might increase longevity. We would be doing no more than the most developed understanding of justice requires, given that the obligation to preserve life carries the weight Kohlberg assigns to it. But that is ridiculous. Sometimes the obligation to preserve life matters more than anything else and sometimes it does not. To accept this we need not abandon the language of justice and rights and adopt some alternative orientation. What we need instead is the commonsense recognition that contextual sensitivity is crucial to the interpretation of rights. To criticize Kohlberg for the inordinate abstraction of his theory of justice exposes no limitation in justice itself. The real limitation is in his understanding of justice.

Although Kohlberg commonly appealed to Rawls as a source of validation for his own theory (e.g. Kohlberg 1986: 497), the virtue of justice as it is understood in Rawls's liberalism is very different than Kohlberg's. What interested Kohlberg in Rawls was his theory of justice as fairness and especially the elaborate thought-experiment he used in constructing that theory. Kohlberg's use of Rawlsian ideas involved more than a little distortion, but that is peripheral to my concerns.[2] What interests me is the understanding of justice as an ideal of reasonableness, an ideal intrinsic to the political conception of the person and logically prior to the case for justice as fairness. Whether justice as fairness amounts to an adequate theory of the just society is a separate issue, as I think Rawls would himself admit.

Rawls's understanding of justice as reasonableness is not vulnerable to the same charge of excessive abstraction that damns Kohlberg's. This is clear given the account of Rawls's conception I gave in Section 9. The reciprocity I extend to others in evincing the reasonableness of the citizen who is just in Rawls's sense requires a sharp sensitivity to the cultural and historical context in which the virtue is to be exercised. If I am ignorant of the way my perception of a particular moral conflict, as well as my perception of my interlocutors, is coloured by burdens of judgement that arise from cultural disparities, say, or different historical (mis)understandings, I will not be able to respond as justice requires. That being so, Rawlsian justice requires of me a way of thinking that is 'contextual and narrative' in a sense that Gilligan should commend. If it is a way of thinking that is also abstract, it is only so to the degree that the goal of reasonable consensus among interlocutors prompts us to abstract from what would deflect effort away from that goal.

The fulcrum of Kohlberg's proceduralism is a role-reversal test in which dilemmas are supposed to be resolved by playing a form of 'moral musical-chairs'. The moral agent imagines herself in the role of each affected party and one role 'wins', although how the winner emerges is fraught with difficulties (cf. Kohlberg 1981: 199; Brook 1987). But such tests are vulnerable to the criticism that they fail to call into question the moral presuppositions of roles into which people have been successfully socialized. Where unreasonable pluralism plays no small part in socialization, many learn only too well to accept their subordination as just and to desire no more than the domination of others will permit them to have (Calhoun 1988: 455). The perspective of such people, when we take it up in 'moral musical-chairs', will be implicated in their own oppression. But Kohlberg's procedure provides no way of showing that this is so.[3] The paradox of Kohlbergian justice is that although it harbours abstractive tendencies that would wrench us away from many morally relevant features of our lives, the procedure it prescribes threatens to leave us mired in other contingencies that distort moral vision. Alternatively, Rawls's distinction between reasonable and unreasonable pluralism lends itself to a moral critique that would challenge the presuppositions of established roles and the possible distortions in judgement and desire among those who have been inducted into them. The ideal of reasonableness is contextually sensitive not only in acknowledging that cultural and other situational variations make a difference to what justice requires; it can also alert us to the injustice that many contextual factors will obscure.

This takes us to the last of Gilligan's distinctions between the orientations of care and justice: the supposed gap between an ethic that revolves around relationship and one that follows the path of rights and rules. Annette Baier has focused on this as the heart of the distinction between the two orientations:

there is at least a difference of tone of voice between speaking as Rawls does of each of us having our own rational life plan, which a just society's moral traffic rules will allow us to follow, and which may or may not involve close association with others, and speaking as Gilligan does of a satisfactory life as involving 'the progress of affiliative relationship' where the 'concept of identity expands to include the experience of interconnection'. (A. Baier 1994: 25; quoting Gilligan 1982: 170, 173)

The force of this contrast can be brought out through Nancy Sherman's illuminating notion of 'virtues of common pursuit'. Sherman points out that much modern moral philosophy has been grounded in the assumption that ethics is exhausted by the question of what we owe to others and—more controversially—ourselves. The assumption overlooks the fact that in addition to caring for others and ourselves, we also care about the things we do together (Sherman 1993: 277–8). The virtues we need so that our caring for the things we do together might flourish—what Sherman calls virtues of common pursuit—are different than the ones needed for the other ethically important kinds of caring. So far as I understand it, Baier's claim is that justice as Rawls conceives it is the master-virtue for what we owe others. The self who punctiliously observes the rules that tell us what is owed is free to think of them, and the people whose interests they protect or advance, as altogether extrinsic to what gives purpose to his own life. Gilligan's voice of caring captures instead the idea of virtues of common pursuit that can thrive only in a setting of 'affiliative relationship' that connects our very identity to the good of others. To possess and practise virtues of common pursuit is to participate in a way of life to which justice and its traffic rules are essentially alien; it is to become someone for whom caring for the things we do together is basic to personal identity.

But justice as Rawls conceives it is a virtue of common pursuit. His political conception of the person does not say that the self is constituted only by a capacity for a conception of the good and the powers of reason necessary to its implementation, leaving justice to operate merely as so many external constraints on the pursuit of the good. The idea of the reasonable is as fundamental to Rawls's conception of the person as the idea of the rational. The development of the sense of justice that occurs under the auspices of the reasonable is a matter of growing competence and commitment to something we can only do together—the reciprocal determination of terms of cooperation that we could agree to be justified. To be just in Rawls's sense is necessarily to care about others as partners in an enterprise of making justice that would be unintelligible without their reciprocal engagement.

These ideas are as prominent in Rawls's earlier work, before the shift towards political liberalism, as they are in his more recent writings. In *A Theory of Justice* he sketched a developmental moral theory in which the beginnings of the sense of justice are evoked by parental love, it then expands to embrace wider associations, including the political community as a whole, and then finally it takes the 'principled' form that includes both full moral understanding of the basis of justice and the motivation that befits that understanding. At the last stage as much as the first, justice is firmly rooted in identity-conferring connections with others because the emphasis throughout is on 'the forming of attachments as final ends'(Rawls 1971: 490–6).

The fact that Rawlsian justice is tied to identity-conferring connections also undermines the opposition between autonomy and dependence that commonly surfaces in the literature on care, including Gilligans's work (e.g. Gilligan 1982: 98; 1987: 29). Autonomy as it figures in the development of justice as reasonableness is a necessary companion to that virtue of common pursuit. For autonomy is the inevitable consequence of serious imaginative engagement with the lives of those with whom we seek to live together in justice; it is the very antithesis of the retreat to some inner citadel that the contrast with dependence would suggest. Feminist political theorists have been right to decry ideals of autonomy that conduce to an alienated independence, and right also to stress the theoretical and practical influence such ideals have had. But the most astute have also realized that the criticism does not apply to all interpretations of the concept (Nedelsky 1989).

The impetus of Gilligan's own recent views would seem to lead her towards a position on justice and autonomy that is close to Rawls's own, even if she would not describe it in those terms. She now distinguishes between a 'feminine ethic of care' and a 'feminist ethic of care' on the grounds that the second would rectify the complicity in patriarchal oppression of the first. The feminist ethic shows that its feminine ancestor promotes 'a faulty notion of relationship' that would trap women in attachments that thwart and silence them (Gilligan 1995: 122–5). But what is the morally superior notion of relationship that the feminist ethic of care would offer to correct the faults of its feminine precursor? A cogent answer would surely have to say at least this. Feminist care is a virtue of common pursuit whose cultivation would empower women to address issues of domination and manipulation in their lives and to think and speak for themselves about the good and the right, against the grain of patriarchal socialization.[4] Yet that is what justice as reasonableness might enable us to do, notwithstanding Rawls's unjustified complacency about justice in the family.[5]

Justice cannot be understood as the whole of public virtue. The grounds for saying this are explored further in Section 26 where I discuss Rawls's theory of moral development at greater length. But to forstall misunderstanding, the chief reasons are worth stating briefly here. The feasibility of eliciting a justice that is sufficiently wide in scope for political purposes seems remote unless that process proceeds via emotional identification with the particular political community in which justice is to be enacted. Furthermore, even if justice could take root alone, the connection to others it entails is likely too austere and fragile a bond to ensure by itself the solidarity that an adequate public morality must encompass. But none of this affects the point at issue here: if we want a moral orientation that expresses the centrality of human connection to our moral identity and gives pride of place to virtues of common pursuit we need not forgo the voice of justice.

## 24.  Care and the Circumstances of Justice

Care is basic to justice, given at least one plausible conception of what justice requires of us. Once that point is granted, much that seems to constitute care as an alternative moral orientation disappears. But the care internal to justice as reasonableness is patently not the only morally relevant kind, and it may be some other kind that gives the distinctive content and tone to the 'different voice' that Gilligan and others have championed.

That possibility might seem to be confirmed by the paradigms of moral conduct typically invoked in feminist literature on care. These differ dramatically from the standard examples of mainstream moral and political theory. Instead of men keeping their promises and honouring their contracts, we find women caring for children or friends without a thought for rights or duties (e.g. Ruddick 1987; Noddings 1984). Perhaps the best politics would assign a far more modest role to justice than the one I have claimed for it. The interpersonal capabilities and emotions that liberal justice tends to consign to families and voluntary associations might then enliven our public morality, giving us a richer, more elevating politics than what Hume called 'the cautious, jealous virtue of justice' can provide (Hume 1983 edn.: 21).

An argument for that conclusion might proceed in this way. Suppose human relationships at their best are found in the unselfish love of parents for their children or close friends for each other. The caring for the good of others that abounds there does not have to end at the borders of intimacy; it can be evinced, for example, in emotional solidarity with strangers in the midst of suffering (Gilligan and Wiggins 1987: 288–93). Consider the explanation of one man for his conduct in saving Jews from their Nazi persecutors: 'Everyone else is basically you' (Monroe, Barton, and Klingemann 1990: 122). From the rescuer's perspective the misfortune of the stranger does not differ in weight as a reason for action to limit suffering than misfortune that might directly befall himself. Heroic benevolence is by definition extraordinary. But the blurring of boundaries between self and other as distinct loci for the experience of hardships and evils, so vividly evident in this case, is also apparent in the less spectacular examples of unselfish love and concern to which the exponents of care appeal.

The extent to which an ideal of vicarious participation in the good of others can be projected beyond the narrow borders of intimacy is to some

extent an open question. But even if it could loom large in a psychologically feasible public morality, we still have to worry about relationships or
transactions in which the ideal can gain no purchase, its influence is too
weak to restrain the disruptive power of non-moral motives, or we must
balance conflicting interests between those for whom we care strongly.
Moral agents need virtues in addition to the care expressed paradigmati-
cally in the love of family or friendship, and their political education must
encompass those additional virtues. In particular, the limits of care have to
be rectified by a sense that others may have pressing claims on one's aid
or forbearance, irrespective of the indifference or antipathy one may at
any given moment feel towards them. Hume's cautious, jealous virtue
comes to the rescue when his warm and generous sisters have run out of
steam.

Notice that to accept this argument is effectively to have given up the
idea that care and justice are rival moral orientations. The argument trans-
forms them into complementary virtues in a common moral life. But this
is not the same as the traditional view that caring should prevail in the
domestic realm while justice reigns in politics. What is distinctive of the
argument is its insistence that a care independent of justice is properly the
highest civic virtue, with justice operating in what Sandel calls a merely
'remedial' role (Sandel 1982: 31). The function of justice is to remedy the
evils that afflict our lives when caring responses are absent, dangerously
weak or otherwise ill-suited to maintaining cooperation on morally
acceptable terms. However, the restoration of order that justice brings
about may still be a poor substitute for the harmony whose collapse creates the need for justice. If I have grown indifferent to someone I once
cared for as a friend, then my sense of justice might restrain me from violating her rights, and thus mutually respectful cooperation could continue.
But that may be a distant second best to the sense of communion which
was possible when I did care. Furthermore, if justice is nothing more than
a remedial virtue, approaches to education that pretend otherwise
threaten to mutilate our moral lives. Once children learn to import justice into situations where a higher form of caring is psychologically feasible, they will give up the best feasible moral response in favour of one
that is inferior. A justice-centred approach to education may also foster a
tendency to interpret all moral encounters in adversarial terms. If conditions of conflict are what appropriately evoke justice, social practices that
suggest it has ubiquitous moral relevance will tend to make relations
increasingly conflictual (Sandel 1982: 32–5).

Rawls's understanding of the virtue of justice is not Hume's. But his
liberalism is developed against the background of a broadly Humean
account of the circumstance of justice. The facts of reasonable and

unreasonable pluralism that are basic to his conception expand Hume's sparser list of the social and psychological conditions that supposedly create the need for justice. For Rawls and Hume alike, justice presupposes conflict (Rawls 1971: 126–130, 1993: 4–22; Hume 1983 edn.: 20–3). But if justice is the virtue that keeps us safe from conflict generated by limited altruism, scarce resources, and the collision of rival ethical beliefs, an alternative strategy for achieving concord would be to pre-empt or mitigate the conflictual conditions that create the need for justice in the first place. Call this the integrative strategy.

A strategy of this sort seems to be at work in the thought of an 11-year-old respondent in Gilligan's research who refused to take for granted the circumstances of justice that Kohlberg's Heinz dilemma presupposes. As Kohlberg frames the dilemma, Heinz's only alternatives are to respect the pharmacist's right to property and allow his wife to die or else steal the drug and save his wife. But Gilligan's Amy refuses to accept the terms in which the dilemma is framed: 'if Heinz and the druggist had talked it out long enough, they could reach something besides stealing'. Older and more morally sophisticated women in Gilligan's research showed a comparable unwillingness to accept the conflict that the Heinz dilemma insists we take for granted (Gilligan 1982: 29, 101–3). All exemplify Gilligan's claim that caring enjoins us to enter moral situations with the intent of ensuring that 'all the needs' are met instead of standing back and asking whose rights should prevail at whose expense (Gilligan 1987: 27). No doubt it is naive to think that enough friendly conversation could always dissolve the circumstances of justice. But there is a parallel, and equally dangerous naivete in the thought that a satisfactory political morality would permit us to be indifferent to the scope and severity of conflict that divides us so long as justice can tell us who has a right to what. Indifference would be self-defeating, since the more extensive and severe the range of conflict the more numerous and strong will be the reasons people have not to do what justice requires of them.

The realization of civic forms of mutual care that would pre-empt or moderate the circumstances of justice is the aim of the integrative strategy. A commitment to some such strategy is common ground between communitarians, such as Sandel, and feminist exponents of ideals of care that purport to be both independent of justice and politically applicable. This is highly ambiguous common ground because the strategy can take so many different forms. The integrative strategy of mass schooling in nineteenth-century America was to forestall social discord by inculcating a shared civic identity that combined patriotic fervour and a Pan-Protestant orthodoxy (Janowitz 1983: 78–85). A very different example is John Dewey's advocacy of an education dedicated to 'democratic progress', by which he meant the increasing ascendency of a certain kind of culture that included but extended far beyond the political institutions of democracy. The education designed to advance that culture would cultivate common interests across entrenched divisions of ethnicity, religion, and class and diffuse broadly scientific habits of mind among all citizens that would determine how these common interests would be harmoniously pursued (Dewey 1916: 81–99, 1932).

Neither of these examples might be appealing to feminist exponents of care. But both reveal a moral hazard that any version of the integrative strategy must reckon with. The hazard is that the strategy might disguise the circumstances of justice by uniting all (or a large majority) in ways that impose unjust burdens on some. This is easy to see in the case of the ethnic chauvinism and sectarian bigotry that often contaminated the rhetoric of mass schooling since the nineteenth century. But the problem also affects Dewey's educational progressivism. His emphasis on the orchestration of cultural and individual differences within the massive solidarity of democratic culture consigns rights to a dangerously marginal role, at best, in public deliberation. If Dewey's philosophy of democracy is the cure to rights-obsessed liberalism, the cure may be worse than the disease (cf. Ryan 1995: 365).[6]

I want to press two closely related claims about the integrative strategy. First, the virtue of justice is necessary as an expression of the interpersonal recognition that befits moral relations among equals, even when caring attachment is enough to motivate action that defuses conflict and gives everyone the liberty and other resources to which they have a right. Therefore, no tolerable use of the strategy could eclipse our sense of ourselves as beings to whom justice is owed. Second, acceptable forms of the strategy cannot promote bonds of caring and community at the expense of the capability and inclination to stand up for our rights where these are under substantial threat. That is necessary if the strategy is truly to ease, and not merely mask, the conflictual conditions in which talk of justice and rights becomes urgent.

## 25. Intimacy and Community

I begin with an example of care in the context of intimacy. That is where we are supposed to find intimations of an ideal of care that might be devised as an alternative to a political morality in which justice reigns as the cardinal virtue. But if justice proves to be as vital to moral relations there as liberal theory suggests it is in politics, the case for reducing justice to a remedial role will be undermined.

My example is from Rose Borris's story about learning to read in her mid-forties. When Rose first tried to enrol in reading classes, she was opposed by Albert, her illiterate husband.

It's hard to get out of home when your man doesn't want you to do this. You're lucky if you can get out the door. That's why I didn't start in September. I had to fight with Albert all the time because he wanted me at home. He said I was never going to learn. Maybe he was afraid. But one day he said, 'It's no use Rose. I can see what you want. I can't stop you.' (Borris with Jiles 1989: 141)

Albert's words might express nothing more than the knowledge that his wife's will was stronger than his. Then again, 'I can't stop you' could be the outcome of a painful process of deliberation in which his resistance to her plans gradually came to seem repugnant. Suppose Albert loves Rose as more than one-half of a cherished relationship. He cares for her as someone whose good matters for her own sake. This is the unselfish care that Gilligan and others would have us celebrate. Given its presence in a sufficiently potent form, this could be enough to overcome the motivational pull of his fears so that eventually he must say 'I can't stop you'. The change of heart might also be prompted in part or whole by a sense of justice: Albert comes to feel that Rose has a right to pursue an education outside the home, and that he has a corresponding duty not to interfere.

Suppose we question Albert about his change of heart. He tells us he relented in his opposition to Rose simply because he cared for her. Thoughts of rights and duties did not enter his head, and he does not see how his response would have been any better if they had. If we say that a care independent of justice is the highest virtue, then Albert's response, on this interpretation of his conduct, is beyond reproach. His unselfish caring operates as an integrative moral strategy, obviating the need to appeal to the remedial language of justice. Moreover, we cannot criticize his response on the grounds that it denies Rose the freedom to which she has a just claim. Some instances of the integrative strategy might work by reconciling an individual or group to less freedom or property, say, than they have a right to claim. But no such problem arises when Albert relents in his opposition to Rose out of sheer unselfish love.

Now consider a case that parallels Albert's hypothetical caring response. A slave-owner knows that the slave he loves will leave him as soon as she is liberated, and that thought grieves him. But he also knows that the slave will never be happy without freedom, and because he cares unselfishly for her, he gives her freedom. However, the slave-owner does not think of his relationship with the slave in terms of moral (as opposed to legal) rights and duties. He does not think of the slave's freedom as something to which she has any right, and he conceives his act of manumission as a matter of benevolence above and beyond the call of moral duty. Now if the slave understands the oppressive character of slavery, she will think that so long as her right to freedom is not accepted, the full measure of her worth as a person has not been taken. Persons have a worth that is not reducible to the relationships in which they are embedded, and their worth creates peremptory claims on the aid or forbearance of others, moral rights in other words, whose significance does not wax and wane according to the affections they may or may not elicit from others. The slave-owner does not see the slave in that way, and for that reason his love, although unselfish, is still degrading.

All this applies equally to the relationship of Albert and Rose on the assumption that his resonse was a matter of care without justice. So long as Albert does not think of Rose's freedom as something to which she has a right, his love too bears the same defect, even when the concern for her good implicit in his love is enough to ensure that to which she has a right. And if Rose is duly conscious of her own dignity, she will regard his attitude as contemptuous. The problem is not that Albert's love is fine as it is and that another, quite separate attitude—respect for Rose as a bearer of rights—needs to be added to make his moral response complete. If a fundamental part of our self-conception is a worth we possess that does not depend on the affections of others, we will want a love that is informed by a recognition of that worth, and anything less will be a flawed and demeaning love.

What may obscure this truth is the common error of thinking that some deep antipathy holds between the attitude of love (or lesser forms of direct concern for other's good) on the one hand and respect for the other as a bearer of rights on the other. That thought is fundamental to Sandel's notion of justice as a remedial virtue; it is basic also to Kant's understanding of friendship: 'For if we can regard love as attraction and respect as repulsion, and if the principle of love commands friends to come together, the principle of respect requires them to keep each other at a proper distance' (Kant 1964 edn.: 141). Ideas such as these may incline us to cling to the idea that a loving rather than a dutiful change of heart on Albert's part would be for the best, at least in some respects. For if the intrusion of a concern for rights and justice into the motivational context of action comes at the cost of a diminished or suppressed love, it seems at best an ambiguous achievement.[7] But why should we think justice would impose any such costs?

Two arguments might pull us towards a broadly Kantian view on friendship and respect. One arises from the fact that justice requires Albert to see Rose as an instance of the universal, a bearer of the right to freedom, and in that respect like anyone else. Even if the conception of justice we favour stresses the need for contextual sensitivity in the interpretation of rights, that does not undermine the universality of the perspective it requires us to take; it only shows that the universality of any satisfactory conception of justice cannot be the mechanical application of highly general rules. But love among intimates and kindred forms of caring, such as patriotic love, require that the object of attachment be cherished in its particularity, not as a mere instance of the universal. Feelings of love for an individual or a community cannot 'abstract from the individual situation and attach themselves to impartial notions of what is just and right' without losing their distinctive character. 'Although there is no doubt some feature of James which is the reason why I love him, I am not obliged to love William as well, just because he shares that feature' (Scruton 1980: 526). Indeed, to 'love' William and anyone else just because they share the same feature would not be to love at all but to adopt some more impersonal attitude of admiration or the like instead. Justice and love are irreconcilable if we identify the first with what Seyla Benhabib calls 'the standpoint of the generalised other', which abstracts from the individuality of those to whom we respond justly, and the second with 'the standpoint of the concrete other', in which the individuality discarded as irrelevant to justice now engrosses our attention and affect (Benhabib 1987: 163–4).

All this goes to show that there must be more to love than seeing another as an instance of the universal. The argument unravels once it purports to establish that love is in any conflict with such seeing. An analogy may help here: If I gaze on a picture in an art gallery and say 'That's a wonderful picture' I am regarding it as an instance of the universal—a token of the type 'wonderful picture'. But I do not at that moment cease to be enthralled by the unique, particular thing it is. Similarly, to whatever extent Albert's change of heart might stem from the virtue of justice, it does not require him to perceive Rose in any way that is at odds with the particularism proper to love.

The second, more interesting argument is the one that appears to have motivated Kant. He thought the deep psychological appeal of friendship lay in the feeling of release and dissolution that friendship gave the self: 'It is sweet to feel a mutual possession that approximates to a fusion into one person' (Kant 1964 edn.: 142). The phrase 'mutual possession' signals the obvious moral danger. To think of someone as a possession is to regard the other as an object one is free to use. But that is to lose sight of the moral inviolability of those to whom justice is owed. Therefore, the coincidence of respect and love must be an unstable ambivalence: love attracts while respect repels, and to love honourably is to be torn by opposing motivational forces.

There is real insight here. If love makes some kinds of morally required conduct easier than they would otherwise be, it might also tend to make other kinds harder. Albert's change of heart would not have been necessary in the first place if he had cared nothing for his wife. Human love often harbours tendencies that may countervail the demands of respect. The mistake in Kant's view is the assumption that a diminished love is the price that must be paid to secure a respect attuned to the inviolability of the other. If Albert's change of heart is prompted by a sense of justice, it would be arbitrary to suppose that any such price must have been paid. The crisis in his relationship with Rose might entitle us to infer that he loves her less possessively than before, assuming that his change of heart became a settled disposition. But a less possessive love is not the same as a lesser love.

Justice has a role in our lives that extends beyond any merely remedial function. The recognition of the other as one to whom justice is due matters profoundly even when a care independent of justice can secure for us that to which we have a right. It matters so long as we want to think of ourselves and others as having an inviolable worth that does not depend on those affective attachments which connect our lives to particular others. That thought is basic to the moral sensibility of post-Enlightenment political culture. And it is a thought that feminist political theorists will hardly wish to repudiate so long as they are concerned with the moral vulnerability of women in caring relationships that threaten to engulf the very sense of self. So if there are civically relevant kinds of caring that justice does not entail, these will supplement rather than supplant the moral primacy of justice, and educational practices that might seek to nourish such caring cannot permissibly do so in a way that would relegate justice to a merely remedial role.

This takes me to my second major claim about justice and the integrative strategy. If the recognition of others as beings to whom justice is due is internal to any caring attachment worth having, no matter how unselfish and loving the attachment might be, then we must take a more generally favourable view of that particular expression of justice—standing up for one's rights—than many devotees of the ideals of care and community tend to take.

Here is Sandel on the 'more or less ideal family situation' in which the circumstances of justice are virtually irrelevant:

Individual rights and fair decision procedures are seldom invoked, not because injustice is rampant but because their appeal is pre-empted by a spirit of generosity in which I am rarely inclined to claim my fair share. Nor does this generosity necessarily imply that I receive out of kindness a share that is equal to or greater than the share I would be entitled to under fair principles of justice. I may get less.

The point is not that I get what I would otherwise get, but simply that the questions of what I get and what I am due do not loom large in the overall context of this way of life. (Sandel 1982: 33)

Sandel imagines a decline from this state of domestic tranquillity as affections wane, interests diverge, and family members stand up for their rights against each other. The story is supposed to have a political message. Like loving families, the institutions of civil society and even national communities themselves may be held together by 'more or less clearly defined common identities and shared purposes, precisely those attributes whose presence signifies the relative absence of the circumstances of justice' (Sandel 1982: 31). We have reason to protect and strengthen the bonds of mutual care that push justice towards the edges of public life just as caring families have reason to protect the spirit of loving kindness against divisive talk about rights and duties.

What does Sandel's story suggest about those who stand up for their rights in a situation of established familial or civic harmony and in so doing trigger a descent into the fallen state of justice? The story does not actually say they are to blame for initiating the process. Sandel could concede that people who get less than they have a right to under the rule of loving kindness might have been badly exploited. I assume that is why he wishes to rule out the case in which 'injustice is rampant' from his domestic idyll. So when victims of rampant injustice have had enough and stand up for their rights, responsibility for the loss of harmony would fall on those who had used them. But even in that case the victims must weigh the evil of their continued exploitation against the ethical loss all must incur when the dispensation of care is undermined by demanding justice. Then the victims must decide that their rights are more important than the collective loss their moral assertiveness would precipitate. A parallel dilemma would occur on the civic plane for groups who have traditionally been given less than their rights but who would have to challenge 'more or less clearly defined common identities and shared purposes' that are somehow nobler than justice in pressing their demands for justice. Therefore, if the integrative strategy is paired with the thesis that justice is only a remedial virtue, those who are taught to think of justice and community in the prescribed manner will believe they generally have good, though not necessarily decisive moral reasons not to stand up for their rights. The risk then is that the integrative strategy will not really undo the circumstances of justice but only disguise their presence in ways that enable some to persist in the caring exploitation of others.

The truth in Sandel's view is the fact that it is often admirable to waive one's rights or act for the sake of others in ways that exceed the duties that derive from their rights. A world without generosity and spontaneous altruism would be wretched, and a world in which people were only motivated by either narrow self-interest or respect for rights would be just such a place.[8] But it is a huge mistake to suggest that those who stand up for their rights, and in so doing disrupt some established social harmony, are forfeiting a precious collective good and harming themselves and those with whom they share community. That mistake cannot be avoided so long as the integrative strategy is harnessed to the view that justice is only a remedial virtue.

On the alternative view of care and justice I have elaborated here, not only is the mistake avoidable; we can also see why it is such a bad mistake. I said that morally worthy love or similar caring attachments to particular others will include the recognition of the other as possessing the inviolability of those to whom justice is owed. That being so, intimates or members of larger-scale caring communities will often have a powerful reason to stand up for their rights that derives in part from their caring attachment to others, given an understanding of the attachment that includes the values of justice. If Albert says he allowed Rose to attend her evening classes out of generosity, and Rose replies that she had a right to go anyhow, this may be a way of telling Albert about the only kind of caring relationship that is acceptable to her. We do not have to see her words as discharging some duty to maintain her self-respect—that might be quite secure already—much less as an unfortunate attempt to introduce the language of justice where that has been obviated by some transcendent solidarity. The language of justice is needed here if Albert is to learn to care for Rose as he should. In the state as in the family the same point will apply: the language of justice will often be needed if we are to care about our fellow citizens as we should.

## 26. Retrieving Patriotism

The integrative strategy is not divested of its appeal merely by showing that it commonly takes forms that conflict with justice. What may underpin the strategy is a concern with protecting justice rather than marginalizing its role in public life. The severity and frequency of conflict under pluralism threatens the perpetuation of justice. The bond of mutual care justice embodies may have to be allied with other ways of harmonizing the lives of citizens if justice is to hold. More controversially, many will regard ties of solidarity that obviate conflict as intrinsic goods whose absence mars our lives, no matter how completely and securely justice is realized. So far as we are swayed by either or both of these arguments, we may be drawn to educational and other political practices designed to create or strengthen ties of fellowship that would mitigate conflict.

At the end of Section 25 I alluded to the possibility of a patriotic allegiance that does not marginalize justice, and my main purpose in the next chapter and the remainder of this one is to explore that possibility. I do not suggest this is the only, or always the most important way in which interests are reconciled in a liberal democracy. Many associations that develop in the background culture will be defined by ideals that function in integrative ways. Practices of charity and public service encouraged by many religious confessions are an obvious case in point. The experience of successful cooperation in economic and other spheres generates over time a 'social capital' in the form of shared trust and goodwill, and this will underwrite new cooperative activities, which in turn add to the store of social capital if all goes well (Coleman 1991: 163–4). Furthermore, where many associations proliferate, the antagonism between some can be eased by membership in others that cut across rival affiliations (Feinberg 1990: 107–8; Macedo 1996: 254–6). Sheer contempt for those who belong to the political party I detest is a lot harder to sustain when some of its members belong to the church I love.

The means by which potential conflict may be reduced within what Macedo calls the 'moral infrastructure' of liberal societies are important and well-known (Macedo 1996: 247). No doubt the relevant processes will often work to disguise exploitation and injustice, as left-leaning social scientists will be quick to note. But it would take an overwhelmingly jaundiced view of civil society to think that that was always the consequence. And once the possibility of reconciling interests in morally innocent ways is granted, it becomes hard to see why the state can permissibly play no role in nourishing the associative ties that undergird a civically reliable sense of justice. Suppose part of the argument for encouraging investment in depressed urban neighbourhoods is to encourage the rebirth of social trust in places where it has virtually ceased to exist. No credible understanding of liberal politics could support the view that the argument is inherently illiberal. If minimally virtuous citizens cannot be expected to grow up in environments devoid of any real community, then nurturing community where that is needed is as urgent a task of liberal politics as any other. On the need to maintain the vitality of civil society, liberals can and should make common cause with communitarians, even if they may disagree on the range of permissible political measures that might be taken to meet the need.

Yet all these considerations pertain to the background culture of public reason. The idea is that interests are often harmonized in the vigorous associative life of the economy and civil society, even if political intervention is commonly needed not only to correct injustice but also to create or protect social conditions conducive to reconciliation. But it may be a bad mistake to suppose that once public-spiritedness and much else that is morally laudable thrives in the background culture, then interests will be adequately reconciled in the polity as a whole. A revealing study in this regard is Robert Wuthnow's recent research on the still strong tradition of moral volunteerism in America. The strength of that tradition attests to the fact that many continue to identify strongly with ends that transcend the fulfilments of private life. Yet what is striking about this phenomenon is that the ends with which individuals tend to identify have a narrowly parochial focus: it is the success of some specific community or the aims of some special interest group that matter. The good of the republic and all its citizens is often a remote and bloodless abstraction. Wuthnow notes the virtual indifference to questions of social justice that many volunteers exhibit: 'Their compassion had focused on people much like themselves, or they saw the people they helped only as individuals, not as symptoms of some larger problem in American society. When they thought about injustice, the notion was therefore more distant, less charged with emotion, like a concept they had read about but not experienced directly' (Wuthnow 1991: 254–5). If the integrative strategy is to serve the ends of justice, one might hope that it could play some role in the foreground of public life. The virtue of patriotism has commonly been understood to play just such a role. How might it fit together with justice as reasonableness?

For some ordinary citizens the ideal of patriotism exerts an emotional power, especially in times of civic crisis, that makes the allure of justice seem faint in comparison. For others, patriotism seems too deeply stained with the excesses of chauvinism for it to be invoked without shame. But even in their case, the shame may overlay emotional fidelity to the particular political community within which their civic identity was formed and continues to find expression, a fidelity properly described as patriotic.[9] The importance of such fidelity is eloquently affirmed in Jeremy Webber's account of what he takes to be the basis of democratic community:

The core of any democratic community is not ethnicity or language or some catalogue of shared values. It is the commitment to a particular debate through time. The specific character of that debate is of real importance to individuals. Members come to care about issues through the terms of that debate. It sets the framework for the positions they take on questions affecting the community as a whole. Using those terms they define their place within society. Their arguments are not, in any simple sense, dictated by the community. But the framing of the issues, much of the range of argument, and the background of experience against which arguments are judged are inherited . . . The vernacular of the debate is crucial in the formation and expression of political opinions. The reflection of that vernacular in political decision making is central to the member's feeling of engagement and participation. (Webber 1994: 223)

At first glance, this might suggest the outlines of a view of political education that differs from mine. Webber could be taken to imply that the main business of creating citizens is ensuring mastery of the political vernacular that will inform the role of citizen in a given polity; coming to care about the issues that preoccupied earlier participants in the ongoing conversation in which that vernacular lives; and learning to care as well about the future all current participants and their children will share together. Political education is thus conceived as an essentially parochial enterprise, determined by the uniqueness of a received civic vernacular and the history of the political community into which future citizens are to be inducted. The process I have been emphasizing—the cultivation of a justice proper to any polity that would claim to be a liberal democracy—seems at first glance remote from all this.

Webber is right to insist on the centrality of historically particular conversations to democratic politics, and his point has obvious educational significance. Creating citizens in Canada cannot be the same thing as political education in Ireland or South Africa, and the differences surely reside in those matters of vernacular and local attachment that he stresses. But it would be wrong to infer that the socially specific elements of political education must displace the generic dispositions that I have stressed under the rubric of justice. The necessary role of those dispositions is discernible in Webber's own argument.

Webber's point about the cohesive power of inherited attachments and historically contingent conversations is made to support an argument about the complex structure of political attitudes in federations like Canada, where loyalties to political entities other than the federation coexist, often uneasily, with allegiance to the federation itself. He contends that our constitutional impasse stems largely from our failure to appreciate the complexity of these attitudes, and the ways in which local political attachments can vary in strength from one part of the country to another without undermining the possibility or desirability of authentic commitment to the federal political community itself. In a word, Canadians have failed to understand and respect the variety of their own political vernaculars (Webber 1994: 222–59).[10]

Whether or not this is true, it is obvious that even to assess the argument as a Canadian I am required to exercise a certain empathy in the manner I interpret the lives of fellow citizens. I must be capable of entertaining the possibility that the characteristic structure of political attitudes elsewhere in the country might be rather different from my own in the robustness of provincial political loyalty, say, without thereby precluding a real shared identification with the pan-Canadian political conversation. And to be capable of this, I must actively accept some of the burdens of judgement—in particular, I need to acknowledge the ways in which differences in historical experience may yield profound differences in political judgement and loyalty without compromising the reasonableness of those who differ or the good faith with which they might continue to seek just terms of cooperation within a shared political community.

A political conversation sustained over time among a particular people may or may not be rightly characterized as genuinely democratic or liberal, and even when it is, the conversation may contain voices that threaten to subvert that characterization or, just as dangerously, voices that are faithful to the liberty and equality worth having but are widely regarded as subversive. Whether our most divisive social controversies can be resolved in a manner that keeps faith with the regulative ideals of the conversation we claim to want—that is, a conversation affirming the liberty and equality of all—depends on whether we can conduct the conversation as reasonable citizens, and not just as emotionally absorbed patriots. Political education cannot only be a matter of immersion in a civic vernacular because we always have to worry about the corruption of the vernacular, and the avoidance of corruption depends on the acquisition of those virtues that enable us to conduct the kind of conversation we should want to have. Nevertheless, to say all this is not to deny but only to qualify Webber's thesis that particularistic attachments are characteristically central to the cohesion of democratic societies.

Rawls's liberalism bears an interesting but ambiguous relationship to these ideas about the formation of civic identity. The idea of the well-ordered society as a political community played an important role in Rawls's attempt to account for the stability of just institutions in *A Theory of Justice,* and elements of that earlier view are reaffirmed, somewhat incongruously, in the concluding chapter of *Political Liberalism* (Rawls 1971: 520–9, 1993: 320–3). The reaffirmation is incongruous because the notion of an overlapping consensus is now supposed to carry all the weight of the case for stability. The suggestion that political society is a community is explicitly rejected on the grounds that this implies the enforcement of some comprehensive doctrine: 'Liberalism rejects political society as a community because, among other things, it leads to the systematic denial of basic liberties and the oppressive use of the government's monopoly of (legal) force' (Rawls 1993: 146 n.).

The argument of Chapter 2 shows that this cannot be true, since Rawls's conception of a just society is itself committed to a partially comprehensive doctrine of autonomy. Furthermore, by tying the concept of political community so tightly to matters of shared belief, Rawls obscures the important ways in which attachment to a political community can intensify or slacken for reasons independent of such beliefs. As many commentators have noted, the rise of Quebec separatism coincided with a process of secularization in that province that made its inhabitants' basic beliefs and values far more like those of other Canadians than they were before (e.g. Taylor 1993: 156–7; Norman 1995: 141–2). Yet at another level, Rawls's entire political theory tacitly appeals to the unifying power of political community. The boundaries of a well-ordered society are fixed by 'the notion of a self-contained national community' (Rawls 1971: 457). Rawls continues to need that assumption because the justice of the society he envisages depends partly on people not being strongly disposed to leave whenever they would benefit more from the distributive principles that apply elsewhere (Rawls 1993: 277). And the stability of the society depends in part on ethnic or other subgroups being disinclined to pursue secession (Nickel 1990: 215–16).

Although Rawls's recent work is often misleading on the issue of community, the conception of community and moral development outlined in *A Theory of Justice* still offers an attractive picture of the connection between the psychological growth of justice and the formation of particularistic political attachments. That connection emerges at the second and third stages of development, as the sense of justice moves beyond its original form as a kind of filial piety to operate within wider social settings, including civic relations.

At the second stage—the morality of association—the individual moves through a 'succession of more demanding roles with their more complex schemes of rights and duties'. The overall scheme of cooperation within which these roles are assigned is held together by affective ties created through the exercise of reciprocity by those who participate within the scheme: 'Thus if those engaged in a system of social cooperation regularly act with evident intention to uphold its just (or fair) rules, bonds of friendship and mutual trust tend to develop among them, thereby holding them ever more securely to the scheme.' To occupy the role of citizen in a well-ordered society is to come to think and feel about the society in this way, and hence to regard one's fellow citizens as 'friends and associates' joined together in 'a system of cooperation known to be for the advantage of all and governed by a common conception of justice'. The well-ordered society is a 'social union' whose 'institutionalized forms are prized as good in themselves' by those who grow up and live in a world structured by them (Rawls 1971: 469–72, 527).

Notice that the process Rawls is describing here is really the development of a liberal patriotism, although the vocabulary of patriotism is not used at all in the description. Induction into the role of citizen and the growth of affective attachment to fellow citizens are essentially tied to the particularity of the polity within which moral learning occurs: it is *this* scheme of just social cooperation to which the individual becomes attached, *these* fellow citizens with whom bonds of trust and affection take root. The only alternative interpretation is to suppose that in the morality of association individuals become attached to just schemes of cooperation in general and to all who might conceivably participate in them. But that is as absurd as supposing that within the morality of authority children become attached to loving parents in general, as opposed to the particular ones who love them.

The ideal of citizenship applicable in the well-ordered society obliges us to comply with the demands of justice. But so long as we are confined to the morality of association, Rawls says that our motivation to be just remains imperfect. The motivation of someone who is thus limited 'springs largely from his ties of friendship and fellow feeling for others, and his concern for the approbation of the wider society.' At the final stage of moral development, the citizen becomes attached to 'the highest order principles [of justice] themselves' (Rawls 1971: 472). The phrase 'attachment to principles themselves' misleads us if we take it to imply any contrast with attachment to the good of others. But that is very clearly not what Rawls intends. The principles he has in mind are 'agreed ways of advancing human interests' and they matter only because the interests they advance matter. The distinctive motivation of principled morality is 'the desire to act on the natural duty to advance just arrangements . . . for the good of the larger community' (Rawls 1971: 474–6).

In contrasting the morality of association and the morality of principle, Rawls has at least two important points to make. First, acting in accord with justice so as to be esteemed by others is not the same as acting justly. The distinction is necessary because acting justly might sometimes require forfeiting the approval of those whose approval one craves. Second, duties may obtain in circumstances where one is unable to muster much fellow feeling for those to whom the duty is owed, and a fully developed sense of justice will motivate right conduct even then. But to concede these limitations of moral motivation as it tends to operate in the morality of association is not to discard its distinctive motivational propensities altogether. Within the morality of principles, 'our natural attachments to particular persons and groups have an appropriate place'. The ties of friendship and trust intensify the moral feelings that attend the virtue of justice, and enlarge the obligations we owe to others. And although the motivation of some at the principled stage might conceivably rely only on 'general sympathy and benevolence' rather than particularistic affections, Rawls thinks it 'would be surprising if these attachments were not to some degree necessary' (Rawls 1971: 475–6, 486).

Yet even here Rawls shows a certain blindness to the importance of patriotic loyalty that his own argument discloses. He notes that the institutional structures of a well-ordered society may be so large that 'particular bonds never get built up'. This is supposed not to matter anyhow because what holds the society together are shared principles of justice (Rawls 1971: 474). Unless Rawls wants to repudiate his own theory of moral development, this makes no sense. For what the theory says is that identification with the role of citizen is the culminating point of the morality of association, and the particular bonds established through that identification form the psychological bridge to the morality of principle. If the bonds that constitute the bridge are never 'built up', then we cannot be sanguine about the emergence of a principled morality that citizens might endorse together.

Rawls's careless remarks here may betray a common misunderstanding of the sense in which patriotic loyalty entails bonding between the lives of fellow citizens. The particularistic ties of intimacy grow through face to face contact. This will be true to some degree of somewhat larger associations as well if they are morally thriving communities. The problem that evidently worries Rawls is that the sheer scale of contemporary national or multinational states makes the paradigm of intimacy or even the kindly neighbourhood irrelevant. But if we think of the bonds of political community on the model that Webber suggests, these paradigms are irrelevant anyhow. No doubt it may be necessary, as Rawls's theory suggests, to see oneself and those one loves as beneficiaries rather than victims of the political community into which one is initiated, so that one's feelings towards it become coloured by a sense of gratitude and belonging. But face to face contact and specific acts of mutual benevolence are certainly not necessary in the case of all or even most fellow citizens.

## 27.  *Trust, Patriotism, and Pluralism*

The conception of moral development outlined in *A Theory of Justice* is a relatively neglected corner of Rawls's political theory, and it belongs to a part of that book whose alleged deficiencies prompted Rawls's move towards political liberalism in his writings over the past decade (Rawls 1993: pp. xv–xvi). But nothing here depends on all the details being right.[11] What is crucial is the general point that so long as we endorse justice as reasonableness, any credible account of its development and stability will take the formation of particularistic political attachments as critically important. That is so because of the dependence of justice on established relations of trust within a given polity and because such attachments provide a potentially powerful bulwark against the centrifugal tendencies inherent in pluralism.

The reciprocity through which reasonable citizens give and receive justice can only function adequately given strong and warranted ties of trust that connect their lives together via the institutional forms of a just society (R. Dworkin 1989: 501–2). If trust is weak, then we will be inclined to interpret the judgements of those who disagree with us, rightly or wrongly, as instances of unreasonable pluralism, and the compromise and moderation appropriate to justice will likely be blocked. The absence of trust deprives us of the mutual regard we need if we are to interpret our moral differences charitably, as honourable disagreements that inevitably occur when reasonable people deliberate together in good faith. Distrust will also incline us to see any accommodation to opposing viewpoints as an unfortunate capitulation to folly or the desire of others to dominate us. Nevertheless, when that moral stalemate has been reached, it cannot be overcome just by cultivating trust without regard to history. For we also know that if trust is strong and undeserved, then we may cooperate harmoniously, but misplaced trust will leave those who do the misplacing exposed to certain abuse. All this means that the reservoir of earned trust that a just society must rely on is necessarily the historical achievement of a particular polity; it cannot be a ready-made moral resource that inheres in the very idea of a liberal democratic constitution, irrespective of historical contingencies. We come to draw on that reservoir of trust only thorough initiation into a just polity, and coming to care about the people and the particular institutions it encompasses.

The importance of the marriage between justice and patriotism in civic virtue can be revealed from another direction. The political culture that occupies the foreground of public life even in a well-ordered society is in two important ways in tension with the pluralism that obtains in the background culture. First, the many differences in creed, ethnic affiliation and the like that divide citizens in their roles and experiences outside politics will affect the judgements they make inside. That is so because of the inevitable influence of such differences on even the fully competent exercise of moral reason. Common acceptance of the burdens of judgements is supposed to allay the potential divisiveness of this predicament by ensuring respect for reasonable differences. But common acceptance may yet coincide with a strong residual conflict between the political judgements we are inclined to make by virtue of credal of other commitments vital to our identity outside politics and the more capacious perspective that we must try to occupy as reasonable citizens. The argument of Chapter 2 suggests that this conflict goes much deeper than Rawls acknowledges. The clear danger is that over time the conflict might be resolved in favour of a politics in which respect for reasonable differences is steadily eroded by conflict among divergent identities that thrive in the background culture.

Second, even if the pressures of pluralism do not directly corrupt public deliberation by reducing it to a cacophony of unyielding and hostile voices, the very vitality of the background culture may draw energies and emotions away from the common civic life on which the perpetuation of justice depends. That was the worry Tocqueville famously expressed in the nineteenth century: 'Private life in democratic times is so busy, so excited, so full of wishes and of work, that hardly any energy or leisure remains to each individual for public life. I am the last man to contend that these propensities are unconquerable . . . I maintain only that at the present day a secret power is fostering them in the human heart, and if they are not checked, they will wholly overgrow it' (de Tocqueville 1945 edn.: 310). So even if pluralism does not transform democracy into a kind of tribal warfare, democracy may yet perish through a process of affective withdrawal as citizenship becomes a tedious distraction from the real business of living. The two processes of civic decay might even work to reinforce each other. As citizens turn away from civic participation, politically engaged tribalists will be quick to fill the ensuing silence, and their clamour may persuade others to turn away in disgust or indifference, and so the process of tribalization feeds withdrawal and vice versa.

The problem of stability that pluralism creates for the well-ordered society has to do with the fragility of any reconciliation between the good of citizens and the political virtue they must evince if the justice of the basic structure is to endure. The ideal of a liberal patriotism suggests a way in which that reconciliation might hold fast against the divisions and disharmony that pluralism, even at its reasonable best, will tend to arouse. So far as citizens come to think of justice as integral to a particular political community they care about, in which their own fulfilment and that of their fellow citizens are entwined in a common fate, then the sacrifices and compromises that justice requires cannot be sheer loss in the pursuit of one's own good. They cannot be sheer loss because for liberal patriots the flourishing of a just community has become a central constituent of their own good. The idea of liberal patriotism is thus a way of integrating the twin aspects of reason that inhere in Rawls's political conception of the person: the rational pursuit of individual good and the reasonable pursuit of justice. And in the absence of that integration, the centrifugal pressures of pluralism itself should make us worry about the durability of any over-lapping consensus on a conception of justice.

## 28. *Two Objections*

An objection sure to surface here draws on a point that was crucial to my argument earlier against Sandel's ideal of community. To see others as justice requires is to regard them as possessing an inviolable worth that is independent of the degree of fellow feeling we have towards them. But patriotic sentiment commonly operates so as to obscure the basis and the content of our obligations even to compatriots. The history and likely future of patriotism is not a story of convergence between justice and fidelity to established or hoped for political communities; it is a story of enduring conflict, or so the detractors of patriotism are likely to say.

Daniel Weinstock's recent assault on the morality of nationalism is relevant here, since much of his critique is also applicable to the idea of a patriotic loyalty that might obtain in multinational and national states alike.[12] Weinstock says that once we agree that rights have moral weight irrespective of the feelings of those who must respect them, we cannot consistently say that emotional attachment among co-nationals has moral value. If we continue to advocate its inculcation for the sake of justice, this could only be 'a concession to human frailty . . . a way of rigging the incentives to get people to do what they ought to do for other reasons'. Furthermore, the appeal to our 'affective reactions' is unwise anyhow since these as often make us resentful as sympathetic towards those whose rights we must respect. The real guardian of rights is 'liberal legalism', which in the form of tax laws, bills of rights, welfare legislation, and the like, conspires to correct the capricious affinities of national feeling (Weinstock 1996: 92–3).

Suppose we agree that the basic justification of rights has nothing to do with feelings of solidarity that compatriots may or may not evoke in a given moral agent. That does not mean measures intended to instil patriotic loyalty can be no better than a manipulative process of getting people to do what they ought to do for other reasons. The reasons that properly motivate us as moral agents are not necessarily confined to the ones that apply at the most basic level of moral justification. The very idea of common citizenship in a world of different polities entails the principle that a more substantial set of rights and duties links the lives of fellow citizens than connects those who lack that common status. That being so, it becomes rational to nourish a sense of solidarity among those who share that common status so far as solidarity makes it more likely that the relevant rights and duties will be honoured. People who are motivated by patriotism will act on a morally relevant motive, even if it has no place in fundamental moral justification.[13] This is just what Rawl's theory of moral development would suggest. The most basic level of moral justification is only fully grasped within the morality of principles, but even there moral conduct need not rely exclusively on the motivating force of reasons that are supposedly unique to that level. Indeed, Rawls suggests that other motives may continue to have some psychologically necessary role (Rawls 1971: 486).

But this does not touch Weinstock's other argument. That argument says national or patriotic sentiment will not in fact reliably support justice, and liberal legalism is the remedy we truly need. But the contrast between political sentiment and legalism is confused. Legalism will have the corrective role Weinstock assigns to it only where it becomes an established part of the regnant civic vernacular. Otherwise we should expect liberal legalism to have all the efficacy of international human rights law in Pol Pot's Cambodia. The fact that national or patriotic emotions often operate against the claims of justice is important, and more will be said about it in Chapter 5. But that problem is not solved by a legal order altogether alien to our socialized emotions that must be pitted against them. What it needed in the first instance is an education that would align patriotic feeling with the claims of justice.

But another, much more formidable objection can be pressed here. So far my discussion of the relation between justice and patriotism has ignored the large moral complexities of societies that are only very imperfectly just. I said that the exercise of justice in a well-ordered society has a historical dimension in that the give and take of just cooperation draws on (and replenishes) a reservoir of warranted social trust. But this condition does not straightforwardly apply to any extant polity. Indeed, the history of any real society under pluralism is not the story of ever deepening trust among a single people; it is typically a bundle of intersecting stories of several different peoples, and the stories may overlap in episodes of conquest and oppression, glory for some and humiliation for others. The legacy of distrust that such episodes bequeath to the present creates a large obstacle to the kind of political education I have commended. The problem is that a failure to examine the legacy threatens to blur the crucial distinction between warranted and unwarranted trust, and to obscure as well the moral urgency of historical injustices that persist in the present. On the other hand, a pedagogy that dwells relentlessly on the past moral failings of the society threatens to leave prospective citizens alienated from its future.

A revealing example of the way in which a morally critical approach to the past may founder on the problem of political alienation is found in John Hope Franklin's observations on the history of race relations in America:

Perhaps the first thing we need to do as a nation and as individual members of society is to confront our past and see it for what it is. It is a past that is filled with some of the ugliest possible examples of racial brutality and degradation in human history. We need to recognize it for what it is and not explain it away, excuse it, or justify it. Having done that, we should make a good-faith effort to turn our history around so we can see in front of us, so that we can avoid doing what we have done for so long. If we do that whites will discover that African Americans possess the same human qualities that other Americans possess, and African Americans will discover that white Americans are capable of the most sublime expressions of human conduct of which all human beings are capable. (Franklin 1993: 74–5)

The question begged here is how the unqualified revulsion towards the past that Franklin wants to elicit could possibly fuel the hopeful orientation towards the future that he also recommends. Our history is the repository of the moral resources we might put to good use in the future. But if there are no such resources, out of what do Americans forge the bright new beginning Franklin directs them towards? If history tells Americans that they have been consistently incapable of valuing the common human qualities that transcend race or marveling at the achievements of those who are racially different, on what grounds can they believe they will be capable in the future? Against the background of history as moral wasteland, there can be no rational belief of that kind. If we present history to students in this way, they might be forgiven for preferring a disengaged cynicism to a hope unjustified by all the past tells them about who they are. This is not to say that Franklin overstates the magnitude of American racism; it is to insist rather that even if he were entirely right about that, a pedagogy that triggers only the moral horror he thinks history should teach us would block rather than support the shared commitment to building a just community that he wants to accompany that horror.

As we shall see in Chapter 5, it is easy (and perhaps rather more common) to go wrong in political education through an error that is just the opposite of Franklin's by supposing that a morally sanitized history is the foundation of civic virtue. But we need to look much more closely at that particular error before we can see how it might be avoided without lapsing back into the kind of mistake that Franklin makes.

# CHAPTER 5

## Patriotism and Sentimentality

### 29. Introduction

The development of justice in citizens' lives is threatened by the very fact of pluralism. The many conflicting convictions and loyalties in the background culture incline us to disagreement that runs counter to respect for reasonable differences, and the vigour of that culture may draw individuals away from the civic engagement on which the maintenance of just institutions depends. These problems are exacerbated once substantial injustice exists within the basic structure and is recognized by many. The project of constructing an attachment to political community that would contain the centrifugal tendencies of pluralism without betraying justice may appear futile when political relations are often poisoned with the enmity and distrust deposited by histories of oppression. But the appearance of futility may often be deceptive, or so I shall claim. My argument will concentrate on these problems as they are manifest in the United States, although the argument will be more widely applicable.

The American example is revealing for several reasons. The claims of patriotic loyalty still have great emotional force for many Americans, even if its most vocal adherents sometimes seem dangerously susceptible to the more virulent moral pathologies of patriotism. But that loyalty is also more often self-consciously tied to the constitutive principles of liberal democratic government than it is elsewhere, and in that respect at least, American political culture might seem a relatively fertile ground for the growth of the liberal patriotism I delineated in the previous chapter. On the other hand, as John Hope Franklin reminds us, American history is replete with 'some of the ugliest possible examples of racial brutality and degradation' (Franklin 1993: 74). The many discourses of what Rogers Smith calls 'American ascriptivism', which suggest that 'the nation's political and economic structures should formally reflect natural and cultural inequalities', have powerfully shaped the past and continue to endure in the present (R. M. Smith 1993: 550). Some may think Smith's argument overblown, but that is nothing to the point here. The relevant question is how can a liberal patriotism be sustained when political institutions and attitudes remain affected by a past that is in many important respects morally sordid, and it would require prodigious historical myopia to suppose that this was not true of the United States.

At the end of the previous chapter, I suggested that the question cannot be rationally addressed, as Franklin supposes, by renouncing the past as a moral wasteland, and then urging our children to create a polity of free and equal citizens, as if out of nothing. Once that error is recognized for what it is, it becomes tempting to construe civic education in the manner that William Galston has recommended:

On the practical level, very few individuals will come to embrace the core commitments of liberal societies through a process of rational inquiry. If children are to be brought to accept these commitments as valid and binding, it can only be through a process that is far more rhetorical than rational. For example, rigorous historical research will almost certainly vindicate complex 'revisionist' accounts of key figures in American history. Civic education, however, requires a more noble, moralizing history: a pantheon of heroes who confer legitimacy on central institutions and constitute worthy objects of emulation. It is unrealistic to believe that more than a few adult citizens of liberal societies will ever move beyond the kind of civic commitment engendered by such a pedagogy. (Galston 1991*a*: 243–4)

In place of the politics of apathy, cynicism, or divisive tribalism, we can forge the unifying politics of sentimentality. The state will have legitimacy in the eyes of ordinary citizens because they have been taught to see it as a great inheritance they receive from people who inspire awe and admiration. Political life will be animated by an education that gives pride of place to rhetoric over reason, an education that is moralizing rather than morally critical. The integrity of the polity will be safe against the divisions of pluralism because citizens have learned to live within the reach of ennobling public emotions that ensure the necessary political cohesion.

The proposed remedy is hardly an unfamiliar one. In America the shaping of civic memory, mainly by political and economic elites, has been driven since the nineteenth century by the goals that Galston champions, and even if local resistance or indifference to that process has been an enduring fact of history, its distorting effects upon public understanding of the past can scarcely be doubted (Kammen 1991; Bodnar 1992). Moreover, the remedy is not uniquely American or modern. Galston's argument is substantially the same as the case for selective historical forgetting famously advanced by Ernest Renan, the nineteenth-century liberal French historian. Renan declared that nation-building requires 'getting one's history wrong' on those unseemly matters which imperil our sense that the nation is indeed a suitable object of pride and devotion (quoted in Miller 1995*b*: 34). And Plato's suggestion that citizens in his ideal republic be told a 'myth' to 'increase their loyalty to the state and each other' anticipates Galston's proposal by a couple of millennia (Plato 1955 edn.: 160–1). Yet Galston's argument is of special interest because he is far more candid about the abridgement of reason that sentimental civic education requires than many of its other contemporary proponents, and unlike his ancient philosophical precursor, he offers an argument that is developed within the framework of a theory of liberal democracy. If his argument were sound, then much that I have already said about civic virtue and political education must be wrong. The sentimental patriotism he espouses is at variance with the rationalist spirit of the virtue of justice as I have depicted it and severely curtails autonomous reflection in politics.

Galston's endorsement of sentimental political education depends in part on an offhand pessimism about the ability or desire of ordinary citizens to understand the rational grounds for the political institutions under which they live. If we reject the pessimism, it is tempting automatically to discard the sentimentality as well. But that would be rash. The question whether sentimental civic education is a good thing is at least partly independent of the question of whom its recipients should be. One could take the view that everyone ought to receive such an education, and that revisionist history and rational enquiry into the justification of liberal politics are optional extras for those with peculiar intellectual tastes. So there can be egalitarian as well as elitist species of sentimental civic education. Although I argue later that the elitist species is less obviously unreasonable than its egalitarian counterpart, my critique will rely mainly on grounds that apply equally to egalitarian and elitist species of the genus.

The task of debunking sentimental civic education may look deceptively easy. The antipathy between sentimentality and certain core values of liberal democracy will quickly become clear in what follows. Yet even if that were established beyond doubt, the case against what Galston recommends would remain incomplete. That is because the problem he addresses does not disappear merely by exposing the liabilities of his proposed solution. A civic education that is rational rather than rhetorical and morally critical rather than moralizing is not obviously a powerful instrument for the arousal of those political affections whose maintenance seems especially difficult in large, pluralistic democracies whose present and future are overshadowed by a morally ambiguous past. In fact, it might be suspected that a spirit of untrammelled social criticism is commonly corrosive of such emotions, and hence an education that gives it free rein will not be compatible with practices that evoke whatever public emotions we rightly prize. Until that compatibility is established, people who recognize the problem Galston addresses will have reason to be attracted to his solution.

## 30. Sentimentality and Unearned Emotion

I have dubbed Galston's approach to political education 'sentimental', although that is not how he names it. The epithet is at least faintly derogatory, and so it requires some justification.

Oscar Wilde said that sentimentality is emotion one has not paid for (Wilde 1962 edn.: 501). That is a revealing metaphor. It says there are some emotions we earn the right to feel with the consequence that they are truly our own—emotions we have paid for, so to speak, in thought and experience—and others that have in some way been illicitly appropriated or aroused so that they do not belong to us in all but the shallowest sense. This in turn suggests that 'sentimentality' belongs among the antonyms of 'autonomy' and its cognates: to succumb to sentimentality is to echo others' emotions in ways that forfeit ownership of one's affective life. Now political education can be conducted in ways that evoke powerful public emotions while inhibiting the psychological context that might make them our own. That is obscure as it stands, but it is as good a beginning as any.

When I was a child during the 1960s in Ireland, a central text in virtually everyone's political socialization was Pádraic Pearse's funeral oration at the graveside of O'Donovan Rossa, a distinguished republican buried with great ceremony in 1915. The oration had a significance for many Irish nationalists comparable to the Gettysburg address for patriotic Americans. Pearse was the central figure in the pantheon of heroes who conferred legitimacy on Irish republicanism and the state he helped to usher in. The oration is almost as rhetorically concentrated as Lincoln's speech, although its restrained ferocity stands in the sharpest contrast to Lincoln's elegiac tone. Pearse exalted republican martyrdom in words that have come to haunt the history of Ireland in subsequent decades: 'Life springs from death; and from the graves of patriot men and women spring living nations' (Pearse 1966 edn.: 136–7). The orator was a man of his word. In 1916 he was among the leaders of an abortive insurrection against British rule and was executed. It was impossible for a child to read the oration in the 1960s without seeing it in the context of what happened in 1916, and for some at least, the oration and the recollection of the insurrection and executions that followed were enveloped in powerful public emotions. We looked back to these events in our past in a way that partly approximated Yeats's perspective in the wake of the tragedy of 1916: 'All's changed, changed utterly | A terrible beauty is born' (Yeats 1937).

Were these emotions we had earned the right to feel? I just suggested that the patriotic fervour an Irish child of the 1960s might feel in looking back towards Pearse and his fellow republican martyrs only partly approximated Yeats's words about the momentous significance of the insurrection. For Yeats's words express an ambivalence that forecloses any facile sentimentality.[1] He was taken by the beauty of the insurgents' uncalculating heroism. But the rebellion and its immediate bloody aftermath also filled him with terror. Subsequent events have revealed the prescience of his terror. My main purpose here is not to deride the emotions that fuel militant Irish republicanism; it is to suggest rather that certain feelings can be elicited and instilled as patterns of political response in ways that obstruct any serious reflection on whatever might show them to be apt or otherwise. The simple, fervent pride in the republican tradition of Pearse that was encouraged in me as a child at school certainly fitted that pattern. When public emotions are evoked and shaped in these ways, we have no right to feel them because we have made them 'our own' only in the thin sense that applies when we thoughtlessly replicate the emotional stereotypes of our culture. Given Wilde's aphorism, we can call the process of arousing and shaping such emotions sentimental civic education.

It will be objected that my example is tendentious. The inculcation of sentimental political attitudes that indirectly support political violence is without doubt wrong. But the problem here is with the evils sentimentality is contingently associated with rather than political sentimentality as such. A sentimental adulation of Abraham Lincoln or Martin Luther King Jr., say, is hardly open to the same moral criticism, or so the objection suggests. One might infer that political sentimentality and the educational practices that promote it are in themselves ethically neutral phenomena. When sentimental political education supports laudable values it too is laudable; when it secures the psychological entrenchment of evil it is rightly condemned. After all, Galston does not say that we can recruit anyone we want to the pantheon, regardless of moral credentials. Candidates must be morally qualified to belong to a truly liberal and democratic pantheon, even if some blemishes and lapses have to be ignored to secure their status there. I believe this objection is badly mistaken. But to see that it is, we need a more exact characterization of sentimentality than Wilde's suggestive remarks can furnish.

## 31. Fictions of Purity and Political Vice

A common thesis about emotions in contemporary philosophy is that they characteristically involve evaluative judgements of some sort and are differentiated on that basis (e.g. Greenspan 1988; Nozick 1989: 87–93). Patriotic pride, say, is not some unique inner thrill to be identified through its peculiar sensational qualities. Intrinsic to patriotic pride are evaluative judgements about the nation or multinational polity with which one identifies, judgements about the impressive accomplishments of its past or the hopeful prospects for its future. Only by virtue of such judgements can we distinguish patriotic pride from other emotions that have a positive subjective valence.

Emotions are subject to rational appraisal precisely because they have a component of evaluative judgement. The judgement at issue in the occurrence of a particular emotion may be ill-considered, unimaginative, betraying a blindness to the complexity of what it purports to be about, in which case the emotion itself warrants rational condemnation. This immediately suggests an appealing line of thought on the nature of sentimentality. Some emotions are in various ways agreeable to us—pleasurable, consoling, inspiring, and the like—and these create a standing temptation to distort our judgements so as to yield the emotional experiences we crave. Refining Wilde's striking aphorism, we might say that emotions are unearned, and hence sentimental, if they come about through some misrepresentation of reality in the evaluative judgements they involve.

But as Mark Jefferson has persuasively argued, not every agreeable emotion indulged at the cost of misrepresenting the world is correctly viewed as sentimental. He asks what distinguishes the sustaining fictions of sentimentality from other species of emotional indulgence, and the answer he gives is a useful half-truth:

Well, chiefly it is their emphasis on such things as the sweetness, dearness, littleness, blamelessness, and vulnerability of the emotion's object. The qualities that sentimentality imposes on its objects are the qualities of innocence. But this almost inevitably involves a gross simplification of the nature of the object. And it is simplification of an overtly moral significance. The simplistic appraisal necessary to sentimentality is also a direct impairment to the moral vision taken of its objects. (Jefferson 1983: 526–7)

The misrepresentation distinctive of sentimentality is no trifling matter because it involves a coarsening of moral vision. Nevertheless, Jefferson draws the boundaries of the concept too narrowly. The qualities he specifies under the rubric of 'innocence' make it clear he is using the word in a sense that contrasts both with moral culpability and the wisdom of experience. His 'fiction of innocence' neatly captures the sustaining ideology of domestic sentimentality as it has flourished in Western societies since the beginning of modernity. The alleged sweetness, dearness, littleness, blamelessness, and vulnerability of women and children, so long as they perform their assigned roles in the conventional family, have long been staple subjects of sentimental discourse. But there is another, complementary sentimentality that revolves around such things as manly greatness, glory, and the lustre of a morally invulnerable heroism. It will not do to subsume all this under the fiction of innocence because the object of emotional indulgence is here misrepresented through a fiction of masterly accomplishment in the world of experience, a world that stands in severe contrast to the sphere of innocence. Yet common ground does link the two kinds of sentimentality. In both cases there is a sustaining fiction of moral purity. The only difference is that in the sentimentality of glory and greatness, moral purity struggles with the contaminating forces abroad in the world of experience and triumphs over them, whereas purity is something to be protected from those same forces in the sentimentality of innocence.

On this understanding of what makes an emotion sentimental, the inculcation of strong and abiding beliefs in certain fictions of moral purity becomes the primary task of sentimental civic education. These will be fictions about the pantheon of heroes who confer legitimacy on political institutions, and that legitimacy will hinge on the conviction that the moral purity of those who created the institutions is embodied in their creation. But the primary task cannot be prosecuted with any hope of enduring success unless certain subsidiary tasks are undertaken. Psychological dispositions that buttress faith in the relevant fictions are needed, and traits that might undermine the faith have to be checked. The moral liabilities of these subsidiary tasks pose difficulties for the defence of sentimental civic education. I address three such liabilities.

First, to protect faith in the relevant fictions it is necessary to constrict the historical imagination in ways that impair what might be called civic self-knowledge. The need for this can be brought out by considering some recent remarks of Stuart Hampshire about the general relationship between self-knowledge and how we understand our own individual histories. Hampshire suggests that we necessarily view our lives retrospectively, as a thin track between two margins (Hampshire 1989: 100–1). Across one margin are the possible things that might have happened to us but did not; across the other lie the possible choices we might have made but did not. Suppose I want to take pride in the life I have led, but that pride is in truth unwarranted by the story of my past. I do not necessarily have to lie to myself about the choices I actually made; it may suffice to evade the truth about certain possibilities that lie beyond the margins of what might have been. So I can ignore the possibility that the friend who turned away from me would have remained if I had been more empathic or that a fulfilling careeer could have been mine with more self-discipline on my part. A sentimental reading of my own past does not necessarily require sheer fabrication. The necessary misrepresentation may be effected through a constricted imagination regarding possibilities that lie just beyond the margins of what might have been.

The same point applies to sentimentality in teaching the history of a political community. There may be no need to lie outright about the past, although that often helps greatly. Constricting the imagination regarding missed possibilities may be enough. A militant pride in Irish republicanism, for example, is a lot easier to sustain by ignoring the possibilities that the choices of Pearse and his fellow insurgents pushed beyond the margins of what might have been in 1916. Might the politics of patience and compromise have secured Irish independence—or as much independence as could decently and realistically be hoped for—without a blood sacrifice? However one answers that question, to explore it seriously and imaginatively is to pursue history in an unsentimental spirit, and whatever public emotion can survive that process is emotion one has paid for. Moreover, the dangers of a sentimentality induced by a constricted historical imagination are abundantly clear in a case of this sort. For if my pride in the blood sacrifice of 1916 hinges on disregard of the political potency of patience and compromise, I will hardly be sufficiently alert to their possible potency in the present.

It is important to be clear about the significance of my example here. I am not just saying that a sentimental civic education might sometimes hinder our appreciation of patience and compromise by blocking development of the historical imagination. That is patently an evil sentimental civic education will not always produce, and so it is not even relevant to the objection that such an education might be practised in support of the right values—such as patience and compromise perhaps. My point is rather that in order to insulate politicized fictions of moral purity from ready falsification, the historical imagination must be truncated in ways that blind us to the possible values that were rejected in the choices not taken, and this will tend to blind us to the contemporary relevance of those same values. This is a liability that sentimental civic education must incur, irrespective of the particular values it is made to subserve.

Second, the simplification of reality necessary to fictions of moral purity will remain precarious at best unless judgements that relate even indirectly to the object of emotion undergo a supportive simplification.

Faith in a pantheon of historical heroes will not be durable if the people they contended with and the institutions they created, destroyed or reformed are seen in ways that register moral complexity and ambiguity. A sentimentality of glory and greatness requires sheer moral polarities, and the apotheosis of historical figures cannot be secure unless the people and the causes they opposed are diabolized.[2] So the coarsening of moral vision that sentimentality entails cannot be localized around an isolated object of emotional indulgence if it is to survive at all. There will be strong pressure to teach other fictions in order to insulate adherence to the central fiction from challenge and refutation (Jefferson 1983: 527–8).

Third, sentimental civic education will tend to be conservative in a sense that even conservatives should find troubling. The fiction of moral purity is eroded so far as we acknowledge any defect in the political accomplishment, or at least the political vision, of those who belong in the pantheon, and so to resist erosion it becomes necessary to deny or palliate any defect. That is the point of Galston's rejection of revisionist history. But this means that the outcome of sentimental civic education will tend to be a debased conservativism. The recipients of that education must be inclined to see themselves as inheritors of political projects which, in conception at least, are perfection itself, so that any significant innovation becomes treachery to perfection.

It does not follow that a sober and judicious conservatism or attempts at its cultural transmission are inevitably sentimental or that radicalism and its educational expression are immune to political sentimentality. Some versions of conservatism, and derivative conceptions of civic education, do not rely on fictions of purity about the past or anathematize serious political criticism (e.g. Oakeshott 1989; Simpson 1989), and some versions of radicalism do both. The political sentimentality of the left is expressed in fictions of purity about the members of its pantheon, and it too is conservative in the influence it seeks to exert when the completeness and perfection of what the pantheon achieved or envisioned is assumed as educational dogma.[3]

The three moral liabilities I have attributed to sentimental civic education help to clarify the curtailment of reason which Galston admits is part of the cost we must pay for its benefits. Galston does not himself specify the cost as I have tried to do here, and perhaps he would balk at the price that must be paid when it is spelled out. A truncated historical imagination, a propensity to filter complex political problems through a network of mutually supportive moral fictions, and finally, a debased conservatism, would each seem to be a rather grievous vice, and any conception of political education which implicitly endorses their inculcation would appear fundamentally flawed.

## 32. Borrowing from Plato

The moral liabilities I have ascribed to sentimental civic education presuppose that certain psychological traits among its necessary aims will
function as vices in the lives of ordinary citizens. That presupposition is
open to challenge. A disposition is only a civic vice when it tends
adversely to affect performance in whatever roles are assigned in a just
polity. If a role that excluded its occupants from the exercise of power
could be justly constructed and assigned, then the fact that a certain disposition would undermine their competence in political judgement
would not make it a vice for them, since they are not supposed to make
such judgements anyhow. Their role would be simply to obey, and political judgement would be an impertinent attempt to second-guess their
betters. That was the kind of role Plato assigned everyone outside the
guardian class in his republic. Therefore, my strictures on sentimental
political education would be brushed aside by a disciple of Plato, or any
other partisan of oligarchy. That move is not so readily available to
Galston because he recommends sentimental civic education as a way of
achieving political cohesion in a liberal democracy.

Yet the concept of liberal democracy is contested intellectual territory,
and among the issues of contention is the optimum balance of representation and participation in the design of political institutions. Where participation is extensive, the exercise of political judgement must be prominent
in the lives of ordinary citizens, and the corrupting effects of educational
practices that morally coarsen judgement will be magnified. So educational theorists who favour participatory politics, like White or Gutmann,
predictably insist on a civic education in which the emphasis falls squarely
on moral criticism and reason rather than emotional uplift (White 1983:
91–2; Gutmann 1986: 95–107). Given the distinctive values of participatory democracy, the roles of ruler and ruled intersect to a degree that
makes the appropriate virtues and vices of each virtually interchangeable.
Conversely, so far as a conception of democracy favours representation
over participation, a disparity will emerge between the role requirements
of ordinary citizens and those assigned to rulers. A part of the disparity
may be marked differences in the virtues and vices that befit the occupants
of the contrasting roles. This makes it possible to launch a quasi-Platonic
defence of sentimental political education within a certain kind of liberal
democratic context. What I have said are the distinctive vices of such an
education would obviously wreak moral havoc were they evinced to any
substantial degree by those who govern. But among the governed the
same putative vices serve the useful function of bolstering affective civic
commitment, and their potentially noxious consequencess are avoided to

the degree that political participation is minimized. One implication of this is that only the elitist species of sentimental civic education remains a viable option: those who govern cannot receive such an education, or at least they must learn to outgrow its effects before they can acquire the virtues of wise governance. Galston seems at least attracted to the quasi-Platonic argument. He insists on a distinction between the political virtues of participation and those that safeguard representative institutions; he chides Gutmann for giving the former pride of place; and he approvingly quotes Thomas Jefferson's view that the genius of democracy consists in the way representative government differentiates the authentic *aristoi* from the *pseudo-aristoi* (Galston 1991*a*: 225, 247– 8).

The thesis that democracy at its best is a superior version of aristocracy is controversial. But there is no need to dispute the thesis here to show the inadequacy of the quasi-Platonic argument. The argument fails because even when representation is massively emphasized and participation correspondingly slighted, a substantial overlap remains between the virtues of the ruler and the virtues of the ruled. As a result, the political sentimentality that militates against the virtue of the ruler will be similarly destructive of the virtue of the ruled. This becomes clear by looking at the significance of two of the virtues Galston says ordinary citizens must acquire in a liberal democracy: the ability and inclination to choose wisely in the election of officials, and political loyalty.

The efficacy of representative institutions in elevating the *aristoi* to political office and keeping out the *pseudo-aristoi* depends on what ordinary citizens do in that sphere of political participation, modest though it might be, that representation entails. The supposed superiority of democratic aristocracy over plain old aristocracy requires that citizens have the ability 'to discern the talent and character of candidates vying for office, and to evaluate the performance of individuals who have attained office' (Galston 1991*a*: 224). Now the development and effective exercise of that capability depends in turn on what Michael Walzer has identified as a form of 'play' essential to the political culture of a democracy (Walzer 1980: 159–76). This is the making of vicarious anticipative and retrospective judgements, sometimes in deliberative solitude but more often in dialogue with others, about the proper conduct of public officials—on these grounds Clinton should adopt protectionist trade policies, for that reason Ford should not have pardoned Nixon, and so on. A comparable activity could be practised by people who are wholly and permanently excluded from political participation, although it would then be an utterly pointless pastime, like wondering what kind of weather there would be if one were God. In representative democracy, vicarious anticipations and retrospections regarding the decisions of office holders are a profoundly serious endeavour. That is largely because the skill and insight we develop in playing the game are what we rely on to evaluate the performance of office-holders and to measure the talent and character of candidates for office. The talent and character of candidates has to do with the quality of the decisions they are likely to make, just as the merit of current office-holders depends on the quality of the decisions they have made. So citizens who are inept participants in Walzer's democratic play will be in no position to tell the difference between the *aristoi* and the *pseudo-aristoi*.

But once that conclusion is granted, it cannot be sensibly said that the dispositions instilled through a sentimental political education can be reconciled with the virtues that underpin representative institutions. Vicarious anticipations and retrospections of political decisions are as vulnerable to corruption by the traits I have said are part of such an education as are the judgements of office-holders themselves. A citizen afflicted with the debased conservatism that political sentimentality involves is in no position to assess the credentials for office of candidates who promise meaningful innovation. Of course, an ordinary citizen who lacks a historical imagination, interprets ethical distinctions according to sheer moral polarities and is conservative in the degraded sense I have specified does far less harm than the elected official who displays the same vices. But the cumulative harm wrought by an education that produces many such ordinary citizens is great precisely because the more there are the less likely it is that representative institutions will in fact differentiate the *aristoi* from the *pseudo-aristoi*.

The corrupting effects of sentimental civic education on ordinary citizens are also evident once we reflect on the character of political loyalty in a liberal democracy. As Galston admits, political loyalty in that setting necessarily hinges on commitment to the constitutive principles of the liberal democratic state (Galston 1991*a*: 221). That loyalty will certainly encompass a strong predisposition towards law-abidingness, and in even moderately favourable circumstances, it may be evident in a judicious trust in established institutions and a reverence for received civic rituals. But to confuse loyalty with these properly subordinate habits and attitudes is like mistaking erotic love for its typical expressions and patterns of behaviour. There is the permanent possibility that law may be enacted or administered in ways that betray the fundamental values of liberal democracy, that institutions other than the law may be implicated in the same betrayal or that received rituals may cease to be a fitting expression of adherence to those values. Here again skill in Walzer's democratic play, and a serious delight in such play, may be viewed as ensuring the vitality of public virtue in its deepest aspects; and to the extent that sentimental political education impedes the development of that skill and delight, it will impair the kind of political loyalty that is desirable.

In the light of all this, it is not surprising that Galston seems less than comfortable with the neat distinction he initially makes between philosophical education, which gives critical reason unfettered scope, and a civic education that restricts its exercise for the sake of affective political commitment. The distinction is drawn with hard outlines that are immediately softened: 'In principle and in practice, liberal democracy does exhibit a degree of openness to philosophical education, and to its social consequences, that is probably without precedent in human history' (Galston 1991*a*: 243). But the issue is not about what educational processes a liberal society should be open to; it is about what processes it cannot do without to preserve and enrich its public culture. A liberal democracy cannot merely be hospitable to the exercise of critical reason as it is open, say, to the virtues that support certain religious or aesthetic ideals. If it is to thrive from one generation to the next, even in forms that stress representation over participation, civic virtues informed by critical reason must be widely and deeply diffused among the citizenry; and that being so, sentimental civic education in all its forms cannot be an appealing option.

Nothing I have said means that Galston's offhand pessimism about the ability and desire of ordinary citizens to think deeply about their political institutions is misplaced.[4] What my argument so far suggests is that to whatever extent his pessimism might be warranted so too is pessimism about democracy being any better than a species of oligarchy in which we cannot even expect the oligarchs to be well chosen. But I think we have grounds to take a less bleak view than that. The fact that American political culture often seems inimical to the kind of deliberation that is proper to a free people is reasonably viewed as in large part a consequence of alterable social practices (Gutmann 1993: 143–4). If success in American elections now seems to depend far more on who concocts the cleverest sound bytes than on who has the most thoughtful moral arguments, that is surely something that might be changed through a better educated citizenry rather than a consequence of the fixed limits of reason in people's lives. At any rate, to embrace the pessimistic alternative is to make it a self-fulfilling prophesy.

## 33. The Uncertain Role of Critical Reason

An option may cease to be appealing to us, and still we continue to think it is the best we can do. I introduced sentimental political education as a widely prescribed remedy to the problems of tribalism and political disengagement in a society where individual and group interests come to eclipse any affective attachment to the political community. Although some may infer that the cure is worse than the disease, others may continue to prefer the cure in the absence of alternative therapy.

The unavailability of alternative therapy might seem inevitable so long as we think that history stands exposed as a moral wasteland once we give up on Galston's remedy. The aim of encouraging patriotic attachment would then depend on our ability to inspire a desperate leap of faith in a political future that is radically discontinuous with the past, and any such aim seems utopian. The absence of an alternative to Galston's remedy will also seem inevitable so long as an education wedded to critical reason is not understood in the particular moral context that gives reason its political significance. That failure is common. Consider Jeremy Waldron's claim that besides the intellectual formation of a ruling caste, the critical abilities nurtured by the humanities and sciences in higher education have had a primarily apoliticial or even anti-political value:

Beyond [the intellectual training of rulers], if the sciences and humanities have had any sort of mission at all, it has been to educate, respectively, two kinds of non-citizen: first, the cosmopolitan scientist who will identify with his peers around the world rather than his fellow compatriots, and with the scientific enterprise itself rather than the peculiar interest of this or that republic; and second, the dissenting anti-citizens of literature and philosophy, young intellectuals tortured with educated despair and exercised by nothing more civically uplifting than a determination to expose the emptiness in everything they see around them (Waldron 1993*b*: 12).

Waldron is an academic philosopher allowing himself the pleasure of a little journalistic hyperbole here. The hyperbole should not distract us from the troubling insight of the passage: critical reason is often developed within our educational institutions to a dazzling level of sophistication which nonetheless leaves us at a political dead-end. The point is especially troubling regarding the humanities because there we pervasively encounter matters of palpable civic significance.

Critical reason in the shape of an implacable scepticism is politically sterile. But that is the shape it commonly takes, for example, in that congeries of views which are bundled together under the label of postmodernism. Perhaps the most prominent theme in the academic literature which bears that label is the alleged complicity of conceptions of reason that have underpinned the civilization of the West in the oppressive practices of that civilization. The unmasking and subversion of this base complicity is supposed to be a primary task for the intellectual who scorns the cultural heritage of Western modernity (e.g. Foucault 1965). The scholarly practice of unmasking still makes it customary to place a fig-leaf of moral affirmation on the nakedness of what Waldron calls 'educated despair'. (Perhaps moral cynicism or apathy are other attitudes to be decorously disguised, and ones that are even more civically lowering.) Some quick genuflection towards empowerment or 'difference' will usually suffice these days, and the very daring may extol 'transgression'. But the primary institutional function of such gestures often seems to be to provoke others to remove the fig-leaf. Perfunctory moral affirmations enable others to enter the discourse and charge that this or that argument or text was not truly empowering or that empowerment is itself implicated in oppression, and so forth. The ceaseless production of fig-leaves creates ceaseless opportunities to unmask the emptiness or complicity in evil of what other have left unmasked. To be sure, the moral pathologies of educated despair and nihilism are by no means unique to postmodernism, and irrespective of the styles of thought they inform, such attitudes can be psychologically fundamental to achievements of great and abiding value. There would have been no Nietzsche without educated despair. But when academic criticism becomes little more than a self-perpetuating industry of unmasking it can hardly do much to help anyone live within the reach of elevating public emotions.

The difficulties of interpreting the educational role of critical reason so that it might function in politically fertile ways can also be seen from a very different perspective, one that informs Galston's conception of philosophical education. Postmodernist practices of criticism, for all their variety, revolve around a preoccupation with contingency and historicity. But a more ancient philosophical tradition identifies reason with the necessary and the universal. The aspiration here is towards a perspective which abstracts from all the partiality that afflicts our thinking once it is entangled with the contingent and the particular. Through abstraction, we are supposed to attain an objectivity far above the flux and disarray of our everyday experience. Reason so conceived becomes the view from nowhere, to borrow a memorable phrase from Thomas Nagel (Nagel 1986). Galston's chief worry about philosophical education is that there is a radical mismatch between the view from nowhere to which the unconstrained exercise of reason supposedly leads and the historically located stance that is necessary to the political competence and allegiance of citizens. The view from nowhere may or may not be capable of underwriting the constitutive ideals of liberal democracy, and if it cannot, critical reason seems once again to bring us to a political dead-end (Galston 1991*a*: 243). So long as the philosophical jury is out on the rational necessity of liberal democracy, it may seem as if the denizens of the view from nowhere must remain agnostic on the question whether liberal democracy deserves their fealty.

The argument I have traced so far might seem to push us towards a paralysing ambivalence regarding how we are to respond educationally to the problems of political education under pluralism. A cogent line of argument suggests that the values of critical reason must be part of a common civic education if liberal democratic institutions are to be continued in ways that militate against their corruption, regardless of the balance we strike between representation and participation. Therefore, sentimental civic education stands condemned before us as the enemy of those virtues. But when rational scrutiny of a political community's past exposes a history in which oppression is the dominant theme, that very fact gives us strong reason to withhold the identification that a liberal patriotism entails. Moreover, influential conceptions of critical reason in contemporary academic culture seem to aggravate the problems of civic apathy and tribalism or to be at best irrelevant to their solution. That being so, sentimental political education may continue to elicit our grudging approval. Clearly, the only way around this impasse is to elucidate ways of using critical reason in politics, and ways of teaching future citizens to use it, that can be both civically engaged and uplifting while remaining genuinely critical.

## 34. *Emotional Generosity and Historical Imagination*

The possibility of a reason that gives both civic engagement and criticism their due can be approached through an instance of someone reflecting on a moral choice in a manner that expresses powerful public emotions. The patriotic attachment those emotions evidence is also explicitly pitted against politically sanctioned oppression of the most egregious kind. My example comes from a letter of Theodore Parker, one of the early transcendentalists and an important influence on the thought of Lincoln (Wills 1992: 107–18). The passage explains why Parker gave refuge to runaway slaves:

There hang beside me in my library, as I write, the gun my grandfather fought with at the battle of Lexington,—he was a captain on that occasion,—and also the musket he captured from a British soldier on that day—the first taken in the war of independence. If I would not peril my property, my liberty, nay, my life, to keep my own parishioners out of slavery, then I should throw away these throphies, and should think I was the son of a coward, and not a brave man's child. (quoted in Frothingham 1874: 410)

An easily imagined context to these words would make them grossly sentimental. If the 'trophies' Parker alludes to are deployed as reminders of a pantheon of heroes whose politics were irreproachable wisdom, then we have a fiction of purity being used to explain and justify a political act. But then Parker would have to be an ignoramus. The heroes of the revolution countenanced and sometimes practised slavery. Only by extraordinary ignorance or self-deception could one try to explain or justify opposition to slavery by pointing to their shining example. Parker was no ignoramus. Indeed, he noted wryly that when judged against the standard of its avowed fidelity to liberty 'the nation's course [is] as crooked as the Rio Grande' (Parker 1973 edn.: 143). This should hearten the most belligerent revisionists in contemporary American historiography, and so even by their lights, the quoted passage would seem to require a more charitable reading than a quick dismissal as sentimental trash.

From a radically abstract philosophical perspective the passage poses different problems. Those with a fondness for the view from nowhere will have difficulty making sense of the historical specificity of Parker's reasoning. That difficulty arises even if we suppose, for the sake of argument, that the view from nowhere revealed compelling reasons for the belief that all persons have rights to equality and liberty that slavery violates. Then Parker's action was rationally required. But contingent facts about the behaviour of his forbears and what they risked their lives for have no bearing whatsoever on the evil of slavery that the view from nowhere reveals. So from that standpoint, Parker may look like an obtuse man who did the right thing for irrelevant reasons. His thinking would seem not sentimental but only stupid.

I suspect that hardly anyone would be comfortable with this conclusion, including those rare philosophical souls who hanker for the view from nowhere. For even they are unlikely to talk and judge about politics outside the study or the seminar room in a language that effaces history. Like Parker, their everyday political judgements will witness to the precedent of citizens who came before them, traditions those predecessors initiated and symbols they left that continue to inspire, and it is by heeding such judgements that their children will begin to learn about politics long before the view from nowhere gets mentioned. When they criticize Bill Clinton's shift to the right, it will be in the vernacular of the New Deal or the Great Society rather than the lingua franca of the Categorical Imperative. All this is no objection to the abstractions of political philosophy. But it does suggest that whatever the merits of such theory, it must make sense of more historically embedded patterns of political thought, like those Parker evinces, instead of discarding it as so much vulgar raving.

That is a point worth pressing. Even though Parker himself thought there were reasons that decisively condemned slavery always and everywhere, by itself that thought could not explain his decision to shelter runaway slaves and defend them to the last. For the question that faced Parker was not which course of action the view from nowhere would prescribe; the question was what he would do, given the view from somewhere in particular that gave meaning and direction to his life. As Harry Frankfurt has noted, someone may choose to violate a moral obligation 'not because he thinks it is overridden by a stronger one but because there is an alternative course of action which he considers more important to him than meeting the demands of moral rectitude' (Frankfurt 1988: 81).

This casts some light on how we might read the quotation from Parker. He is not explaining why slavery is wrong. That is taken for granted. He is giving reasons why the wrongness of slavery was so overwhelmingly important to him, reasons which show why protecting the slave was something he had no alternative but to do. Since these reasons must come to have their motivating force within the particular story of how he came to be the man he was, they necessarily have a historical dimension. Parker casts himself in the role of inheritor of a certain political project or tradition the adequate understanding of which, at the time he gave refuge to runaway slaves, made any other course of action unthinkable. I want to make three interlocked claims about this self-understanding.

First, although Parker talks about biological kinship with the initiators of the tradition, what really matters is a sense of affective kinship, a love or regard for them that was inseparable from identifying with what they cared for and despised. (After all, if Parker abhorred his progenitors and everything they stood for, his biological ancestry could not begin to explain why he behaved as he did.) Second, the affective kinship that matters here does not presuppose that the inherited project or tradition is to be replicated in its received form. Here is a remote but revealing analogy. Picasso understood himself in part as the inheritor of a great tradition of Spanish painting within which Velázquez stood among his major precursors, and some of Picasso's greatest work of the 1950s is a sustained homage to Velázquez. But Picasso also transformed the traditions of Western art almost beyond recognition, and any surface resemblance between his art and that of Velázquez is negligible. Similarly, a dedication to political change, even radical transformation, is compatible with a sense of deep indebtedness to history. That is why Parker could look to a past that stirred powerful public emotions while maintaining the critical acuity to see a moral course as 'crooked as the Rio Grande'. Third, this melding of powerful emotion and critical acuity depends on a certain way of looking at the past, a way that is both emotionally generous and imaginative. This is the vital point and it bears some elaboration.

At first glance, the idea that we could learn to look at the past of a political community with emotional generosity might seem to be a euphemistic way of recommending sentimental political education. But that is not so. Emotional generosity and sentimentality are not the same thing (Tanner 1977: 139). If we can be politically corrupted by indulging emotions regarding our history that require the manufacture of fictions of purity, we can also be undone by habits of interpretations rooted in fictions of the absence of value. The best alternative to unearned public emotion is emotion we have paid for rather than the despair or nihilism that so easily succeeds the deflation of sentimentality. Public emotions we have paid for can be viewed as the fruit of a sense of history that stands poised as a mean between opposing vices: on one side is the sentimentality that projects values onto the past which belie the truth about who we are; on the other is a despair or cynicism blind to values that the same truth can sustain.[5]

A sense of history disfigured by evaluative judgements that misrepresent the world would not be an intelligible possibility unless we might instead have a historical sensibility free of such distortion. So the very act of disparaging sentimental civic education presupposes that we might try to see the past in ways that are veridical and yet nourish the kind of affective kinship that Parker exemplified. The basis of his affective kinship with the heroes of the revolution was 'Love of Freedom . . . Accordingly, the work providentially laid out for us to do seems this,—to organize the rights of man' (Parker 1973 edn.: 143). But the work providentially laid out was not necessarily the work that had been done. If a love for liberty gave substance and continuity to the love for country that was worth having, and substance also to the ideal of common schooling in which Parker placed his best hope for the nation's future, the historical reality of America in his view as often evidenced the betrayal of liberty as the workings of a shared patriotic love (Parker 1856: 214–44, 1973 edn.: 157–69).

Parker recognized that the very meaning of the constitutive ideals of American politics was open in a way that made them vulnerable to abuse and misinterpretation. The egalitarian spirit of democracy could be celebrated in the mottto 'You are as good as I, and let us help one another'. It could also be sullied in the motto, 'I am as good as you, so get out of my way'. The equality of reciprocal goodwill was faithful to America's democratic tradition in a way that the equality of mutual indifference was not. But this could not be established merely by appealing to what the initiators of that tradition believed or did: ' "Our fathers did so", says some one. "What of that?" say we. . . . We will take their wisdom joyfully, and thank God for it, but not their authority, we know better; and of their nonsense not a word. . . . Let them keep decently buried, for respectable dead men never walk' (Parker 1973 edn.: 154).

Yet if Parker looked to a political past in which wisdom could be taken, while much nonsense and evil could be cast aside, we might ask on what basis the necessary discrimination could be made. What made 'You are as good as I, let us help one another' better than 'I am as good as you, get out of my way'? For Parker, the answer could be determined through a rational apprehension 'that there is such a thing as absolute right, a great law of God, which we are right to keep, come what will come' (Parker 1973 edn.: 152). This confluence of a philosophical and a divine view from nowhere will doubtless impress rather fewer people at the end of the twentieth century than it did during the middle of the nineteenth. But what is essential to the kind of historical sensibility Parker represents can be understood without the idea of a moral lens outside history through which what is valuable in the past can be made perspicuous. What is crucial rather is a view of political tradition in which the pressing question is 'what is the best of this tradition?' rather than 'what are the dominant or most powerful elements in this tradition?' (Herzog 1985; Barry 1990: 369–70). If we are very fortunate, the answer to the two questions will converge. But if we really care about the first question we must not confuse it with the second because what is dominant and most powerful in a tradition may be what occludes and undermines what is best.

The question 'what is the best of this tradition?' does not become meaningless even if we give up on the view from nowhere. Our ability to answer the question may be circumscribed by the critical resources of the traditions of political thought and practice to which we have access, as well as the limits of whatever good sense and creativity we can muster in using them, but it would be absurd to infer that these limits must deprive the question of its point. Moreover, regardless of limitations on our interpretive powers, the best answer to the question may always be contingent in the sense that the answer that was right for Parker may be very different than the one that is right for us. But again, our rootedness in history shapes but does not undermine our critical scrutiny of that history.

Emotional generosity and the imagination are central to the kind of historical sensibility I want to affirm because without them one cannot adequately answer the question 'what is the best of this tradition?', especially in circumstances where the best may have to be contrasted with what has been dominant. Looking to the past without the easy consolations of sentimentality means confronting a story in which evil may loom larger than good, and the good that is perceptible is not instantiated in anyone or anything in pristine radiance. A readiness to be affectively engaged by the

good in that setting requires a certain interpretive generosity, and a corresponding resistance to the meanness of spirit that goes with insisting that
the good must be perfection if it is to be good at all.

The example of Parker is instructive here too. Noting the contradiction
between the doctrine of equal liberty and the ongoing practice of slavery
in the nineteenth century, he ironically suggested a revised version of the
Declaration of Independence:

Now, it is not so strange to find it said that negroes are not 'created equal' in
inalienable rights with white men. . . . So, to make our theory accord with our
practice, we ought to recommit the Declaration to the hands which drafted that
great State paper, and to instruct Mr. Jefferson to amend the document, and
declare that 'All men are created equal, and endowed by their Creator with certain inalienable rights, if born of white mothers; but if not, not'. (Parker 1973
edn.: 152)

One can read the revised Declaration in a couple of ways. First, since
Jefferson was himself a slave-owner, and the political order he helped to
create protected the institution of slavery at the time of its creation, the
revised version unveils the true meaning of the original document. The
status of those whose exclusion was assumed by the author is made plain,
and so we can see the Declaration for the expression of racism it 'really'
is. If the past evokes any public emotion here, it can only be the resentment and outrage that attend the recognition of history as a moral wasteland.

Another reading, and the one that Parker invites, would see the revised
text as a reminder that what is morally elevating in the original depends
on discounting whatever qualifications to its rousing moral universalism
its author's actions or the enduring practice of slavery in America might
suggest. The gap Parker playfully creates between the revised and the original text is intended to disclose the gap between what Americans are and
what they might be at their best. No amount of rationalization about original intentions or authoritative traditions must disguise that gap. Dead
men do not walk, especially if they are as respectable as Thomas Jefferson.
And regardless of his views, the best of a people's moral heritage may still
be obscured in the evil of what they have become.

The second reading requires an emotional generosity that the first
repudiates: without denying the moral ambiguities and partialities that
surrounded the writing of the Declaration, its affirmation of equal rights
is embraced both as a source of continued moral inspiration in the present and legitimate pride in the past. Furthermore, the second response has
the advantage of being coherent whereas the first does not. If we are
indignant because for Jefferson part of the sub-text of the Declaration was

the exclusion of slaves (or women), that can only be because we accept the truth of what is affirmed in the text proper, and unless we were the inheritors of a political tradition in which such texts could have canonical status, we would be in no position to inveigh against the sins of Jefferson. In short, the first response does not merely obstruct the way in which a sense of history may be aligned with the cultivation of civic virtue; it is also a bad case of biting the hand that feeds you.

I said that an adequate answer to the question 'what is best in the tradition?' requires imagination as well as emotional generosity. There is more than a little overlap between the two. The temptation to excoriate the fathers of the revolution because they failed to think as we do (at our wholesome best) about race or gender arises in part from a failure of the imagination—a failure to imagine a historical context for judgement in which what is morally obvious and compelling to us would not be so to others, or where the social costs of acknowledging certain moral truths may be more burdensome than they are for us.[6] But the significance of the imagination extends beyond this. I said earlier that the imagination is important in helping us to retrieve what was lost in the choices not taken at pivotal moments in history, and it will be important too in helping people to understand ways in which what is good and decent in our traditions can be defiled. I turn to an example of that defilement in the following section. However, it should be clear at this stage that we are not compelled to choose between sentimental civic education and a pedagogy that liberates critical reason at the cost of political alienation. That is a false dilemma. The kind of historical sensibility I have described here combines an exacting commitment to reason with a generous susceptibility to those public emotions that bind us to the body politic. A political education that seeks to engender that sensibility is no doubt a difficult undertaking at the best of times, and in the sorry circumstances of contemporary American schooling it will often seem a hopeless undertaking. But it is hard to see another route to political virtue in a liberal democracy.

## 35. *History, Literature, and Political Virtue*

I have tried to undermine Galston's contrast between political education and a pedagogy that gives reason free rein. But the historical sensibility I have characterized as the basis for dispelling the contrast does allow for a distinction between political history as a resource of civic virtue and political history as an exercise cut adrift from any identification with the story it tells. To study history so as to answer the question 'what is the best of this tradition?' in order to use the best in the present is but one way to study it. There is no reason why outstanding historical scholarship should not be the product of educated despair or any other morally sterile attitude one cares to imagine. Galston is right to suppose that history in civic education differs from history *tout court*. His mistake is to think that the distinction corresponds to the difference between the construction of a pantheon of heroes and its demolition.

Yet once we are clear about the specific role of history in political education, we can think afresh about the kind of pedagogy needed to fulfil that role. Here is one idea. If we want for our children a historical sensibility that enables them to understand their political traditions with emotional generosity and imagination, then the processes by which we attempt to achieve that aim might often have less to do with conventional historical scholarship than with literature. For the most powerful and vivid expressions of that sensibility are commonly literary. Consider Eudora Welty's short story about the murder of a civil rights activist in the South during the 1960s, 'Where is the Voice Coming from?' The narrator of the story is the killer himself, and he begins with a brutally direct explanation of why he killed: 'I says to my wife, "You can reach and turn it off. You don't have to set and look at a black nigger face no longer than you want to, or listen to what you don't want to hear. It's still a free country." I reckon that's how I give myself the idea' (Welty 1980: 603). The bitter irony here is the use of the language of patriotic dedication to freedom to explain the violation of all that is decent in the tradition to which the language belongs. The irony is heightened by the fact that the murder takes place in a town called Thermopylae, recalling the great battle of antiquity when Greek liberty was defended against the barbarous hordes of Persian imperialism. Welty's less than subtle point is that the killer gives voice to another menacing barbarism, even as he absurdly poses as a defender of liberty. The depth of her story, however, lies in the way she reaches beyond baffled horror in the face of barbarism, and seeks to understand the voice of the killer. At the end of the story, it is a voice that continues to horrify, but it also evokes a pity grounded in the values of a political tradition the killer cannot understand.

Moments after the murder, the killer approaches the body of his victim and says 'We ain't never now, never going to be equals and you know why? One of us is dead' (Welty 1980: 604). For the killer, the thought that he is someone who matters depends on showing that at least some others do not. Self-respect is a zero-sum game in which success means that others must be made to lose, even at the cost of killing them. But the desperation just below the surface of the narrative reveals a man haunted by the knowledge that he has lost, and the voice he wants to reach out and turn off is really the suppressed inner voice that lays bare his own worthlessness. When his wife mocks him for leaving the weapon near the body, the inner voice rises to the surface: 'Is that how no-'count I am?' The newspaper prints a photograph of the murdered man and triggers a ridiculous self-pity—'I ain't ever had one made. Not ever!'—and the reward it offers for information on the killer arouses an equally ridiculous pride: 'For as long as they don't know who that is, whoever shot Roland is worth a good deal more right now than Roland is.' The unbearable heat of Thermopylae is a motif that runs throughout the story, suggesting a place that is not emotionally habitable even for the killer and his wife. It is a place 'so hot that even if you get to sleep you wake up feeling like you cried all night' (Welty 1980: 606). The voice has not been turned off, and he cannot face where it comes from.

The killer of Welty's story is unable think and feel in terms of the language of freedom and equality he ignorantly abuses, and his failure in that regard is what makes him both pitiful and horrifying. He is pitiful because his self-contempt discloses his inability to comprehend a dignity that would not require the servility of another, and he is horrifying in the way his self-contempt vents itself in a murderous hatred towards those whose servility he thought he could count on. Welty does not invite us to excuse the killer: to understand and pity is not to forgive or palliate the evil that was done. Indeed, to lose sight of the magnitude of the evil—to feel pity without horror—would be to miss the point. To learn to read 'Where is the Voice Coming from?' in a manner attuned to its emotional complexities is to learn to participate in the kind of historical sensibility I have tried to clarify as an alternative to both sentimentality and an alienated scepticism. The story may be about the very worst of America rather than the best, but its moral depth resides precisely in the way it tacitly draws on the best of the tradition to make sense of the worst.

A story such as this is no substitute for dispassionate social analysis of the causes and consequences of American racism. But then again, becoming adept and knowledgeable at scholarly analysis is not the same as coming to see and feel about racism in the way that Welty asks us to, and in the context of political education, the latter outcome may be of greater moment.

## 36. Whose Tradition?

The voices of the historical sensibility I have celebrated—Parker's and Welty's—belong to people from the culturally dominant group within the American story. They are voices of white, prosperous America, and so, it might be said, they only speak for and to those who have benefited the most and suffered the least in the story. For those outside that privileged circle, this point might be elaborated in two very different responses that are commonly confused.

The less radical response would note that pride in the best of a tradition, and the emotional generosity that enables us to discern the best alongside the evil and betrayals with which it is confusedly entangled, comes easily to people who have most reason to be grateful for the good the tradition has bestowed. But the situation is different for those who have enjoyed little of that good and suffered much of the evil. Where there is no reason to be grateful there is no reason to be generous. An African-American child trapped in urban poverty could not decently be asked to pity the killer in Welty's story or to take from it a renewed emotional attachment to the values of American liberty and equality which give that harrowing tale its ethical setting. A civic education for those who have suffered the most cannot take as its aim the cultivation of a sense of history so drastically at variance with their own experience. The first response tends to slide into a second, more radical view. For those who have suffered the most, the American political ideals of liberty and equality are simply not part of their tradition at all. They should turn away from the alien culture of their oppressors, and find their moral and political bearings from other sources. The second response captures the thrust of Afrocentrism, for example, where that is offered as a virtually self-contained alternative to all that Eurocentric civilization represents (e.g. Asante 1980, 1991).[7]

The less radical response expresses an important truth. So far as a group of future citizens live without the benefits of what is best in the traditions of their society, it is preposterous to expect them to identify with what is best and make that the basis of constructive political participation. The child who lives in the squalor of a neighbourhood where a Hobbesian war of all against all is daily enacted may in fact grow up to be an ardent political activist in the name of American liberty and equality. But there we see the fruit of an extraordinary strength of spirit. That is not something we can sanely expect as the routine outcome of education in so hostile an environment. But to see all this is not necessarily to give up on an education for all that seeks to engender the kind of civic virtue I have espoused. Instead, one might infer that where the circumstances of some children's lives make that education seem grossly inappropriate and utopian the circumstances need to be changed to make it otherwise (e.g. Darling-Hammond and Ancess 1996). To say this is simply to repeat a truism that is endlessly uttered by educators, and endlessly ignored by others: we cannot reasonably hope for educational success above a rudimentary level for children who are not adequately cared for both outside and inside their schools (e.g. Graham 1993). The truth of the truism holds whether the relevant criterion of educational success is creating a highly skilled workforce for a global economy or transmitting the political virtues on which free government depends.

Notice that the interpretation I have offered of what is true in the less radical response depends on not allowing it to slide into the more radical response. The interpretation hinges on the claim that what is best in the tradition is the rightful inheritance of all children. Where social conditions systematically obstruct certain groups from securing that inheritance, and that fact is viewed by many with equanimity, the fitting response is outrage and a determined effort to change those conditions. The more radical response precludes this line of thought. It may share a sense of outrage at the plight of marginalized groups, but whatever considerations inform the outrage cannot come from the liberal democratic tradition of Western modernity since that has been disowned. That tradition is not *theirs*. What reasons might be given to people who have endured much of the worst and enjoyed little of the best of the tradition to choose between the less and the more radical response?

To make some progress with that question we need to be clear about what is at stake in claiming a political tradition is or is not one's own. There is some temptation to think of such traditions on the model of real estate which can only be passed from the possession of the original proprietors on the basis of ties of blood. Those who do not have the relevant ties might be lured into a false sense of ownership if they were given rented accommodation, so to speak, on the property. But after enough exploitation at the hands of the real owners, they will realize their mistake. Then they must take off to find some other real estate to which they can claim ownership on the basis of blood ties. This is an absurdity in which we quickly become trapped once we reduce questions of the ownership of tradition to questions about the geographical location of ancestors. The current academic respectability of terms like 'Afrocentric' and 'Eurocentric' tends to disguise the absurdity, though that is reason to regret their respectability rather than grounds to ignore the absurdity. To claim ownership of a political tradition is to make a claim about one's *moral identity*; it is to commit oneself to continuing a particular story because one thinks it is morally worthy of continuance. This means that even though ownership always entails a sense of history, the history it draws on may have little or nothing to do with ties of blood. The men and women slaughtered in Tiananmen Square were inspired—some would say duped—by principles of liberal democracy that originated in Western cultures, but whether they were inspired or duped, it is grotesque to suggest that they all died for values that were not their own.

So when ownership of American political tradition with its European roots is disavowed in educational discourse, this must be understood as a claim about the moral identity of those who disavow it, and the moral identity they want for their children. But the content of that identity cannot be intelligibly reduced to facts about race or ethnicity. To disown the stories that Parker and Welty tell simply because the storytellers come from the wrong race or ethnic group makes as little sense as suggesting that the dead of Tiananmen Square did not perish for their own values because their skin colour did not match the ideals to which they mistakenly laid claim. But once we understand the disavowal of ownership as a claim about moral rather than racial or ethnic identity, the problem of biting the hand that feeds you surfaces again. For the values which give content to the rejection of the tradition—respect for cultural diversity, the demand for an authentic rather than a spurious political equality, and the like—are internal to that tradition (e.g. Barber 1992: 144–50). It is also well to remember that the hands that are bitten are not uniformly white. The liberal democratic tradition is a complex narrative that weaves together stories of philosophical reflection, social activism, political accomplishment and failure, all revolving around the ideal of free and equal citizenship. The African-American tradition of agitation for civil rights is as much a part of this grand narrative as any other.

## 37. Patriotism and Communitarianism

My endorsement of liberal patriotism implies at least some qualified approval of the political structures of modern states, since under current conditions these will typically demarcate the political communities that might command the loyalty of patriots. American patriots may be strongly and rightly critical of their government at any given moment in time, and critical too of many features of the basic political institutions under which they live. But if their criticism is consistent with an American patriotism, then the one thing they will not renounce is the continued existence of the American state. Thus moral scepticism about patriotism intersects with moral scepticism about the state itself. The criticism commonly takes a communitarian form.

MacIntyre claims that liberal morality and patriotism are inherently antipathetic (MacIntyre 1995). Much of the supporting argument founders on the same obfuscating dichotomies that undermine Galston's argument. His distinction between liberal morality as a system of rules binding on all rational agents, without regard to historical contingencies, and a patriotic loyalty whose security requires the curtailment of reason parallels Galston's account of the supposedly divergent ends of philosophical and civic education. But the two arguments differ on one critical point. Galston thinks patriotic loyalty remains an important virtue in liberal democracies. MacIntyre says that the public culture of contemporary liberal democracies is such that the appeal to patriotism is necessarily a sham. A morally cogent patriotism presupposes social conditions which do not hold in our world:

A national community . . . in which the bonds deriving from history were in no way the real bonds of the community (having been replaced by the bonds of reciprocal self-interest) would be one towards which patriotism would be—from any viewpoint—an irrational attitude. . . . Since all modern bureaucratic states tend towards reducing national communities to this condition, all such states tend towards a condition in which any genuine morality of patriotism would have no place and what paraded itself as patriotism would be an unjustifiable simulacrum. (MacInytre 1995: 225)

The modern state is a device for mediating the pursuit of self-interest among people who are invited to think of it in cost-benefit terms. But such a state, were it always seen in merely cost-benefit terms, could expect no loyalty. 'Being asked to die for it is like being asked to die for the telephone company. And yet the modern state does need to ask its citizens to die for it, a need that requires it to find some quite other set of images for its self-preservation' (MacIntyre 1988: 149). But since the state is really no more than a bureaucratic mechanism and typically presents itself as such, these images must be a ludicrous hoax, the stuff from which sentimental political education is made.

Suppose we throw away MacIntyre's caricature of liberal morality as a motivationally inert view from nowhere. Still it might be true that the actual states we belong to are no more than amoral bureaucracies whose precarious survival depends partly on appealing to naked self-interest and partly on fostering the sporadic illusion that the state is more than an instrument of self-interest. If this were the whole truth about our extant, self-described liberal democracies, then this element at least of MacIntyre's argument would be sound. Any such state would be a mere modus vivendi, and whatever compliance to the norms of free government its citizens evinced would have no real moral basis (see Section 15). Reciprocal self-interest is what Rawls calls 'mutual advantage'; it is not reciprocity in the sense fundamental to justice as reasonableness. To be motivated by mutual advantage and that alone is not yet to act morally (Rawls 1993: 16–17). In these circumstances, no political community yet exists in which a shared commitment to justice has any purchase at all, and therefore liberal patriotism would only be possible by concocting a collective fantasy in defiance of that fact.

Notice all that would have to be the case for MacIntyre's depiction of our politics to be fair. It would not be nearly enough to establish that states commonly act as if they were amoral bureaucratic mechanisms and that overweening self-interest routinely subverts political deliberation. What would have to be shown is that the distinctively moral resources of democratic politics—the ideals of free and equal citizenship, and the conceptions of rights and duties derived from these—have been so thoroughly enfeebled in states which lay claim to those resources that they can no longer be invoked as a basis for constructive civic engagement. What is the best of this tradition? becomes an idle question where the tradition is defunct.

But a political diagnosis as grim as this can only be sustained by looking at the past and present of liberal societies without any of the emotional generosity and imagination I have stressed as integral elements of liberal patriotism. Paradoxically, the rhetorical force of MacIntyre's argument depends in large part on the moral vitality of the tradition it purports to discredit. For if we recoil in disgust at the thought of the state as a mere arbiter of egoism and a manipulator of patriotic delusions it is not necessarily due to our sharing MacIntyre's nostalgia for idealized versions of premodern social forms. Many of us surely recoil because we adhere to the ideal of a polity that enacts the justice of free and equal citizens, and honours the claims of self-interest only within limits fixed by the rights of all.[8] The debased politics MacIntyre describes and derides is as remote from that ideal as it is from any polity that would satisfy his yearning for monistic solidarity. But if a deep, latent commitment to free and equal citizenship is indeed the source of widespread disgust with the familiar corruptions of democratic politics, the moral core of such politics cannot be so enfeebled as MacIntyre's own argument suggests.

I said that the endorsement of the modern state that a commitment to liberal patriotism involves need only be a qualified endorsement. I should say a little about what prudent qualifications might be necessary. A commonplace of contemporary politics is that many of the most important problems we face as citizens cannot be addressed within the established institutions of sovereign states. They are problems that require the coordination of action at an international level, and at that level we lack institutions sufficiently powerful to meet the requirement because we are still captive to the ideology of the sovereign state and the vainglorious isolationism that is its usual companion. Another commonplace is that sovereign states are under seige from within as well as without. Increasingly assertive forms of ethnic, linguistic, and religious particularism are social trends that often seem impossible to accommodate, either morally or pragmatically, save through processes of political decentralization. And here again an ideal of patriotism dedicated to the preservation of powerful centralized states may seem an obstacle to desirable, even necessary change. These are very large matters, and it would be foolish to suppose much that is helpful could be said about them here. But I want to say something about why a state-centred patriotism might continue to be an important ideal to perpetuate in our public cultures even if we are often rightly sympathetic to the case for both decentralization within the state and the development of more powerful international institutions outside.

The two commonplaces about the liabilities of the modern, centralized state are fundamental to Sandel's claims about the future of American civic virtue. 'We cannot hope to govern a global economy without transnational political institutions, and we cannot expect to sustain such institutions without cultivating more expansive civic identities.' So an insular American patriotism must be diluted by some larger, more cosmopolitan attachments. Yet American patriotism must also give ground to the decentralizing pull of parochial group identities.

For given the demands of republican citizenship, the more expansive the bounds of membership, the more demanding the task of cultivating virtue. . . . The task of forging a common citizenship among a vast and disparate people invites more strenuous forms of soulcraft. This raises the stakes for republican politics and heightens the risk of coercion.

We supposedly lower the stakes for republican politics and minimize the risks of coercion when the primary sphere for civic engagement becomes communities less vast and disparate than the state itself. The best setting for republican virtue is a society where authority is much more widely dispersed than it now is in the United States and political identities have been transformed to match that dispersal: 'Only a regime that disperses sovereignty both upwards and downwards can combine the power required to rival global market forces with the differentiation required of a public life that hopes to inspire the reflective allegiance of citizens'. Identification with the state qua political community need not disappear altogether under such a regime, but its commanding role in civic life recedes as other objects of loyalty increase in salience (Sandel 1996: 319, 345).

The basic thesis that a dispersal of sovereignty both upward and downward is desirable is one I have no wish to challenge. But if it is desirable, we still need to worry about the moral risks that would attend the process. I want to argue that the maintenance of a strong, state centred-patriotism at the core of Sandel's 'multiply situated' political agent may be needed to

cope with those risks. Sandel's defence of his thesis obscures this important possibility.

Part of the trouble with Sandel's reasoning is that the argument he
makes for the downward dispersal of sovereignty is equally an argument
against its upward dispersal. For if America really is too large and disparate a country for a politics of virtue to be vigorously pursued at the
level of the state, the vastly larger and more disparate global community
will be that much less eligible as an arena for meaningful civic participation. Therefore, the upward dispersal of authority from the state, if it were
feasible at all, would increase the power of institutions from which people
would be even more alienated than they are now from the state, and that
would intensify the very problems Sandel wants to solve. Furthermore,
on any plausible understanding of what the downward dispersal of sovereignty would entail in a country like America, it will empower many
communities no less disparate than America itself. If the politics of civic
virtue must retreat in the face of pluralism, it must abandon the field here
as well. The upshot of this is that the only society in which we might
rationally expect 'civic virtue' of any kind to thrive, given the logic of
Sandel's argument for decentralization, is a society of more or less homogeneous enclaves. 'Virtue' might be on edifying display in everyone's
backyard. At least that might be so in the backyards of those fortunate
enough to occupy enclaves with the resources to support the finer things
in life. But in the wider world beyond our backyards, virtue would have
little or no foothold. That is not at all what Sandel wants. But if his ideal
of the multiply situated political agent is to make any sense, it cannot be
because the scale and diversity of political communities create conditions
that make strenuous demands on civic virtue inappropriate.

Richard Rorty notes that some liberal Americans respond with a special moral outrage to the hopelessness and misery with which many
young blacks live in American cities. The outrage is special in that a
response of comparable intensity is not evoked by suffering of comparable magnitude (or far worse) elsewhere in the world. What gives the outrage its emotional force is patriotism. As Rorty puts it, the thought
fuelling the outrage is that an *American*, someone who is 'one of us',
should live without hope (R. Rorty 1989: 191). The patriotism at issue
here belongs to the tradition of Parker and Welty, a tradition in which the
*patria* that inspires devotion is a community in which justice must be
done despite the opposing pull of racial or ethnic identity. The outraged
liberal will be aware that the resources needed to help urban blacks may
impede the pursuit of other ends she prizes and sometimes champions in
the name of justice—better schools for her own children, or better med-
ical care for her aged parents. Moreover, the ends that give significance to

the lives of her black compatriots may be remote from her own, and yet that remoteness does not detract from the urgency she ascribes to their predicament. So her outrage occurs within the circumstances of justice, and is naturally expressed in the vocabulary of rights and duties appropriate to those circumstances. Still, it is an outrage informed by identification with a political community that the virtue of justice does not itself entail.

The patriotism evident in Rorty's example is a moral resource we would do well to cherish and encourage in our children in a world where some of the powers of the sovereign state might be dispersed both upward and downward. After all, cosmopolitan civic virtue seems no more than a philosopher's figment unless citizens have empathic imaginations powerful enough to sustain a sense of common fate with cultually distant compatriots. If white middle-class Americans, ensconced in their suburbs, cannot feel that hopeless young blacks count as 'one of us', they cannot be expected to care much for the even more distant victims of American foreign policy. Nor can we expect decentralization to help the victims of injustice closer to home when 'one of us' becomes increasingly confined to 'those who are just like me'.

# CHAPTER 6

## The Great Sphere and Rights

### 38. Introduction

The preceding chapters outline what I take to be both the prime civic virtues and the principal ends of political education in a liberal democracy. What is most likely to be contested in all this is not the list of virtues per se but the insistent emphasis on autonomy as a thread running through them. Few will take exception to the bare proposal that we instil justice and patriotism in our children. But when these are understood in ways that entail a stringent ideal of autonomous reflection regarding the right and the good, the proposal takes a radical form to which many will object.

Bruce Ackerman's description of what he calls 'liberal education' captures some of what is likely to provoke the strongest opposition to my own argument:

The entire educational system will, if you like, resemble a great sphere. Children land upon the sphere at different points, depending on their primary culture; the task is to help them explore the globe in a way that permits them to glimpse the deeper meanings of the dramas passing on around them. At the end of the journey, however, the now mature citizen has every right to locate himself at the very point from which he began—just as he may also strike out to discover an unoccupied portion of the sphere. (Ackerman 1980: 159)

Conflict between the great sphere and more parochial views of education is muted but not resolved by the qualifications we might sensibly make to what Ackerman says. Children are hardly well placed even to glimpse the 'deeper meanings of the dramas unfolding around them' until they have some secure grasp of the meaning of their own culture of birth. Nor are they likely to profit from a nomadic curriculum if that wrenches them abruptly away from all that gives meaning to their lives outside the school. A thoughtless application of Ackerman's proposal would forfeit ethical seriousness for the sake of a vapid cultural dilettantism. But to say that is not necessarily to give up on the idea of the great sphere; it might only be to acknowledge the need for a certain gradualism and sensitivity in its implementation, as well as the importance of balancing its requirements against other educational ends. I want now to focus on the normative core of Ackerman's idea of schooling as the great sphere, which the caveats we should enter do not undermine.

The essential demand is that schooling properly involves at some stage sympathetic and critical engagement with beliefs and ways of life at odds with the culture of the family or religious or ethnic group into which the child is born. Moreover, the relevant engagement must be such that the beliefs and values by which others live are entertained not merely as sources of meaning in *their* lives; they are instead addressed as potential elements within the conceptions of the good and the right one will create for oneself as an adult. I characterize the understanding this process is intended to yield as 'sympathetic' not because it entails an indiscriminate embrace of pluralism. My claim is that to understand ethical diversity in the educationally relevant sense presupposes some experience of entering imaginatively into ways of life that are strange, even repugnant, and some developed ability to respond to them with interpretive charity, even though the sympathy this involves must complement the tough-mindedness of responsible criticism.

The understanding the great sphere seeks to engender might be achieved in social settings other than the school; it might even take root inadvertently in a child's life. In Edmund Gosse's memoir of growing up in a Puritan household in Victorian England, an education of the most extreme austerity begins to unravel when Gosse's father gives his son a novel to read, a novel that stirs hopes of a wider and better life beyond the insularity of his home (Gosse 1979 edn.: 141–4). No doubt Gosse's experience is not unique, and it would be foolish to think that schooling as the great sphere is the only way to achieve a kind of understanding that might be reached by other means. But schooling is also likely to be the most promising institutional vehicle for that understanding since the other, extra-familial social influences that impinge heavily on children's and adolescents' lives—peer groups, the mass media of communication and entertainment—do not readily lend themselves to that end.

Some will have deeper qualms about Ackerman's ideal. They will say that a civically sufficient understanding of pluralism is inevitably picked up as children grow up and take their place within the larger world, beyond the formative institutions of childhood and adolescence. The school and the family should turn aside from all this cultural tumult, exerting a steadying influence in a world where other institutions seem to offer little. The most interesting thought behind this proposal is expressed by Galston: 'the greatest threat to children in modern liberal societies is not that they will believe something too deeply, but that they will believe nothing very deeply at all' (Galston 1989: 101).

Two things need to be said about this. First, one might suspect that there is no sense in which 'depth' of conviction is worth having that is properly contrasted with the understanding the great sphere promotes. That understanding will certainly weaken conviction when strength of conviction is simply a product of ignorance. But when believing 'deeply' is just a function of believing ignorantly, it is hard to see any belief worth protecting. It will be hard to see that not only if one thinks the examined life alone worth living; it will be hard to see from the viewpoint of any way of life that takes the demands of truth and understanding seriously. Be that as it may, it is simply wrong to say that the relevant understanding of ethical diversity is picked up in the public world of contemporary pluralistic societies. What is picked up there is a seductive sense of the many glittering variations that a life of heedless consumption and trendy group-think can now take.[1] That is not what any intelligent protagonist of the great sphere could have in mind.

But to warn against some common misunderstandings to which schooling as the great sphere is subject is not to disarm all serious opposition. Opposition takes several shapes, partly because of the different meanings of the 'primary culture' with which Ackerman contrasts the pluralistic curriculum of his great sphere. By 'primary culture' we might mean the family's distinctive pattern of life, as defined by parents. That is what Ackerman seems to mean. Alternatively, we may refer to the culture of some larger group to which the family in some sense belongs but which may nonetheless diverge sharply from parental values and choices. The arguments that can be made for an education that gives pride of place to respect for the primary culture of the family does not entail the priority of deference to more inclusive cultural units because there is no necessary convergence between the policies that the two attitudes would support.

Some educational policies bring the possible divergence between respect for parental choice and deference to group identity dramatically into view. Under Quebec's controversial Bill 101, anglophone parents who did not receive an education in English inside the province, as well as all francophone parents, are denied access to anglophone schools. The whole point of that provision is to ensure the survival among future generations of a linguistically defined community against the threat posed by families whose primary culture might be insufficiently supportive of that wider group project. But notice that the repudiation of the great sphere in the name of group identity is not at issue in Bill 101. Whether the school provides a sympathetic understanding of ethical diversity or not does not depend on whether the primary language of instruction is French or English. The matter would be quite different if cultural developments in Quebec during recent decades had increasingly accentuated religious differences with the rest of Canada, with the consequence that legislation now required Catholic schooling without regard to parental choice. Such legislation could have not a shred of moral justification. The educational provisions of Bill 101 are certainly contestable. But what gives them some credibility is the case for saying that they are designed to sustain a specifically civic identity, rooted in the French language, that is fully compatible with as wide a range of credal and ethnic commitments as might be affirmed anywhere else in Canada.

I focus throughout this chapter on respect for the familial primary culture, and with the friction that may arise between its demands and the imperatives of the great sphere. I do so because parents' rights, unlike ideals of group identity that might conflict with considerations of parents' and children's rights or the proper ends of political education, provide a powerful objection to the imposition of schooling as the great sphere. My principal claim is that although parents might have a right to reject schooling that instils commitment to an open-ended ideal of autonomous development, thay have no right to reject educational provision that would conduce to the degree of autonomous development that schooling as the great sphere, properly understood, would seek to establish.

## 39. Parents' Rights to Educational Choice

The case for schools that adhere closely throughout to the familial primary culture is typically presented as a matter of parents' rights. That is just the kind of argument we should expect if we are asking about possible moral limits on the coercive pursuit of politically desirable ends. For an important point of agreement in recent discussions of rights is that they provide a framework of moral constraints within which a politics of the common good can be practised (e.g. R. Dworkin 1977: 184–205; R. Martin and Nickel 1980: 181; Galston 1991*b*: 249–57). So even if it were agreed that autonomy is an essential element of political virtue, we still face the question of whether a form of schooling that fosters autonomy against the grain of parental dissent could be morally legitimate.

An influential proclamation of the particular right that concerns us is contained in Article 26 of the *Universal Declaration of Human Rights*: 'Parents have a prior right to choose the kind of education that shall be given to their children.' I assume that 'parents' here refers to those who occupy and are morally entitled to continue occupying a particular social role rather than those who just happen to stand in a certain biological relation, even though there is ordinarily (and rightly) a close correspondence between the social role and the biological relationship that procreation establishes. The social role is defined by the primary and more or less permanent responsibility that individual adults may have for rearing particular children as their own.[2]

To claim on behalf of parents a right to educational choice is to say that they have an interest in the education of their children of sufficient weight to warrant the imposition of duties on others regarding the protection or promotion of that interest. To discharge the requisite duties is to respect the corresponding right. Two questions must be distinguished straightaway: Are we justified in thinking there is such a right? What is the moral content or scope of the right and when (if ever) should we set aside its requirements? We should accept the right of parents to educational choice. But neither the first question nor the blunt answer I just gave has much moral interest. The really interesting question is the second one. Moral conflict about the significance of parental choice in education arises from rival answers to the second question, and an affirmative answer to the first does virtually nothing to overcome the conflict. Agreement that there is a parental right to educational choice coincides with profound differences about its scope as well as the conditions under which the right is defeated by other moral reasons.

The scope of any right is indicated by specifying what it is a right to— that is, by enumerating the particular duties it imposes on others, by identifying who these others are, and by noting the general conditions in which the duties have application or might be waived by the right-holder (Nickel 1987: 13–14). The relevant duties are conveniently classified as either negative, when they require only forbearance towards the right-holder, or positive, when some action of support or protection is demanded. Similarly, rights or facets of rights are positive or negative depending on the duties with which they are correlated, although a given right may comprise an amalgam of positive and negative facets.

A negative parental right to choice, which nonetheless comes with some strings attached, forms part of the agreed backround to disputes about parents' educational role in liberal societies. No one supposes a totalitarian state that dictates the course of education in all its fine detail would not thereby violate the rights of parents. Nor does anyone think that someone who makes gravely harmful choices about the education of his children by depriving them, say, of the benefit of language is nonetheless acting within his rights. Yet the content of the duty of non-interference that correlates to the right remains strongly contested. State regulation of home schooling and denominational education curbs parental choice; whether such regulation fails to comply with the negative duties that the alleged right to choice entails is another, and far less obvious matter.

If we lack much consensus about the negative duties we have with regard to parents' choices, we also share little common ground on whatever positive duties might be binding on us. According to libertarians such as Loren Lomasky, parental rights impose negative duties that approach the widest imaginable scope. We can rightfully interfere with parents' choices regarding the teaching and learning of their children in only the most extreme cases of irresponsibility. But Lomasky also argues for positive duties of the most slender scope (Lomasky 1987: 165–87). Conversely, a conception of parents' rights that accords a much narrower range to negative duties than libertarians would accept can also assign exacting positive requirements. Brian Crittenden argues for parity of state funding for students in commmon and separate schools as a requirement of respect for parental rights. Yet he also thinks no one has a right to choose a form of schooling that fails to satisfy substantial educational criteria (Crittenden 1988: 103–37). So even though Lomasky and Crittenden agree that powerful parental rights are the moral basis of educational policy for any free people, their agreement is virtually empty because they conceive the scope of that right in utterly different ways.

Conflicting conceptions of the scope of parents' rights is not the only source of disagreement about their interpretation. We might disagree about the comparative importance of specific duties which (we agree) a given right imposes or we might hold contradictory views about when the right is defeated by weightier moral reasons. That second possibility is especially important. As Judith Thomson has shown, the *infringement* of a right does not necessarily constitute what she calls a *violation* of that right because circumstances arise in which we ought not to fulfil a duty that a particular right imposes (Thomson 1990: 122). Rights are violated only when their infringement is without a sufficient moral justification. The distinction between infringement and violation makes our moral thinking about rights a lot less tidy than we might like it to be. But the distinction is indispensable once we accept both that rights can sometimes conflict—the duties they impose cannot always all be fulfilled—and that when conflict occurs some resolutions may yet be morally better than others.

I have underscored the possibilities of conflict about the scope and defeasibility of the parental right to educational choice mainly because they show that the case for the great sphere as an institution that may trump the choices of parents does not stand or fall with the radical thesis that there is no such right. My purpose here is to make a case for the legitimacy of the great sphere that does not require anyone to accept the radical thesis; in fact, my argument contains strong grounds to reject it.

The tendency to confuse the issue of whether parents have a right to educational choice with questions about its scope and defeasibility is easy to understand because the same arguments that are used to establish the right are just what we need to examine in order to answer questions of scope and defeasibility. Our understanding of the content of any right and the conditions under which the duties it imposes are justifiably set aside depends crucially on our understanding of why we should recognize it in the first place. Two broad strategies of derivation are possible for the parental right to educational choice. The right may be grounded in the interests of children or the interests of parents. Only so far as the right is grounded in the interests of parents themselves is it a basic moral right; otherwise it is only an indirect way of protecting the good of children, albeit perhaps a contingently necessary way of doing so in almost any human society.

## 40.  *Children's Needs and Parental Self-Fulfilment*

How might a parental right to educational choice be justified on the basis of children's interests? Two platitudes give us a good beginning.

First, children need to be cared for by adults as they grow up. The care they need cannot take the form of the merely impersonal benevolence that an ever-changing cast of strangers might give; it is only possible in enduring relationships that occasion regular and affectionate interaction (Goldstein, Freud, and Solnit 1973). These emotionally privileged relationships across generations take on a decisive educational significance because the adults who provide the necessary interaction will thereby exert a powerful formative influence on the child's character and abilities (Thomas 1989: 86–7). That being so, some substantial latitude regarding educational choice becomes a necessary part of the freedom any agent requires in order to discharge the primary responsibility to rear a child. Second, the care received by any child must come from adults who exhibit at least a rough overall consistency in the character traits and abilities they encourage, what they declare to be true and false, worthwhile or trivial, and the like. This is the requirement of 'cultural coherence' in child-rearing that Ackerman and others have rightly stressed, and the requirement holds because given a sufficiently chaotic array of formative influences in the early stages of any child's upbringing, no coherent self could emerge (Ackerman 1980: 140–6; McLaughlin 1984).

But even if children need to receive the care of adults in a culturally coherent setting of enduring intimacy, and this means the relevant adults must enjoy some liberty in educationally significant choice, does it automatically follow that parents must exercise the dominant role in child-rearing that we have tended to take for granted in developed Western societies? Not necessarily. Consider child-rearing among the Inuit:

The bonds between children and adults are quite fluid in Inuit society. Children are commonly seen darting around town visiting several homes, asking for food or seeking attention and then darting off to the next home. They may even decide to live with another related family for a period of time. In this case, the parents can sway the child's decision if they feel it would not be a good idea, but they will likely support the decision if the child is insistent.

While being able to seek attention and favour from any adult may seem like paradise for children, there is another side to it. It can also seem like being surrounded by babysitters as all adults can exercise authority over the child in terms of discipline, instruction, disapproval for inappropriate behaviour etc. (Pauktuutit 1990: 11)

The passage makes it clear that parenthood exists as a distinct and important social role among the Inuit.[3] And nothing here suggests that Inuit parents are less concerned with making good educational choices on their children's behalf than parents elsewhere. However, their role is less salient than it is typically for us because the responsibility to love and care for children is more evenly dispersed among a dense network of kin. The Inuit can very obviously meet the platitudinous needs of children. But the social authority of all adults to discipline, give instruction or reprove misconduct, and the freedom for children to interact closely and without parental supervision with all adults in their community, are practices that only make sense on many assumptions we cannot prudently make, at least outside of increasingly rare conditions. Inuit practice assumes a degree of cultural homogeneity that has long disappeared in most contemporary societies, for example, as well as levels of warranted trust among all adults in the collective pursuit of child-rearing that are hardly to be approached in any but the most stable and harmonious traditional society.

So children need to be loved and cared for in a culturally coherent environment, and in the contemporary world they will typically, if not quite always need parents who take a notably prominent role in meeting those needs. Performing that role requires the making of educational choices. Since the relevant needs are as fundamental as any to individual well-being, the interests they constitute are important enough, if any are, to give rise to appropriate constellations of rights and correlative duties. This generates the child-centred case for the parental right to choice in education. The point of the argument is to suggest that certain morally basic interests of children cannot be adequately served without some protected realm of choice for parents in educational and other matters that may be invaded, say, by a meddlesome state that seeks to advance those interests directly and ineptly, without the necessary mediation of parents, or that discounts those interests altogether in its pursuit of other goals (e.g. Houlgate 1988: 175).

Suppose child-centred considerations alone determined the parental right to educational choice. The relevant question then is whether the option of repudiating schooling as the great sphere is included in its scope. If it is included, what has to be said is that such schooling poses some serious threat to the satisfaction of the elementary needs of children. That cannot be said with any show of reason. Critical thought of the kind that the great sphere seeks to elicit may lead to psychological conflict, and eventually to estrangement from parents, along with the burden of suffering that estrangement is likely to bring in it wake. But these possible outcomes do not frustrate the needs that ground the child-centred argument, even if they would preclude the realization of ideals to which many people subscribe. The coherent self whose development would be blocked in an incoherent cultural setting is not the same as the seamlessly integrated self, whose development may well require a far more cohesive supportive environment than mere cultural coherence will ensure. The value of close psychological integration is intrinsic to many influential conceptions of the good, such as those that include the ideal of simple integrity I discussed in Sections 19 and 20. These will certainly be called into question by the great sphere, given the ethical dissonance and conflict essential to its curriculum. But so far as the child-centred argument goes, that is nothing to the point.

The failure of the child-centred argument to support the choice of parents who would reject the great sphere does not entitle us to infer that the choice must be beyond the scope of their rights. In fact, we have good independent grounds to suspect that the argument cannot be the whole story because the argument cannot adequately protect choice in some of the most flagrant cases of repression. In the Soviet Union, children of adults who belonged to certain Christian denominations were sometimes taken away from their parents (Fishkin 1992: 154). No doubt this had disastrous consequences for the children on many occasions. But often this may not have been so. If the children were taken away early enough, and placed in homes where their basic needs were met, then we can make no strong case for a violation of parental rights that derives from those needs. Furthermore, the kinds of interference that families endured whose children were not taken away—compulsory schooling that enforced a contemptuously anti-religious curriculum and the legal prohibition of denominational education outside school—imposed indignities whose moral significance cannot be captured by the child-centred argument. So long as governmental meddling did not frustrate the elementary needs of children, or did not seriously threaten to do so, no parental right to choice was even infringed that the child-centred argument could warrant.

This outcome might prompt us to devise more ambitious variants of the argument so as to widen the scope of the duties it imposes for the sake of a suitably protected sphere of parental choice. In the modest version considered so far, the scope of these duties is fixed by the platitudinous and minimal character of the interests they protect. Therefore, alternative uses of the child-centred strategy might try to ground parental rights of wider scope in premises about the best interests of children, rather than their minimal developmental needs. One large difficulty here is the contestability of any particular interpretation of the best interests of children. Our understanding of their best interests depends on our particular vision of the good life, and if our interpretation of the child-centred argument demands agreement on that, the fact of reasonable pluralism suggests that agreement will never be forthcoming. But suppose, against the odds, we could secure a reasoned consensus on premises about children's best interests. Although we might then agree to an expanded scope for parents' right regarding certain choices, the very same considerations that support expansion in some matters would necessarily require a severe contraction in others.

The point can be illustrated by a much discussed American legal case, *Mozert* v. *Hawkins* (1987), that pitted a group of conservative Christian parents against their local school board. The parents wanted their children exempted from a reading programme that allegedly instilled beliefs that were in conflict with their fundamentalist faith. Their case was eventually unsuccessful, but it has remained a flash-point of scholarly controversy (Dent 1988; Gutmann 1989: 81–7, 1995: 570–6; Gutmann and Thompson 1996: 63–9; Stolzenberg 1993; Burtt 1994; Macedo 1995*a*). What motivated the parents in their litigation was largely a concern that the mandatory reading programme would lead their children to damnation, and hence they had a right—indeed, a solemn duty—to protect their children from its evil influence. Suppose we agreed with the parents' judgements about their children's best interests. That certainly seems to give us a child-centred case for siding with the parents against the school board. The trouble is that we now have a child-centred argument that must carry equal weight for denying all children access to the controversial reading programme, even when the parents might want access, because the programme is contrary to the best interests of the children no matter what their parents would choose. In fact, this is not what the plaintiffs in

*Mozert* wanted at all (Burtt 1994: 65–6). So a charitable reading of their position cannot be along child-centred lines. The point of considering that reading here is only to reveal the likely repressive character of the child-centred strategy once we adopt one of its ambitious variants. Any such variant will tend to invite interference with parental choice once interference seems likely to advance whatever interpretation of the child's best interests we happen to favour, even when the parents in whose lives we meddle are conscientious, loving, and competent by any widely acceptable measure of competence in child-rearing.

This does not strictly rule out the possibility of developing an argument that would support deference to parental choice in most cases on the basis of premises about the best interests of the child, including decisions to repudiate the great sphere (e.g. Burtt 1994, 1996). The problem here is finding credible premises that would fill the bill. A former student of mine taught English for many years in secondary schools in rural Canada. Although many parents prized his teaching, others often complained about his habit of using literature to provoke discussion of serious moral, religious, and political questions. But what premises about the best interests of his pupils could warrant the claim that his provocative teaching was both good for the students whose parents admired his teaching and contrary to the interests of those whose parents complained? The contradictory reasons that parents actually gave in support of their admiration or condemnation give no hint of what the necessary premises could be. Some thought adolescents should be encouraged at school to think independently about moral, political, and religious questions, and some thought this was demoralizing. They could not both be right.

The child-centred argument can at best support a parental right to educational choice of alarmingly tenuous scope. So the obvious next move is to ask what interests parents might have that could warrant an enlargement of the right beyond those severe limits. Consider certain general facts about the rearing of children. The role of parent is typically undertaken as one of the central, meaning-giving tasks of our lives. Success or failure in the task, as measured by whatever standards we take to be relevant, is likely to affect profoundly our overall sense of how well or badly our lives have gone. Although the measures of success that we might honourably accept are highly variable both within and across cultures, they almost always include broadly educational ends of one sort or another (Lomasky 1987: 175). Parents hope to rear children who will possess certain prized skills and virtues, or who will live by a certain religious creed or sustain a cherished ethnic identity. Finally, despite its emotional rewards, the pursuit of success in child-rearing is also liable to be burdensome to us, by taxing our capabilities and absorbing our resources. As many feminists have rightly insisted, child-rearing is work. The reward we seek from the work is perhaps opaque in its deepest aspects, but much of it surely has to do with the gradual realization in the life of the child of those educational ends that give content to our understanding of success in child-rearing. That is as true of the devotee of J. S. Mill who hopes to rear a shining example of iconoclastic individuality as it is for the religious fundamentalist who prays and works to raise a zealous follower of the one true faith.

The moral importance of this point is established by the continuity between the educational purposes of parents and the interests that give rise to some of the core rights of liberal democratic societies (Fishkin 1992: 154; Strike 1996). The rights to freedom of conscience and association are widely accepted as among the necessary requirements of any recognizably liberal regime. But the freedom to rear our children according to the dictates of conscience is for most of us as important as any other expression of conscience, and the freedom to organize and sustain the life of the family in keeping with our own values is as significant as our liberty to associate with others outside the family for any purpose whatsoever. No one could reasonably propose or rationally accept terms of social cooperation that did not provide strong protection for freedom of conscience and assembly, and any regime that failed to provide such protection could not but be repressive.

The educational hopes and ambitions of parents do not mean that they are typically, much less properly fixated on moulding the child to fit some predetermined image. An obsession with the adult-in-the-making strikes us as a pathology of parenthood rather than an authentic human good to which we should defer. Indeed, one reason to deplore that obsession is precisely its tendency to frustrate the achievement of intimacy that others have identified as fundamental to the psychological significance of families for their members (Schrag 1976; Schoeman 1980). If my thoughts qua parent are driven by incessant concern for the child qua adult-in-the-making, then I cannot be engrossed by the sheer fulfilment of sharing a life with my child now, nor can the child enjoy that good either since my conduct is coloured by my purely instrumental approach to our relationship. This perversion of the expressive interest in child-rearing is the source of the tragedy in Gosse's *Father and Son*. Gosse's father was so obsessed with the godly adult-in-the-making that he was incapable of sharing a life with his child in the present.

Nevertheless, even if we say that the parental interest in child-rearing inheres primarily in the value of intimacy, rather than success in whatever broadly educational tasks parents set themselves, the good of intimacy cannot be divorced from concerns about the adults that children will become. Intimacy is threatened by the fear of estrangement. Parents who feel strongly alienated on religious grounds from the public culture of their society may view with something akin to terror the possibility that their children will be assimilated to that culture. Assimilation would mean the parents could no longer share a way of life with their children that is for the parents a condition of intimacy.

Yet if child-rearing characteristically has this deep significance for parents, the rights that properly belong to them cannot be determined by an exclusive concern for the interests of children. We do not experience the rearing of a child merely as unilateral service on behalf of a separate human life; we experience it as the sharing of a life and a cardinal source of self-fulfilment (W. Ruddick 1979). The child-centred strategy, when it purports to be the whole moral truth about parenthood, flies in the face of our ordinary understanding of what rearing a child signifies because it does not accommodate that task's momentous expressive significance in parents' lives. By the 'expressive significance' of child-rearing I mean the way in which raising a child engages our deepest values and yearnings so that we are tempted to think of the child's life as a virtual extension of our own.

Consider Robert Nozick's remarks on the connection between parent and child.

There is no bond I know stronger than being a parent. Having children and raising them gives one's life substance. To have done so is at least to have done that. The children themselves form part of one's substance. Without remaining subordinate or serving your purposes, they yet are organs of you. . . . The connection to a child certainly involves the deepest love, sometimes annoyance or anger or hurt, but it does not exist solely at the level of emotion. It is not accurate or illuminating to say that I love my . . . hand. (Nozick 1989: 28)

The point of the analogy in the last sentence is to remind us of the depth of our expressive interest in child-rearing. Nozick's analogy is as dangerous as it is illuminating, and his allusion to filial subordination shows that he is alert to the danger. I return to that point a bit later. But the analogy does help to expose the importance of what gets hidden by the child-centred argument once we set the argument in the broadly egalitarian setting of rights talk.

A moral theory of relationships in the family that says only the interests of one or both parents count is despotic. That is the sin of patriarchy, which entails that all members of a family are properly subject to the father. Patriarchy is no less gross a denial of the truism that we are all free and equal citizens as moral doctrines that argue for the subjection of one race to another. But a moral theory of the family that says only the interests of children really count merely inverts the despotism of patriarchy. No one would now deny that if a moral theory interprets the child's role so as to make individual children no more than instruments of their parents' good it would be open to damning moral objections. But parallel objections must be decisive against any theory that interprets the parent's role in ways that make individual parents no more than instruments of their children's good.

We should want a conception of parents' rights in education that will not license the oppression of children. But we should also want a conception that will do justice to the hopes that parents have and the sacrifices they make in rearing their children. Neither desideratum can be discarded if our interpretation of rights in the family is to accommodate the moral equality of its members.[4]

## 41. Parents and Sovereignty

The problem here can be approached by asking how claims to a zone of personal sovereignty might include the parental right to educational choice. By a 'zone of personal sovereignty' I mean a sphere of conduct in which individuals are rightfully free to make their own way in the world, even if the exercise of that freedom might often warrant censure (Feinberg 1986: 47–51). Personal sovereignty is the social space where the traditional freedoms of liberal politics apply, such as freedom of conscience, and for the purposes of the argument that follows I do not need a more precise characterization than this.

Suppose the parents of a musically talented and interested child face a dilemma. They can either buy a piano for the child or take her on an expensive holiday, but they cannot afford to do both. They go off to Disneyland. If the scope of their right to educational choice were fixed by the best interests of their child, a strong case would exist for saying that the parents had no right to this particular choice. After all, the holiday does not benefit the child educationally, and the likely atrophy of her musical passion is a clear educational loss. Yet I think scarcely anyone would think the parents were not within their moral rights in choosing as they did, although many might also say—I include myself here—that their choice was unfortunate, even stupid.

Why say the choice was within their rights? If we have no moral duty to respect the decision of parents in circumstances like these, which is one implication of denying that the choice was rightfully theirs, the door is open to tyranny of an especially invasive kind. The thought of agents of the state with enough power to compel the parents to buy the piano should repel everyone. A bureaucracy with the authority to second-guess any significant decision that parents might make is an unappealing prospect, to say the least (Schrag 1980). But other reasons for upholding the parents' right to choice have nothing essentially to do with fears about the likely ill effects of an overweening state.

A conception of rights in child-rearing that accommodates the expressive significance of the task for parents must protect their sincere judgement about what is best for their children in many situations where their judgement looks just plain wrong to outsiders. Moreover, if the moral burden of rearing children is not to engulf entire lives without residue, the burden must be curtailed by the recognition that parents have lives beyond the service they give their children, and that some discretion in how they balance that service against responsibilities that flow from other projects and roles, as well as the claims of self-interest, rightfully belongs within their sphere of personal sovereignty. Within some limits set by child-centred reasons, finding the balance between parental responsibilities and other values must be a matter for the judgement of parents because otherwise parenthood becomes a state of bondage, and any zone of personal sovereignty to which parents are entitled would evaporate.

The Disneyland case is intended to show that just because a particular option is educationally bad it does not follow that parents have no right to choose it. Once we grant that point, *Mozert* appears in a fresh light. Suppose we agree that what the plaintiffs in *Mozert* wanted for their children was educationally bad. The Disneyland case shows we might still have a duty to respect the choice of parents to exempt their children from an educationally beneficial reading programme. And to acknowledge that duty is not necessarily to presuppose a patriarchal conception of the family, or some gender-neutral descendent thereof. We do not endorse parental despotism the moment we say parents have a right to make a choice that is bad for their children. That being so, the heart of the matter is how to distinguish bad educational options that are within the scope of parents' rights from options that are bad in a way that puts them outside, all the while avoiding both parental despotism and its child-centred inversion. Only on the basis of that distinction can we decide whether parents who repudiate the great sphere on their children's behalf have a right to do so or not.

This point is easily overshadowed by a big difference between my Disneyland case and *Mozert*. The highly protective upbringing that the plaintiffs in *Mozert* wanted for their children, with its scrupulous avoidance of all that conflicted with the parents' fundamentalist faith, might obstruct the long-term development of civic virtues that are essential to mutually respectful cooperation in a diverse society (Macedo 1995*a*;

Gutmann 1995). No comparable frustration of the process of political education occurs in the Disneyland case. But if this is all that could be said for denying the wishes of the plaintiffs in *Mozert*, the grounds for denial would remain indecisive. For it would be unclear whether the denial of choice is a justified infringement of parents' rights for the sake of a compelling collective goal—the diffusion of civic virtue—or whether the option of rejecting the great sphere belongs within the scope of their rights to begin with. The ambiguity is important because the case for the great sphere is weakened if it must be presented as a justified infringement of parents' rights. Whether or not schooling as the great sphere effectively conduces to civic virtue will never be a sure thing, and so any trade-off that might be recommended between its uncertain political benefits and the certain evil of infringing parental rights would be doubtful. The legitimacy of the great sphere thus depends importantly on whether the option of rejecting it is within the scope of parents' rights to begin with.

## 42. Children and Sovereignty

I said that the zone of sovereignty to which parents are entitled will include the right to make some choices on their children's behalf that others regard, perhaps with excellent reason, as bad. Yet to avoid parental despotism, the scope of the right must be circumscribed by the moral parity of the prospective interest in a zone of personal sovereignty that children possess. Since children are numerically identical to the adults they will be when they grow up, securing the rights they will acquire as adults requires that we respect their claim to be treated in ways that safeguard the developmental preconditions of adult rights, whatever the preconditions might be (Feinberg 1980; Lomasky 1987: 157–67). A grim but uncontroversial example makes clear the general point: if the integrity of one's body is a precondition of personal sovereignty in sexual matters, the genital mutilation of female children in some cultures is a gross violation of their prospective interest in sovereignty. The practice is indefensible because it cannot be squared with the moral equality of the child's prospective interest and the adult's realized interest in a zone of personal sovereignty.

Can we argue that parents who wish to veto the great sphere are making a choice that is not merely educationally bad for their child but rather denies the moral equality of the child's prospective interest and the parent's own realized interest in personal sovereignty? An interesting way of saying yes appeals to the ideal of autonomy from which the rights that constitute each person's zone of sovereignty are commonly thought to derive (e.g. Richards 1981 and 1986; Ingram 1994). This I shall call the autonomy argument. I am autonomous to the degree that I have developed powers of practical reason, a disposition to value those powers and use them in giving shape and direction to my own life, and a corresponding resistance to impulses or social pressures that might subvert wise self-direction. The concept of autonomy is open to different interpretations. But regardless of which interpretation is best, a tight link seems clear between the development of autonomy and the kind of understanding that schooling as the great sphere makes available. That should be clear in the light of what is said about autonomy in Chapters 2 and 3. On any barely defensible conception of the powers of practical reason and the motivational and affective propensities that attend their exercise, the open-ended growth of autonomy will require at some point an education that encourages the kind of learning promoted by the great sphere. To be denied a sympathetic understanding of ethical diversity by parents who seek to preserve unswerving identification with the primary culture of birth is to be denied the deliberative raw material for the independent thought about the right and the good that a developed autonomy necessitates under the conditions of pluralism. The upshot of the autonomy argument is that the option of rejecting the great sphere cannot belong within the scope of the right to educational choice that parents could defensibly claim because that right derives from an interest in autonomy which, once we accept the fundamental moral equality of persons in the family, entails the child's right to an education that would include the great sphere.

At first glance, Rawls's political conception of the person might seem to lend some support to the autonomy argument, even if that involves applying the conception in ways he does not anticipate. Rawls argues that the basic liberties to which we have a right under a just constitution are those essential for the 'adequate development and full and informed exercise' of the two moral powers that define the political conception of the person. These powers are the capacity for a conception of the good and a sense of justice. Moreover, it is the requisite development and exercise of these over a 'complete life' that the basic liberties are intended to support (Rawls 1993: 293, 322–3). In Chapter 2 I argued that the conception of the person harbours a much more substantial ideal of autonomy than Rawls explicitly grants. Therefore, we might be tempted to construe the basic liberties that sustain the moral powers of citizens in part as rights designed to conduce to the optimal realization of autonomy. And if we have to understand these liberties in the context of the fruition of our moral powers over a complete life, we need to construct an account of the rights of children, as future citizens, that would protect their prospective interest in the development and exercise of autonomy. Therefore, a right to veto the great sphere could not belong in the scope of parents' rights, since children would be morally entitled to such schooling by virtue of its vital role in the development of their autonomy.

But this would be an abuse of Rawls's argument. The ideal of autonomy is part of the political conception of the person in the sense that it is basic to the understanding of civic virtue that conception implies; it does not fix the content of the rights that properly belong to all citizens. According to Rawls, we do not specify the liberties which justice compels us to respect 'so as to maximise anything, and in particular, not the development and exercise of the moral powers' (Rawls 1993: 332). So we cannot infer that the scope of actual and prospective rights to personal sovereignty under a just constitution would be designed so as to conduce to the maximal development of autonomy. More is at stake here than Rawlsian exegesis. Acknowledgement of the great variety of lives that people permissibly lead under free institutions is fundamental to our prereflective under-standing of liberal politics. But we cannot square that acknowledgement with a reading of personal sovereignty that protects only lives that aim to meet the maximal demands of autonomous reflection and choice. I think the point of trying to understand rights in relation to the 'adequate' rather than the maximal development of the moral powers is to seek a reasonable threshold that would be responsive to the range of lives that a free people could accept as worthy of political protection. Rawls's idea of the 'adequate' development of the moral powers is unhelpfully vague, but that does not detract from the moral importance of the distinction to which it points. And once the need for some such distinction is conceded, the autonomy argument cannot be a satisfactory way of reconciling parents' actual and their children's prospective interests in sovereignty.

The autonomy argument is correct to the extent that it affirms children's right to an education that liberates them from cultural domination, whether it be in the family or in some larger cultural unit. I shall say more presently about the content of the right and its implications for the scope of parents' claims to educational choice. But taken just as it stands, the argument blurs the relationship between children's and parents's rights in education by construing the moral significance of personal sovereignty too crudely.

## 43. Sovereignty and the Limits of Autonomy

The first thing to notice here is that many parents who seek to veto the great sphere are unlikely to wish for autonomy in their own lives while discounting any prospective interest that their children might have in becoming autonomous persons. They are guilty of no crass double-standard. On the contrary, the influences they seek to shield their children from are likely to be influences they shun themselves as a threat to the only life worth living. For such parents, the zone of sovereignty to which they lay claim is not an arena in which an autonomous self can operate unhindered by the demands of others; personal sovereignty is rather the social space that permits the godly to slough off the vanities of self. Consider John Wesley's observations on the relationship between the self and its Maker:

If the Will of God be our one rule of action, in every thing, great and small . . . it follows, by undeniable consequence, that we are not to do our own will in any thing. . . . Thus, we are to use our understanding, our imagination, our memory, wholly to the glory of him that gave them. Thus our will is wholly to be given up to him, and all our affections to be regulated as he directs. We are to love and hate, to rejoice and grieve, to desire and shun, to hope and fear, according to the rule which he prescribes whose we are, and whom we are to serve in all things. (quoted in Greven 1977: 102)

Wesley's conception of obedience to God as an unrelenting denial of the self is by no means the only one; other interpretations, far more congenial to the exponents of autonomy, are also possible. Moreover, liberalized conceptions of theism are plainly far more prominent in our world than they were in Wesley's. But we cannot dismiss Wesley's conception as a mere thing of the past either. For its influence continues to be discernible in Christian educational and religious practices, in North America and elsewhere, and comparable conceptions of piety are to be found in currently influential branches of Islam and Judaism. All this leaves those who might be attracted to the autonomy argument with the puzzling phenomenon of many people who seem to prize the rights that constitute their sovereignty as a way of renouncing all aspiration to autonomy.

What does that renunciation mean? Although a literal reading of the passage might suggest that what Wesley enjoins is a spiritual discipline that alienates our very status as agents, that is hardly what could be meant. I assume that in giving his will 'wholly up' to God Wesley remains an agent who chooses to obey God's commands, as he understands them, even if no credit redounds to the agent for that choice or understanding because both are wholly due to the grace of the Lord. But even though this means Wesley tacitly endorses the value of those powers of practical reason that are implicit in the very concept of choice or agency, it would be absurd to infer that an enthusiasm for the development of autonomy is latent in his words. His claim is that we cannot live aright by relying on the growth of our own powers of rational thought and choice towards ever more refined levels of development; we live as we should by relinquishing such foolishness and surrendering the self to the 'Will of God' as it is revealed to us in scripture and prayer. The very idea of wise self-direction would seem preposterous to Wesley because the self can be the source of no wisdom.

For many people this looks like a vast error. But that reaction must not obscure some obvious facts. A life lived in the grip of the creed Wesley proclaims may contain much that we can recognize as good: it may be a serenely happy life, it may be characterized by admirable service to others, it may revolve around some profoundly fulfilling vocation, it may be sustained by emotionally rewarding personal relationships. As I argued in Section 21, on any credible account of the range of good-making features that a life may exhibit, they are a heterogeneous bunch, and many of them might be compossible with a Wesleyan renunciation of autonomy. Even if all such goods would tend to flourish better with a highly evolved level of autonomy, their presence in a life without it may be contingently inseparable from its absence. Someone's happiness may depend decisively on the unquestioning security of her faith.

These thoughts suggest an interesting response to the autonomy argument. Suppose we are right to condemn the choice of some parents to veto the great sphere on their children's behalf because autonomy is stunted thereby. We could be right to condemn the choice only in the sense that we might be justified in deprecating the conduct of the parents in the Disneyland case. That is to say, our grounds for regarding the parents' conduct as wrong may be good enough, so far as they go, but *not* good enough for saying that the choice was not rightfully theirs. We still seem compelled to acknowledge that the child who is denied the great sphere may yet grow up to live a rich and rewarding life, and the educational choices her parents make may be in large part the cause of what becomes good in that life. The chief point is that if the personal sovereignty to which an adult can justly lay claim sometimes protects goods other than autonomy, and we lack any decisive reason to suppose that autonomy must outweigh these other goods, a child's prospective interest in sovereignty cannot be reduced to a prospective interest in autonomy above all else. Therefore, parents who choose to veto the great sphere in defence of a way of life at odds with autonomy do not necessarily deny the moral parity of their actual interest and their child's prospective interest in personal sovereignty.

The autonomy argument founders because we must reckon with the reality of lives, such as that which Wesley exhorts us to lead, in which many goods might be realized and yet autonomy, at least in any strong sense, seems to be rejected. What is not clear is whether this requires a wholesale rejection of the autonomy argument. After all, we are not faced either in child-rearing or the conduct of our own lives with two stark alternatives: make the development of autonomy the prime object of your endeavours or else forsake it altogether. The question I want to press now is *how far* autonomy can be repudiated without spoiling our lives. Recall that even in Wesley's case the notion of pious self-denial presupposes the rudiments of autonomous development. But do the barest conditions of agency suffice if our lives are to be good? Even if becoming a virtuoso of self-rule is far from necessary for a good life, one might rightly think that something substantially above a primitive level of agency is a fundamental human interest. I want to say that the prospective interest in personal sovereignty our children have, even if it must be understood in a way that does not exalt Socratic self-examination as the summun bonum, does entail the necessity of a degree of autonomous development that takes them beyond a condition I call 'ethical servility'. I suggest that the moral importance of overcoming ethical servility supports the right of children to an education that includes the kind of understanding the great sphere would promote, and the option of vetoing that education cannot belong within the scope of parents' rights so long as those rights are construed in a manner that eschews parental despotism. This is my 'servility argument', which might be regarded as a subtler and also, I hope, a more persuasive cousin of the autonomy argument.

## 44. Filial Servility and Parental Despotism

The concept of servility applies to a degraded social status or role or to a vice that may take root in our conduct and attitudes, regardless of status or role. I am interested in servility as a vice. What does it involve?

According to Thomas Hill, servility is a matter of 'misunderstanding one's rights . . . [or] placing a comparatively low value on them' (Hill 1995: 85). But not every failure correctly to identify or care enough about one's rights could warrant the imputation of slavishness that 'servility' connotes; the failure must rather be of a peculiarly grievous kind that cuts to the very core of the sense we have of ourselves as beings with rights. I think that would also be Hill's considered view, since all his examples focus on a gross failure to understand or appreciate one's equal standing in the moral community as a right-holder on a par with others.

Among Hill's examples is the Deferential Wife. The source of her servility is a false moral belief that she has a paramount duty to serve her husband. Thus her servility has nothing necessarily to do with the abuses her husband may visit on her, although Hill's account tends to obscure that fact. Her husband might only want what is good for his spouse and inflict no humiliation or maltreatment. Servility and despotism are mutually reinforcing vices, but there is benign as well as malevolent despotism. Her husband might encourage her to develop her talents or to pursue a career outside the home because he thinks that would make her happy, all the while maintaining his belief that she must obey him if her happiness is to be secure. And she is servile so long as she thinks of these activities as circumscribed by the primacy of her servile role, and hence as things to be abandoned without a thought for herself should her husband wish her to do so.

Imagine a Deferential Child whose servility is a precise analogue of Hill's example: the child believes she has an overriding duty to serve her parents and acts and feels accordingly. Suppose I try to rear such a child for unselfish reasons. I am convinced that without my wise direction she will likely act in ways that ruin her life. This makes me the parental equivalent of the benign Despotic Husband. I must ensure control of my child's conduct on all matters of fundamental ethical significance, and with that end in view, I instil the belief in my child that she must always obey me. I take it that whatever reasons condemn the vice of servility and its inculcation in the example of the Deferential Wife must apply with equal force here. There is no morally relevant difference between the two cases so far as the evil of deferential servility goes.

Now imagine a slightly different scenario in which I rear my child with substantially the same aim and a slightly different strategy. My prime goal is still to ensure permanent control of my child's conduct. But instead of instilling deferential servility, I rear my child so that as an adult she maintains an ignorant antipathy towards all alternatives to the ethical ideal I inculcated during childhood. By an 'ignorant antipathy' I do not just mean a lack of information combined with an aversion to what one does not know. I mean a settled affective disposition to refuse to register whatever reason might commend in the objects of one's antipathy, even if, at some later date, one might acquire much knowledge about them. So long as that disposition persists, the possibilities it banishes beyond the pale of deliberation are rendered ineligible in much the same way that a belief that one must defer to one's parents renders ineligible whatever conflicts with parental commands. In short, instead of rearing a Deferential Child, I can settle for a serviceable substitute: the Ethically Servile Child.

Unlike the Deferential Child, my Ethically Servile Child does not think of herself as under any duty to defer to me. She may enumerate her rights correctly, talk eloquently about their meaning, and prize them as highly as anyone reasonably could. Yet in a deep sense she remains subordinate to my will because the choices I made in moulding her character effectively pre-empt serious thought at any future date about the alternatives to my judgement. Ignorant antipathy regarding those alternatives secures her ongoing subordination in much the same way that the Deferential Child's belief that she has a duty to defer to her parents guarantees her subordination. In each case the field of deliberation in which the agent operates as an adult has been constrained through childhood experience so as to ensure ongoing compliance with another's will. The servility of one mirrors that of the other, even though the means by which it is established is different. No morally relevant difference is discernible between the condition of the Ethically Servile Child and the Deferential Child. Whatever moral reasons we have to decry the production of the one will equally condemn the production of the other.

One final aspect of my variations on Hill's case must be noted. In my story of the Ethically Servile Child, I imagined myself consciously deciding to instil an ignorant antipathy towards all that conflicts with my basic beliefs. That is strictly inessential to the evil of servility itself, although it may be relevant to questions of culpability. In the real world, conscious decisions of this sort are probably rare in the perpetuation of ethical servility. Those who instil that attitude may themselves often be examples of the Ethically Servile Child, in which case their efforts in child-rearing will tend sincerely to be represented to themselves and others simply as the sharing of heart-felt convictions with one's children. Nothing in the vice of ethical servility prevents one from graduating to the role of Despotic Parent without transcending the vice that one's own Despotic Parent inculcated during childhood. A chain of ethical servility may link one generation to another, moving back into an indefinite past, and obscuring for those whose lives it connects the character of their most basic choices and beliefs.

The antidote to ethical servility is the kind of understanding I have associated with schooling as the great sphere. Its point is not to teach children that Socrates was right and Wesley wrong on the question of how people should live. To have that understanding is not to be disabled from choosing as Wesley did; it is merely to be empowered to make that choice for oneself. This is not to deny the fact that Wesley enjoins us to become servile instruments of the Lord's will. But whatever the merits of that prescription, it cannot be the same as being a servile instrument of one's parents' will, even if that distinction is sometimes blurred in the tradition of child-rearing that Wesley represented.[5]

The great sphere certainly requires a level of autonomous development above the condition of mere agency; but on no account does it demand commitment to reasoned self-rule as the apogee of human development. The lesson it teaches is that each of us must learn to ask the question of how we should live, and that how we answer it can be no servile echo of the answers others have given, even if our thoughts commonly turn out to be substantially the same as those that informed our parents' lives. Agreement with those we love, even when it is in large part due to a concord of thought and feeling that love has fed, is not the same as ethical servility.

Those who would argue for the right of parents to veto the great sphere are effectively demanding a right to keep their children servile. But we cannot reconcile their demand with the fundamental moral equality of persons in the family. If the child's prospective interest in personal sovereignty is assigned parity of weight with the adult's actual interest, efforts to render their children servile will constitute a violation of the child's rights, given any credible interpretation of what those interests are. To be reared in a manner that instils ethical servility is not just to be like someone whose parents made an unfortunate educational choice by choosing Disneyland instead of a piano; it is to be denied one of the developmental preconditions of adult rights—viz. a level of autonomous development sufficient to overcome the vice of ethical servility.[6]

Suppose someone objects to the servility argument on grounds that parallel the considerations that earlier proved telling against the autonomy argument. Just as we might repudiate autonomy in a strong Socratic sense, and yet live good lives, can we not also embrace servility and live well? After all, the Deferential Wife may be the very model of domestic contentment, as Hill himself suggests (Hill 1995: 80). Similar possibilities arise in the case of ethical servility. Children who grow up to be ethically servile may be happy, and they may achieve much else that makes a life worth living. The choice their parents make in rearing them to be servile may be causally connected to these good-making features of their lives. If all that is so, how can we claim that parents who instil ethical servility thereby violate their children's rights?

But the analogy between this response to the servility argument and my earlier answer to the autonomy argument breaks down at a crucial point. The autonomy argument presupposes that the development of autonomy matters above all else, and so our realized or prospective interest in a zone of personal sovereignty must be construed accordingly. But a conception of the good in which autonomy occupies this dominant role is only one among others that have some rational credence. There is no reason to suppose that autonomy must trump all rival goods. People should be free to adjudicate among conceptions of the good for themselves, unless we have decisive moral reason to rule out some conceptions. An interpretation of any right, such as parents' right to educational choice, which arbitrarily assumes that autonomy or any other particular criterion must be everyone's paramount concern is oppressive. Now this line of thought cannot be plausibly adapted to rebut the servility argument. For a necessary assumption in that argument is that human beings have a right to order the diverse possible constituents of the good life in their own way, to choose a life in which autonomy is pursued at the expense, say, of secure religious conviction or to reverse those priorities. The trouble with ethical servility is that its inculcation denies the individual precisely that freedom.[7] Therefore, not only are we unable to parry the servility argument by adapting the moral reasons that undermined the autonomy argument; those very reasons are what condemn the inculcation of servility.

One might still coherently say that a servile happiness or intimacy is a substantial human good. But that is nothing to the point within a rights discourse where the child's prospective interest in personal sovereignty carries equal weight with any adult's. Within that context, the accommodation of efforts to instil ethical servility makes no sense at all because to be made servile is effectively to forfeit one's sovereignty to another. A moral perspective in which we cease to think of servility as a vice that spoils our lives is possible, but it is not one we could reconcile with our considered judgements. Consider Augustine's remarkable apostrophe to 'the Catholic Church, Most True Mother of Christians':

It is You who make wives subject to their husbands . . . by chaste and faithful obedience; you set husbands over their wives; you join sons to their parents by a freely granted slavery, and set parents above their sons in pious domination . . . You teach slaves to be loyal to their masters . . . You bind all men together in the remembrance of their first parents, not just by social bonds, but by some feeling of their common kinship. You teach kings to rule for the benefit of their people; and you it is who warn the peoples to be subservient to their kings. (quoted in Brown 1967: 225)

The point of the quotation is not to berate Augustine for failing to anticipate the Enlightenment and liberal democracy; my purpose is only to show how utterly alien from our own moral universe is a world in which servility does not count as a vice. For reasons too obvious and numerous to be worth mentioning, Augustine's conception of filial servitude as the moral cement of society is repellent to us.

Yet at one point Augustine's words impinge uncomfortably on our own sensibilities. I claimed earlier that the expressive significance of child-rearing for parents must be recognized in any morally defensible conception of their rights in education. Nothing I have said subsequently retreats from that claim. If the particular ends to which schooling as the great sphere is wedded cannot rightfully be rejected by parents, this still leaves the education of any child underdetermined in countless important ways. Many educational questions it leaves unanswered are still within the scope of parents' rights and will properly be settled in any particular case in a way that expresses their distinctive vision of the right and the good. But because the expressive significance of child-rearing is so profound for parents it is tempting to inflate the moral claims it can support and to defend in the language of rights relationships of despotism and servility—versions of the parental 'domination' that Augustine celebrated. That is the seductive side of Nozick's thought that I am connected to my hand as I am connected to my children. My argument has been an attempt to show that taking rights seriously in the family forbids us from succumbing to that seduction.

## 45. *From Principle to Policy:* Mozert *Reconsidered*

Children have a right to an education that is at least infringed when ethical servility is inculcated. The provision of a form of schooling that would work as an antidote to such servility does not infringe the rights of parents. The argument of the preceding chapters suggests that it can also be endorsed in the name of civic virtue. Therefore, public policies designed to ensure that the schooling children receive adheres to the pattern of the great sphere may often be an effective, even a necessary way of safeguarding their rights while at the same time honouring the rights of parents and contributing to the proper ends of political education. To see how that abstract conclusion might apply in guiding policy, it will help to take a closer look at *Mozert*.

What complicates the case is the fact that the plaintiff parents' objections to the reading programme prescribed for their children confounded reasons of extremely uneven merit (Stolzenberg 1993: 596–7). That makes it easy for those who are unsympathetic to their demands to address only what was foolish or deplorable in their reasoning, and easy also for sympathizers to stress what might have had substance in their case while ignoring the very real moral hazards of acceding to their demands. I begin with the strongest reasons for not accommodating their demands, and then I turn to what may have been legitimate grievances. My interest in the case is not in whether the correct legal decision was made but in what the facts might reveal about the limits of parents' moral rights to educational choice.

Some of the parents' objections to the reading series were expressed in terms of how the material could be interpreted as a denial of their faith. Once such an interpretation was deemed possible by the parents, the required reading was claimed to constitute a violation of their own and their children's religious liberty. Limited exposure to certain ideas that contradicted their faith might be acceptable, but only so long as these were labelled as wrong and the faith they contradicted explicitly upheld as right. On the other hand, some ideas, such as evolution and 'false supernaturalism', were so radically inimical to the faith that all reference to them had to be eliminated from the classroom. The plaintiffs claimed it was 'occult practice' to use the human imagination beyond the limitations of scriptural authority (*Mozert* v. *Hawkins County Bd. of Education*: 1062–4).

These facts make it reasonable to infer that part at least of what disturbed the parents about their children's required reading was the obstacle it posed to the inculcation of ethical servility. To claim that schooling consistent with their rights must be rid of virtually all that could be understood as inconsistent with their faith is to assume they were entitled to mould their children's abilities and desires so as to make alternatives to the creed they prescribed more or less unthinkable. Moreover, in denying that the parents had such a right, the court did not tacitly renounce the doctrine of biblical inerrancy that was central to their faith.[8] Many of the plaintiffs' co-congregationists were able to reconcile belief in biblical inerrancy with a willingness to see their children participate in the controversial reading programme. The basis of that reconciliation is easy to see. For it is one thing to believe that the Bible contains no error and another to say that any exercise of thought beyond the boundaries of scriptural authority, as the plaintiff parents understood that authority, is damnable impiety. If the court's refusal to accommodate the parents' objections tacitly repudiated a doctrine of inerrancy, it was a doctrine that affirmed the inerrancy of parents rather than the Bible, and on that count at least, the court could not be faulted.

Children have a right to an education that includes an understanding of ethical diversity that the parents in *Mozert* wrongly wished to block. But nothing follows immediately about the stage at which schools should attempt to engender that understanding. The attempt might be conducted prematurely or insensitively, and the younger the children, the higher those risks are likely to be. If the attempt were to leave children feeling merely confused, demeaned, or frightened, then some real harm might be done. And serious reflection on alternatives to our established ethical convictions is perhaps unlikely to be fruitful—even if it is no worse than pointless—until they are indeed securely established, and in the case of younger children, that can not be assumed. These are weighty considerations, and I return to them in Chapter 7 when the case for state-sponsored separate schooling is examined.

Reasonable disagreement about what counts as judicious timing or sensitive pedagogy in controversial matters is to be expected under pluralism, and once we heed the moral importance of parents' expressive interest in child-rearing, a strong case is available for deference to parental choice within that area of reasonable disagreement. To be sure, these were not the terms in which the parents in *Mozert* framed their objections. The exposure to diversity they inveighed against was condemned as sheer wickedness rather than premature or insensitive teaching. But we should still ask if a temporary parental veto on schooling as the great sphere for children of elementary school age might have been warranted on moral grounds that the parents' own reasoning failed to adduce.

The general point that deference to parental concerns about timing and tact is often morally required is unassailable. By the same token, we also have reason to worry that efforts to evoke the relevant understanding of diversity might be conducted too late or too timidly to have much prospect of success against the pressures of an upbringing that leans heavily towards ethical servility. The seriousness of that particular worry has to temper our willingness to delay exposure to diversity out of respect for parental scruples about timing and tact. That worry must surely weigh heavily in *Mozert*. The kind of education the plaintiffs wished for their children was plainly one that at least carried a severe risk of making them ethically servile. Furthermore, the particular encounters with diversity they objected to—for example, stories of women whose accomplishments outside domestic roles were impressive, or a tale of a Catholic community that did not proclaim the error of Catholicism—would often appear to be a gentle way of stirring some rudimentary appreciation of beliefs and values beyond the boundaries of a fundamentalist faith. On no reasonable interpretation could such experiences be seen, for example, as surrendering children to the seductive power of an aggressive secularism or as enforcing the onerous ideal of autonomy entailed by active acceptance of the burdens of judgement. But they might be plausibly read as making some important contribution to that modest, but morally critical degree of autonomy that the supersession of ethical servility would require. And even if there were a large gap between that modest autonomy and the reasoned self-rule intrinsic to full-blown civic virtue, that modest autonomy is an important support to a basic tolerance of religious and other differences.[9]

But this is not the final, or even the most interesting word on *Mozert*. The plaintiffs had another argument that was unfortunately overshadowed by their plainly illiberal demands. At one point, the most prominent of the plaintiffs testified that her main objection was directed to 'the [reading] series as a whole' rather than the offensive or seductive impact of specific texts. The series as a whole, according to the parents, was pervasively biased against their beliefs. The series constituted required reading for the entire duration of elementary school, and yet its references to religion were allegedly tilted heavily towards exotic faiths, and its sparse allusions to Christianity included not a single example of Protestantism.

Notice that complaints that the reading series failed to excoriate or ignore Catholics and other infidels are entirely irrelevant to the charge of bias. Those complaints only make sense on the assumption that an educationally appropriate series would have been biased against everyone except evangelical Protestants, and because that assumption was completely untenable, so too were the complaints it motivated. But the charge of bias carries weight on the assumption that an acceptable reading series would have included respectful depictions of Protestant Christianity alongside representations of other ways of life. This second line of argument in the plaintiffs' case was not about the evils of reflection on diversity but the alleged failure to initiate such reflection in a context where the way of life which the parents and their children shared was given due respect and recognition.

The court gave short shrift to that second argument. Judge Lively noted that 'balanced' textbooks might be desirable, but added that trying to 'cure the omissions' in the required reading series would not satisfy the parents (*Mozert* v. *Hawkins County Bd. of Education*: 1064). But the important question was not what would have satisfied the parents but what would have redressed any legitimate grievances they had. No doubt the case for 'balanced' textbooks easily degenerates into a foolish plea for an education that will say nice things about everyone and give offence to no one. But the foolishness of that must not obscure the force of the demand that public education not be systematically biased against ways of life that deserve our respect or at least our toleration under pluralism. The facts of the case in *Mozert* do not make it sufficiently clear that the charge of bias was justified.[10] Unfortunately, the reasoning of the plaintiffs and their critics hid that issue almost completely from view.

In a study of bias againt Protestant Christianity in commonly used American textbooks, Paul Vitz reached a conclusion that reveals the importance of the issue that *Mozert* both exemplifies and obscures. According to Vitz, educational bias of one sort or another is inevitable, and so it is wrong to think we could ever create a 'balanced' educational environment in which all children would be accepted without systematic prejudice against some. 'In short, it is intrinsic to any monopolistic school system that it will be oppressive and coercive—especially in a country as varied as the United States. America is truly pluralistic, and we must finally recognise that today's pluralism in American life requires pluralism in American schools' (Vitz 1986: 90–1). The fact of pluralism here becomes the rationale for educational fragmentation. Fragmentation is supposedly necessary because any single institution that attempts to embrace the pluralism of the larger society will be oppressive and coercive towards somebody or other. After all, the idea that common schools could justly accommodate the full range of ethical diversity may seem merely foolish when the expressive interest in child-rearing is tied to so many different and incompatible values. Vitz's own defence of that idea is inept.[11] But the idea should still disturb us. So even if the parents in *Mozert* were right that the prescribed reading series was biased against their way of life, that is just what we should expect from schools that purport to serve everyone equally well. Any attempt to correct that bias will come at the price of bias against some other group. The conclusion will be congenial to many who now espouse 'choice' as the panacea to the ills of schooling in many liberal democracies. I think Vitz is dangerously wrong here. But to see why we need to look much more closely at the institutions of common and separate schooling under pluralism and at how the political control of both might be informed by regard for the proper ends of political education and the rights of parents and students.

# CHAPTER 7

## Common Schools, Separate Schools

### 46. Introduction

A hundred years ago John Dewey announced that the progressive teacher was the 'prophet of the true God, and the usherer in of the kingdom of God' (Dewey 1897/1972: 95). His theistic language is not to be read at face value. Dewey's divine kingdom was no more than a utopian ideal of democratic society. Progressive teachers in the common school were cast in the roles of prophets and creators of that utopia, and Dewey would provide them with the necessary script for wise prophesy as well as the right pedagogical methods to do their sacred work.

Dewey's faith in schools as the route to democratic salvation will seem quaint and foolish to many as this century draws to a close. Indeed, his own sense of the power of schooling as an instrument of social progress became more muted later in his career (Westbrook 1991: 508–10). But we have taught ourselves to expect far less of schools than Dewey hoped for, even after those hopes had been duly chastened. The common school in particular has come to be widely regarded as an institutional anachronism that must give way to educational arrangements more responsive to private preference and cultural diversity. Of course, the decline of the common school is still viewed with alarm in some quarters. One concern is that many policies purporting to respect individual choice will have a damaging effect on the education of the poor by deflecting resources away from the schools to which they send their children. But typically this argument seems to defend the common school by warning us against policies that might make a bad situation worse. The disdain for the institution among its detractors is almost matched by the disenchantment of its defenders. Both lack the faith that inspired Dewey and the leading educators of his generation.

Our collective loss of faith in the common school is perhaps one of the most significant shifts in educational thought during this century. But I suspect our current attitude may look as wrong to our descendants as Dewey's democratic ardour seems to us. For our current attitude attests to a crude and unambitious understanding of what common education might be and a blindness to the difficulties of supplying the common education worth having without truly common schools. In these respects at least, Dewey's visionary idea of an education for all that ennobles the common school is preferable to our own pessimism. That is not to accept the specific content of his communitarian vision. My point is only that he posed the right question by asking what suitably rich and inspiring view of a shared educational venture could inform common schooling in a free society. I do not offer here anything like a comprehensive vision of what that venture now should be. But I argue that an adequate conception of common education for the citizens of a liberal democracy warrants a sober faith in common schools as a potentially powerful instrument of social good, and it should also make us wary of policies that would undermine them. However, I hope to develop an argument for common schooling that is sensitive to considerations supporting the acceptability, even the desirability, of some kinds of separate schooling.

## 47. Education and Schooling

The cardinal distinctions in the argument that follows are between common education and common schooling on the one hand, and separate education and separate schooling on the other. The distinctions matter because rival policies for common or separate schooling are confusedly entangled with competing conceptions of common or separate education.

A conception of common education prescribes a range of educational outcomes—virtues, abilities, different kinds of knowledge—as desirable for all members of the society to which the conception applies. How members might differ in religion or gender, for example, is irrelevant to the basic content of common education in a liberal democracy. A school is common if it welcomes students of an appropriate age, without regard to differentiating factors of a particular kind. The relevant factors are what James Fishkin calls 'cleavages' in the body politic. A cleavage is 'a polarization among self-identified groups' such that to participate in the relevant self-identification is typically to see one's group in at least some social competition or conflict with other such groups (Fishkin 1992: 130). A school that discriminated on the basis of race, social class, religion, or first language would be a separate school, given the strength of such criteria as cleavages within pluralistic societies. But since not all possible bases for distinguishing students are cleavages, some common schools might have specialized purposes of many different kinds.[1]

I want to make two further stipulations about what counts as a common school. Such a school must welcome the children it serves not only in the formal sense of forswearing any explicit appeal to cleavages in its admission criteria or curriculum; it must also offer a learning environment that is genuinely hospitable to the credal and cultural diversity the society exhibits within limits fixed by the constitutive political morality of that society. That is to say, common schools have a distinctive ethos that makes them open to the pluralism of the larger society. Schools that lack that ethos are only de jure common schools. Second, I assume that genuinely common schools will, to some degree at least, actually mirror in the composition of their student bodies many of the major cleavages of the society itself. No real school will be an exact microcosm of the society within which it exists, and the range of pluralism in large democracies makes it certain that some important cleavages will not be represented. To that extent, the best we might feasibly hope for is quasi-common schooling. But quasi-common schooling might be a very useful institution for all that.

A conception of separate education prescribes a range of educational outcomes as desirable for some particular social group distinguished according to religion, ethnicity, or the like. A school is separate if it welcomes only members of the society who belong to groups that are distinguished by such criteria. A de jure common school may be a de facto separate school if the absence of differentiating criteria in admission requirements coincides with a pedagogy and ethos that are contemptuous of particular groups. Conversely, a de jure separate school may grow more like a de facto common school as it relaxes doctrinal or other selective criteria of admission and develops a pedagogy and ethos that are no longer appropriate only to the social group for whom that school was originally intended. That is more than a notional possibility. Admission policies to Catholic high schools in the United States often give no consideration at all to students' religious background (Bryk, Lee, and Holland 1993: 128–9). These schools tend to exhibit a degree of diversity in ethnicity and social class, and to a lesser extent, in race, that compares favourably to state-sponsored public schools (Coleman and Hoffer 1987: 31–2). More important perhaps, their success in educating children from disadvantaged groups and organizing school life around institutional norms that affirm 'a shared responsibility for building a just and caring society' stands in sharp contrast with the rather dismal failures of much de jure common schooling in these regards (Lee, Bryk, and Smith 1993: 230).

The importance of that example must be stressed. In North America, the debate about the future of education has become framed largely in terms of the contrast between a system dominated by publicly funded and publicly governed schools, formally open to all, and alternative schemes that would create a more or less regulated market in educational services. The contrast that shapes the debate is between schools that are funded and controlled in different ways. But the difference between common and separate schools has to do with institutional ethos and what is taught to whom. To assume either that the common schools worth having are necessarily safe once the pattern of governance and funding historically associated with them persists or that the ideal must be abandoned under any alternative to that pattern is simply irrational. We still lack a good understanding of the educational consequences of different patterns of funding and governance for schools in varying social conditions. But we obscure the hard questions that need to be asked about that when common schooling is thought to stand or fall with the preservation of organizational systems that have often included schools far less common in the ways that really matter than many schools outside.[2]

Furthermore, the possible connections between the two categories of educational conceptions on the one hand and common and separate schooling on the other are more complex than they might initially seem. To begin with, the success of common education in a diverse society does not necessarily require common schooling. The clearest example of this is easily imagined: a society with an overwhelmingly powerful and pervasive political tradition supporting the ends of common education has no need to make any special institutional provisions to promote them. In that case, any partiality towards common schooling in state policy would be arbitrary at best and discriminatory at worst. Similarly, the success of separate education need not require separate schooling in all circumstances. The prospects of success in Catholic separate education were perhaps rather better for the typical Catholic family under Communist rule in Poland than they were for comparably devout families in the seductively secularized societies of Western Europe during the same period, despite the ready availability of separate Catholic schools in Western Europe and their absence in Communist Poland.

Common schools might even become a vehicle of separate education while retaining an overarching commitment to common education. The provision of optional language programmes for linguistic minorities, or even specialized religious instruction, are ways in which common schools may attempt to create an educational environment that instantiates substantive and not merely de jure commonality. The success of common schooling will depend crucially on whether it can elicit trust across the cleavages that divide the society it is supposed to serve. That trust is unlikely to be given unless common schools can be responsive to some degree to the demands for separate education with which cleavages will tend to correlate.

The distinctions I have made help to formulate two claims that should be widely acceptable. First, what is finally important is success in whatever common or separate education is worth having, and the practices of common and separate schooling matter only derivatively as they promote or hinder that success. To think otherwise makes as little sense as supposing that hospitals are good or bad in a way that is independent of their effects on the health of patients. Second, any morally defensible approach to education under pluralism must acknowledge *both* the necessity of some common education and the acceptability of at least certain kinds of separate education for those who would choose them. The necessity of a common education for all follows from the need to secure a sufficiently coherent and decent political culture and the prerequisites of a stable social order. The acceptability of at least some kinds of separate education follows from the need to respect the many different convictions and ways of life that flourish under pluralism and the divergent educational aspirations that flow from these.

The line I have drawn between education and schooling is not intended to beg the question against those who would insist on a very intimate connection between certain varieties of separate education and separate schooling. Nothing I have said so far rules out the view that a satisfactory separate education of some kind cannot be supplied without separate schooling. I consider a possible way of defending that view in the following sections. Yet once we reject the crazy idea that a common education can be completely repudiated, the partisans of separate schooling must do more than talk of what is needed for separate education; they must also show how a satisfactory common education can be given to children who do not attend common schools.

My initial focus is on separatism as it applies to state-sponsored schooling. First, I examine the case that has to be made in defence of public support for separate schooling, and how that case might be weighed against the educational value of common schooling. I ask whether the argument for separatism can be reasonably made on the basis of parents' rights to educational choice, and my answer is that it probably cannot, although it might often succeed on other grounds. The issue of tolerated but unsponsored schooling is addressed in Section 54. Finally, I return to common schooling, and I consider its viability given the controversial ends to which it is properly committed.

## 48. *The Separatist Argument*

I begin with a separatist argument that seems easily to satisfy the criteria of common education, on any credible reading of what those criteria might be.

The French-speaking population of New Brunswick—the Acadians—have been strong supporters of Canadian bilingualism and the federal commitment to a multicultural polity. But they have also argued against fully bilingual schools for their children because the cultural fragility of French in a society where the power of English is immense requires some institutional enclaves where their language can be safe against erosion that no one really wants. That was the gist of the case they made to Canada's landmark Commission on Bilingualism and Biculturalism in the 1960s: 'Their environment was, they argued, already saturated with English. They feared that if the Acadian schools emphasized English as much as French, the balance would be tipped decisively towards English' (Webber 1994: 243).

There is no question here that the Acadian position signalled any alienation from the civic life of New Brunswick or Canada as a whole. The separate schools they wanted were no less committed to whatever ends of common education might be sensibly affirmed than the common, fully bilingual schools they rejected. The case might have been different if French- and English-speaking citizens of New Brunswick had no robust, shared political vernacular and loyalty that cut across their linguistic differences and linked their public life to the larger, Pan-Canadian conversation. Then acceding to Acadian demands might have been disputed as divisive, or at least as a failure to favour educational institutions that might do a little to heal political divisions. But these were not the circumstances of the case. Giving the Acadians the separate schools they wanted helped to protect a politically assimilated cultural community against unwanted encroachment better than the alternative of common schooling, and it did so in a manner that incurred no perceptible social costs in the pursuit of common education.

The Acadian case is revealing because it illustrates what has to be achieved in a successful separatist case. Two independent arguments have to work. It has to be shown that a particular aim of separate education cannot be pursued with enough hope of success without separate schooling. But that is not enough. We also need to know that the separate schooling demanded in the name of separate education is consistent with adequate prospects for success in common education.

That second requirement means that the case for separate schooling tends to become complicated in circumstances of the following kind.

Suppose we choose an educational end for our children which, so far as it is achieved, brings about a near ubiquitous transformation in how they will live. Suppose further that the end cannot be conscientiously endorsed by many members of the society we inhabit so that it must belong to one conception of separate education among others rather than a vision of common education that all could be reasonably expected to affirm.[3] Some religious ends are the most obvious example here. But transformative aims are also adopted when ethnic or racial identity takes on the significance of a unique and virtually all-inclusive worldview, as it does in certain versions of Afrocentric education.

Unlike linguistic accomplishments or ethnic loyalties that are additions to a civic identity essentially unaltered by what is added, transformative educational aims raise obvious misgivings about how they can cohere with the ends of common education. But precisely because they are transformative, accommodating such aims within common schools raises equally obvious difficulties. A truly transformative aim can hardly be effectively pursued in a school that necessarily attempts to welcome all students, regardless of the notions of separate education to which they or their parents might subscribe. The consequences of commitment to the aim must saturate how one studies or teaches literature, how one thinks about the choice of a career or the nature of human intimacy, and virtually any other issue of consequence in a human life. But that is not the kind of environment that common schools can provide.

Susan Rose quotes the following from a handbook expounding the educational priorities of an American Christian fundamentalist school: 'In light of the order God has produced in the material universe . . . we cannot overlook Mathematics as being an instrument for teaching our students concepts of order and logic as a [*sic*] very attribute of God' (Rose 1993: 457). Similar sentiments are basic to the educational ambitions of even the more liberal advocates of separate confessional schooling who resist the idea that religious education might be compressed into one slot in the curriculum among others (e.g. Groome 1996: 107). Faith makes a difference to everything. Therefore, the achievement of any transformative aim would seem threatened in a social setting where one is educated by and with people who do not accept the aim for themselves, however respectful they might be of the convictions of those who do.

Educational scholars often talk of the 'hidden curriculum' of institutions such as schools. The hidden curriculum comprises the attitudes, beliefs, or the like that the very fact of participating in the institution will tend to instil, and which are yet, at least typically, not consciously acknowledged by those who participate (e.g. J. R. Martin 1976). The hidden curriculum of the common school must suggest that at least in this environment one can and perhaps should study mathematics, discuss moral problems, and so on, in a way that sets aside commitment to separate educational values which, for some of their adherents, can *never* be justifiably set aside. Common schools could not expunge that element of their hidden curriculum without ceasing to be common schools because their distinctive ethos requires an openness to pluralism.

A rough but important distinction can be drawn between radical and moderate versions of the separatist case. On the radical version, common schooling poses an unacceptable threat to the transformative aim of separate education at any point in the educational process, and therefore all schooling for those who embrace the aim must be separate. Moderate versions of the argument will stress the need for separate schooling during the early stages of the educational process, when the aim has at best a precarious purchase on the child's life. But the need is regarded as decreasingly urgent as the child grows in whatever understanding and commitment the aim entails. Exponents of the argument in its moderate versions will regard common schooling as acceptable at the later stages of the educational process; they may even be persuaded to regard it as desirable on grounds of common education.

To assess the separatist case in either version, we need to know what the proper aims of common education are. I argue that in one widely assumed answer to that question, the case for even radical separatism looks compelling. But that answer fares very badly under scrutiny.

## 49. Minimalist Common Education

The difficulty of reconciling the separatist argument, especially in its radical version, with the requirements of common education is disguised by the widespread assumption that these requirements are minimal and uncontroversial. Common education can doubtless be implemented with ease in separate schools once we grant that common education is reducible to the inculcation of respect for law, and, only a little less uncontroversially, that all other shared aims derive from a concern with enhancing economic productivity and competitiveness. To interpret common education along these lines is to endorse what I call the 'minimalist conception' of that concept. For adherents of the minimalist conception, the proper content of common education in a free society is given by whatever substantive educational ends can be supported by a more or less inclusive consensus in that society.

Even if empirical research showed that many separate schools were currently ineffective in implementing the minimalist conception, the sensible inference would be that they need to be improved in that respect, not that they must be discouraged, much less abolished. Nothing in the familiar forms of separatist argument and practice is seriously at odds with goals like obedience to law, literacy, and scientific competence. This is not to deny the notorious friction between religious fundamentalism and scientific orthodoxy on many questions. But that is irrelevant to scientific competence of the sort that belongs to the minimalist conception. In that context, scientific competence is understood as a tool for technological exploitation, and since contemporary fundamentalism has made peace with that narrow use of science, where the separatist argument is used on behalf of fundamentalism it still poses no substantial danger to the pursuit of this particular educational aim. You can be taught that God made the world in six days a few thousand years ago—and that Charles Darwin was a harbinger of contemporary moral nihilism—and still grow up to be a model employee in the research division at IBM. Similarly, when literacy is construed expansively to include a command of the imaginative or speculative uses of language, serious conflict with many influential conceptions of separate education will certainly occur. But a far more austere and technical notion of literacy belongs to our minimalist conception.

Once common schools are dedicated to nothing more than the minimalist conception, they will inevitably be unacceptable to the adherents of separate education and uninspiring to those of us who once looked to the common school with strong social hopes. That is so because minimalist common education can include no more than the lowest common denominator in a society's understanding of what its children should learn. The more diverse the society is, the lower that common denominator will necessarily become.

That education must at best be seriously incomplete because as individual citizens we rightly have much more elaborate convictions about what is worth teaching our children than the lowest common denominator can possibly include. Imagine a child who is successfully taught what more or less all of us agree is desirable. But the child is also utterly lacking in everything else that you in particular think worth learning. The sheer paucity of what we all agree to be desirable means it is virtually impossible to imagine someone in these circumstances that *any* of us could recognize as better than negligibly educated. On all the many issues that distinguish and divide us, minimalist common schooling must follow Seamus Heaney's wry advice for conversation across the sectarian cleavages of Northern Ireland: 'Whatever you say | say nothing' (Heaney 1975: 57).[4]

From the perspective of others, common schools attached to the minimalist conception will offer an education that is worse than incomplete; it will be badly distorted. That is so because by excluding all except the lowest common denominator of acceptable learning a mistaken view of even that small common ground is apt to become embedded in the hidden curriculum. A conservative Christian, for example, may think that teaching 'the work-ethic' in an institution where work is not publicly interpreted as ministering to the greater glory of God is profoundly misleading because without that religious purpose the values of diligence and productivity become contaminated by the greed of secular society.

Thus Vitz's claim that common schools are inevitably biased against someone or other under pluralism is hard to disagree with once we assume that common schooling must be restricted to minimalist common education (Vitz 1986: 90–1). So long as anyone believes that mathematical competence or industrious habits only have value as aspects of particular separate educational aims, then common schooling will be objectionable because it wrenches these away from the context that gives them value. But since the whole point of the minimalist conception is to evade whatever disagreements divide us, the inability of common schooling to accommodate all objections must be bias according to the very standard of impartial teaching that the minimalist conception stipulates. Schools can never really 'say nothing' about our differences if by 'nothing' is meant a steady neutrality with regard to our divergent notions of separate education.

If common education is understood in minimalist terms, it is easily reconciled with virtually all the forms of separate education and separate schooling we are acquainted with. And once common schools see their mission as the implementation of that conception, they will become an increasingly unattractive institution under pluralism. So the separatist argument looks persuasive even in its radical version, and our collective disenchantment with the common schools looks inevitable, once it is assumed that the minimalist conception is the best conception of common education.[5] The question now is whether that is true.

## 50. Consensus and Respect

The appeal of the minimalist conception is easy to understand. Since the creation of state-sponsored schooling on a mass scale in the nineteenth century, the problem of creating a cohesive society in the midst of pluralism has typically been addressed by imposing a conception of common education that expresses the culture and advances the interests of politically dominant groups. The imposition has frequently been a grave injustice to those outside the same groups, and our own thought about common education and common schooling is often overshadowed by a sense of collective shame regarding the experience of culturally marginalized groups in de jure common schools.

The character of that experience is intimated in the words of the distinguished American educator Ellwood Cubberley, describing immigrants from southern and eastern Europe who came to America in the late nineteenth and early twenteth century:

Illiterate, docile, lacking in self-reliance and initiative, and not possessing the Anglo-Teutonic conceptions of law, order and government, their coming has served to dilute our national stock, and to corrupt tremendously our civic life. . . . Our task is to break up these groups or settlements, to assimilate and amalgamate these people as part of the American race, and to implant in their children, so far as can be done, the Anglo-Saxon conception of righteousness, law and order and popular government. (Cubberley 1909: 15)

For Cubberley, common education is necessarily and literally an act of cultural conquest: the customs of immigrants must be eradicated and their children absorbed into a single race whose values are as thoroughly Anglo-Saxon as such unpromising human material will allow. His understanding of the purpose of common schools was not eccentric at the time he said these things. Ethnic and religious bigotry has played no small part in shaping the institution of mass schooling from the nineteenth century and throughout much of the twentieth (e.g. Tyack and James 1985; Glenn 1988).

But what was the nature of Cubberley's moral failure? The answer that leads us to the minimalist conception is this. Schools that purport to be open to all and yet endorse values that are not accepted by all are an affront to the dignity of people who think and live otherwise. Oppression is only avoided when common education is recast to include nothing that any minority would repudiate, including those who have traditionally been disempowered and marginalized. This train of thought makes it possible for Nomi Stolzenberg to describe cultural assimilation through education as 'that insidious cousin of totalitarianism' (Stolzenberg 1993: 582). Common education that really eschewed all kinship with totalitarianism could not assimilate anyone, or so the story goes.

But the evil in Cubberley's view is not the bare idea that common schooling is properly committed to educational ends to which some members of society might object. The evil is partly his ugly stereotype of Europeans who do not belong to the 'right' racial stock. He also confuses the public morality of liberal democracy with the ethnic identity of those who first brought it to America. But Cubberley was right to insist that future citizens of a democratic community have to be assimilated to a common political culture that affirms shared understandings of law and government. He was also right to say that they needed to be literate and capable of self-reliance and initiative. We can and should agree with all that and still reject his false and repellent thesis that cultural, indeed racial uniformity is the basis of political order. Cubberley wrongly thought that pluralism is the high road to anarchy. But we make a mistake scarcely less calamitous if we suppose with Stolzenberg that all assimilation is the insidious cousin of totalitarianism.

The inadequacy of the minimalist conception can be brought into clearer view by reflecting on the inevitable incompleteness of any consensus it might capture. As I have defined it, minimalist common education rests on a 'more or less' inclusive agreement on the ends of common education. Complete unanimity would be an impossible requirement because in any large and complex society nothing can be expected to secure that level of support. Not everyone is enamoured with the goal of ceaseless economic growth on which contemporary educational debate tends to be riveted. Less innocent departures from unanimity are also familiar. Some of the members of America's more exotic militias have reservations about law-abidingness. The repudiation of racism and religious bigotry, even on their weakest interpretations, are not congenial to some in our midst. A common education that commands unanimous assent is an impossibility, and therefore minimalist common education must settle for something less than that if it makes sense to espouse common education at all.

Unfortunately, in settling for something less than unanimity, the absurdity of the claim that the minimalist conception embodies the respect due to all citizens is starkly exposed. The claim presupposes that respect is forfeited once common educational aims are imposed by a majority or a powerful elite on others. But that is precisely the imposition endured by racists, for example, whose children might be taught respect for people regardless of race in the name of common education. From the standpoint of the minimalist conception, the only possibly relevant difference between that case and the plight of an immigrant child, for example, whose culture is reviled in the classroom is that the immigrant child *might* belong to a more substantial minority than the adherents of racist attitudes. But why should the mere size of a minority be a relevant, much less the decisive criterion of oppression in the pursuit of educational ends? There is no credible answer to that question. The size of a minority whose way of life is unjustly disparaged through the imposition of a putative common educational aim certainly affects the scale of the injustice. But on the prior question of whether injustice has occurred it is irrelevant.

We are fortunate in contemporary liberal democracies in typically having rather more than a bare majority in support of the ideal of a polity without racism, even if there is much disagreement about just what that means. But a consistent advocate of the minimalist conception would have to concede that if support for the ideal declined so that substantial minorities embraced the most flagrant racism, then it could no longer form part of the minimalist conception, and attempts to promote the ideal through common education would oppress racists. That is ludicrous. What all this really shows is the contingency of the connection between any existing consensus on what all children should learn and a common education that would respect differences where respect is due. A massive consensus on an aim of common education is no guarantee that it expresses the respect due to all. By the same token, an aim that is widely rejected may express a respect for all that those with the power to enforce their will in de jure common schools sorely lack.

The moral poverty of the minimalist conception does not mean that we should be indifferent to whether the best interpretation of common education can win a strong consensus. What it does mean is that we cannot determine the best conception just by asking what would now secure agreement. A consensus on the ends of education that is adjusted to the full range of views that deserve respect cannot be complacently identified with the common ground we happen to occupy at this or any other moment in history. At least that is so as long as we cannot be sure that our pluralism is entirely a matter of reasonable pluralism. Current agreement is one thing; the moral consensus we would have if we lived together on a basis of equal respect is quite another.

The fact that a separate system of schooling should have little difficulty in implementing the minimalist conception does nothing to support the separatist argument because that conception is utterly inadequate. Similarly, the fact that common schooling circumscribed by the minimalist conception is an unattractive institution does nothing to discredit the general practice of common schooling. In the next section, I draw on the content of the previous chapters to specify some of what a morally credible conception of common education would include and how that conception bears on the practice of common schooling. The separatist argument can then be measured against some of the requirements of a defensible common education.


## 51. Political Virtue and Common Schooling

The argument that follows is grounded in the account of political virtue outlined in Chapters 2 through 5. It will help to rehearse the main elements of that account.

Justice as reasonableness is the prime virtue of citizenship for a free people. A certain notion of reciprocity is the nerve of that virtue: the reasonable citizen is disposed to propose fair terms of cooperation to others, to settle differences in mutually acceptable ways, and to abide by agreed terms of cooperation so long as others are prepared to do likewise. Principles that pass the test of reciprocity under pluralism must abstract from many of the divisions that pluralism contains. The importance of this point is made explicit in Rawls's idea of the burdens of judgement. The roots of political conflict about the good and the right are not all to be ascribed to the vices of unreason, such as closed-mindedness, logical bungling, or sheer ignorance. Accepting the burdens of judgement means acknowledging that many others adhere to values at odds with our own without being any less reasonable than we are. The morally relevant acknowledgement is more than assent to an abstract claim about the necessary imperfections of human judgement; it is a pervasive virtue of public reason that inclines us to devise and interpret rules of coexistence so as to accommodate the scope of reasonable pluralism.

Justice as reasonableness is a virtue of common pursuit. That is to say, it requires us to care about something we can only do together: the construction of a political morality that would be acceptable to each of us because it does no violence to the differences that divide us after we have reasoned about them as best we can. But even then the differences that divide us are still a force liable to pull against the common demands of justice. A liberal ideal of patriotism is a way of shoring up the motivational strength of those demands against the pressures of pluralism. The patriotism that matters is no dilution of justice. What it secures is identification with a particular political community as a setting for the realization of justice. Identification makes the flourishing of the community a constituent of our own good, and because liberal patriots think their community's flourishing depends on its justice, conflict is mitigated between the rational pursuit of good and reasonable deference to the claims of others.

Even if all this were granted as an argument about the content of common education at its best, nothing immediately follows about the desirability of common schooling or the limits of even the radical separatist argument. But a case for common schooling begins to emerge if we look more closely at the particular phase of moral development that joins the rudimentary moral life of the child in the family to the role of the just citizen in the public culture of a democracy. The moral learning that links these together takes place within Rawls's morality of association, and the requirements of that learning are the basis of an argument for common schooling.

The end of the morality of association is the virtuous citizen in the well-ordered society. But that end is foreshadowed and gradually approached through a series of roles that require increasing intellectual demands and finer moral discriminations. The intellectual thread of development has to do with what Rawls calls 'the art of perceiving the person' and understanding the intricacies of social cooperation. To grasp one's role within a given association, one must see how it fits together with other such roles in an overall scheme of cooperation, and this in turn requires an evolving ability to see things from the perspective of those who occupy other roles in the scheme. Our first steps into the world of associations are made as neophytes in the art of perceiving the person. 'But this lack is gradually overcome as we assume a succession of more demanding roles with their more complex schemes of rights and duties. The corresponding ideals require us to view things from a greater multiplicity of perspectives as the conception of the basic structure [of society] implies.' But what binds us to particular associations is not the growing subtlety of interpersonal understanding per se. That might only be used to manipulate others more effectively without the affective development that must accompany intellectual growth. The ties that bind are the deepening feelings of trust and affection others evoke as they act towards us with evident goodwill, and we then learn to respond in kind. Our goodwill is channelled through the given structures of duties and ideals that associations furnish, and as we come to see these as operating to the benefit of all, the association itself becomes an object of affection and loyalty (Rawls 1971: 469–72).

Rawls is not talking about the ordinary course of moral learning in our world. He is delineating the shape it would take in a well-ordered society. The associations within which people might come to play some part in that world could not be organized in ways that militate against the ideal outcome of the morality of association. Things are plainly different for us. But the process Rawls describes also yields some important ideas about how we might proceed in a less than well-ordered society.

Schooling has a large place in children's lives across the full span of the transition from membership in the family to membership in the polity. Because schooling has that place, the evolution of the roles and ideals that the institution offers to children as their schooling progresses should be designed with a eye to whatever pattern of moral development issues in the virtue of the citizen. Given Rawls's argument, the appropriate institutional design would pose increasingly taxing intellectual demands with regard to the art of perceiving the person and the understanding of social complexities. At the same time, it would nourish an ever widening web of relations of trust, reciprocal goodwill, and associative loyalty. This is where the educational value of common schooling, at least in the years immediately preceding the accession to full citizenship, comes into focus.

An increasing appreciation of 'a multiplicity of perspectives' is just what we should attempt to engender within the morality of association if the reasonable citizen is our desired end. For without a broad sensitivity to the many reasonable perspectives that acceptance of the burdens of judgement entails, the virtue of reasonableness simply does not exist. The point is connected to the familiar Aristotelian thesis that virtues, like skills, are acquired through their exercise (Aristotle 1980 edn.: 28–9). The thesis is that virtues and skills in their most refined forms are the fruit of educational processes in which we exercise them as more primitive habits, becoming ever more adept and discerning as we practise, reflect, and practise again in the light of what prior practice and reflection have taught us. Now the exercise of reasonableness presupposes deliberative settings in which citizens with conflicting beliefs and ends can join together to ask how they might live together on terms that all might endorse on due reflection. Such settings must straddle the cleavages that divide them from each other. That being so, the Aristotelian thesis would suggest that the growth of reasonableness requires at some stage that reciprocity be practised in dialogical contexts that straddle our social cleavages. Call this the dialogical task of common education. The common school is an obvious way of creating the necessary context for that task prior to assuming the duties of citizen.

The required context might be simulated with some success in separate schools, although a dialogical setting that really includes students and teachers whose diverse ethical voices represent the pluralism of the larger society would as a rule be preferred. When a dialogical setting excludes diverse voices, as a separate school must do by welcoming only those who adhere to its separate educational aims, we are compelled to create imaginary interlocutors if we are to 'practise' reasonableness. But imaginary interlocutors are a pallid substitute for the real thing. They are a pallid substitute because religious and moral doctrines or cherished cultural practices do not enter the world with fixed labels enabling us to classify them as reasonable or not. The reasonableness of such things can only be established on the basis of a searching examination that is open to the possibility that they are worthless. But that possibility is sometimes hard to keep alive when we keep company only with those who agree with us. Acceptance of the burdens of judgement means that even if my own convictions meet the criteria of reasonableness, I must also see that many opposing beliefs of my fellow citizens do so as well, and I must become adept at sifting through these to make sense of what reason does or does not endorse in them. I must come to see how many points of divergence between their political judgements and mine may be hard cases to which the same normative concepts can be reasonably applied in different ways; I must learn how vagaries of personal history may colour choice and belief in ways that cannot be entirely overcome by the development of our common reason; I must come to see how the comprehensive religious or ethical ideal I subscribe to selects from the diversity of human goods and organizes these in ways to which there are cogent alternatives.

We cannot sensibly suppose that this learning ever comes easily to people. As Elaine Scarry delicately puts it, 'we have trouble believing in the reality of other people' (Scarry 1996: 102). But the trouble surely escalates when the associations that dominate our lives during our formative years filter out the perspectives of those who are not like-minded or reduce them to mere imagined alternatives to our own. There is a presumptive case for undertaking the dialogical task of common education in a social environment where there is no such filter, which is to say there is a presumptive case for common education in common schools once an age is reached at which the task might be appropriately initiated.[6]

The presumptive case is also discernible when we reflect on the affective dimension of citizenship. The political community is easy to celebrate as a sentimental icon when all significant associations in which one participates have been more or less cleansed of encounters with fellow citizens—or fellow future citizens—whose lives are led beyond the cleavages that mark the boundaries of one's own parochial loyalties. But real liberal patriotism entails ties of fellowship and a sense of common fate that transcends cleavages. Otherwise patriotism cannot function as a support to an ideal of justice designed to accommodate reasonable pluralism. Here again, we find some reason to favour common schools as associations that lend themselves to the creation of intellectual demands and the forging of affective ties that presage the realized virtues of the citizen.

## 52. Reconciling Separate and Common Education

A successful separatist argument must somehow be squared with the case for undertaking the dialogical task of common education in common schools. But it would be wrong to think that the case is always so compelling that the separatist argument can never be seriously entertained.

The case of American Catholic high schools is instructive. Acceptance of the burdens of judgement inclines us towards a certain modesty about what reason can establish in theological matters that conflicts with official Catholic teachings. But in the Catholic high schools Bryk, Lee, and Holland depict, issues of doctrinal orthodoxy seem largely eclipsed by a preoccupation with questions of social justice and the construction of morally vibrant communities. As I noted earlier, by any impartial judgement many Catholic schools in North America would seem to count as impressive quasi-common schools. Even if the dialogical task of common education were less successfully undertaken in Catholic high schools than elsewhere—and the heterogeneous composition of those schools suggests that even that need not be true—their success in pursuing other ends of common education would have to be balanced against their comparative deficiencies in that particular task. They might be more successful, for example, in developing some sense of affective solidarity across division of class, race, or ethnicity. That should not surprise us. The political virtues I have outlined as a basis for common education are no simple, unitary achievement but a complex amalgam of different abilities, beliefs, and emotional propensities. We cannot expect that any given school in the real world will be uniformly successful in pursuing all the relevant ends.

Yet the very things that make American Catholic high schools look like quasi-common schools might also arouse suspicions about whether the first conclusion of the separatist argument can be supported in their case. Indeed, some Catholics themselves have worried about whether religious schools that are primarily instruments of the common good, rather than vehicles of Catholic dogma and devotion, are distinctively Catholic at all (Haldane 1996*b*: 134–5). The schools that Bryk, Lee, and Holland describe seem no less praiseworthy from the overall standpoint of common education than francophone schools for Acadians. Yet the rationale for their separateness is far less certain.

The prospects for success in the moderate separatist argument are much less ambiguous. The logic of the morality of association suggests that the dialogical task of common education will be addressed appropriately in the concluding years of schooling. Since moderate separatism applies only to the earlier years, it does not need to defeat the presumptive case. Those who subscribe to illiberal ideals of separate education—for example, those who want no truck with the most basic elements of reasonable citizenship—are another matter. They will hardly be attracted to the moderate version of the argument to begin with, and even if they were, a separate schooling of even brief duration which works against the necessary ends of common education is something no state could rightly sponsor. For example, even if the dialogical task of common education is not aptly begun in earnest until later in the process of schooling, the initial stages of education in common or separate schools must lay the foundation for what comes later. As my discussion of *Mozert* in Section 45 showed, the demands of common education during the early years of schooling are important. Some modest exposure to ethical diversity will be desirable even then, as well as the encouragement of respect across social cleavages. But I assume that such requirements will be acceptable to most exponents of the moderate separatist case.

The real difficulty with the moderate case is not in establishing its consistency with common education but in showing why separate schooling is needed at all by those who subscribe to liberalized conceptions of separate education. Yet I think the difficulty will often be surmounted. To see how this might be done, it will be useful to recall the dualistic conception of practical reason that informs Rawls's political conception of the person and to consider how the twin aspects of reason might unfold in moral development.

The idea of the reasonable is only one element of practical reason; its companion is the idea of the rational, which is evinced in individuals' pursuit of their own good. Although Rawls insists that neither virtue of reason can be derived from the other, there is clearly a sense in which the rational is prior to the reasonable (Rawls 1993: 52). If I am to be capable of reciprocity, I must understand what it is to have a conception of the good and to pursue it rationally; otherwise I cannot understand what is at stake for the good of others when we try to settle the terms of cooperation. The logical priority of the rational does not mean there must be a tidy developmental sequence, with rationality reaching a full ripeness before reasonableness can take hold in our lives. On the contrary, it is much more plausible to imagine a tightly integrated process of psychological development, within which an increasingly complex and discriminating reasonableness draws on an evolving rationality, which is in turn enriched by our developing reasonableness.

Reasonableness, as Rawls understands it, is a highly sophisticated virtue, which imposes heavy intellectual and emotional demands on us, and it has obvious origins in simpler dispositional precursors. The mutuality of beneficence a child learns to show and enjoy in a loving family foreshadows the more complex mutuality that develops later, if all goes well, in somewhat larger-scale associations, and this in turn foreshadows the reciprocity of Rawlsian citizens who attempt to create a fair scheme of cooperation in the midst of pluralism (Rawls 1971: 462–79). Similarly, acceptance of the burdens of judgement has obvious antecedents in propensities to recognize the fallibility of one's own judgements, to refine one's prereflective beliefs by taking account of the views of others, and to moderate individual demands in response to conflict. And unless a child's upbringing is an appalling exercise in unrelenting dogmatism, the concept of reasonable disagreement will be introduced early on. At these more primitive levels as well, the antecedents of a developed reasonableness and rationality are subtly interwoven. The young child who learns to temper claims for parental attention because of the needs of a new sibling, and at the same time begins to take some delight in that sibling, is learning to acknowledge both the independent good of another and the way her own good may be enlarged through a new caring relationship.[7]

But notice that these emerging aspects of practical reason will have a cultural context that matters profoundly to the particular shape they take. Relationships in the family are culturally variable, and we should expect some of that variation to persist even in a more fully just society in which familial relations had been largely rid of domination. That is but another way of saying that some variations in roles within families are instances of reasonable pluralism. Rawls's perfunctory discussion of the rational in *Political Liberalism* ignores the ways in which individuals achieve an initial understanding of their good in a specific cultural setting, where the good is conceived according to a received moral vocabulary that fixes the normative content of roles and the social practices they sustain. Although communitarians have tended to argue as if liberalism were fatally compromised by the sparseness of its canonical conceptions of practical reason, the importance of cultural context can be easily absorbed into the fabric of liberal thought and the educational practices it would support. We can acknowledge that initiation into a particular, established view of the good life is indeed the natural starting-point of the development of rationality, and also that whatever goodwill and cooperation characterize that view are the foundation for the development of reasonableness, without thereby giving up on the central political virtues of the liberal democratic tradition and the need to transmit them through common education. Indeed, Rawls's own conception of the morality of association in *A Theory of Justice* remains a powerful and largely neglected account of how that process might unfold.

The claims I have made about the interdependent development of the rational and the reasonable, and its natural starting-point in received roles and traditions, can be put to good use in the moderate separatist case. Separate schooling of limited duration, created for the sake of separate education, may be one useful way of creating the developmental antecedents of the mature liberal virtues. From the standpoint of parents who embrace some transformative educational aim for their children, the early years of schooling may be a crucial stage in securing a deeply felt understanding of what their way of life means. From the standpoint of the state, the experiences that separate schooling furnishes will lay the groundwork for the political virtues by cultivating their psychological precursors; and given the close and mutually reinforcing relation between the values of the family and the ethos of the separate school, it may even be a more solid groundwork than common schools could typically provide.[8]

Yet the force of this argument from the state's standpoint depends decisively on its being a *moderate* separatist argument. Because those who might press this argument are willing to accept a schooling system that is common in its culminating years, their separatist demands are easily reconciled with the need for schools to create the dialogical context for full-blown reciprocity at an appropriate developmental stage and to challenge received ideas of the good and the right in the manner required by acceptance of the burdens of judgement. The two conditions necessary to a cogent separatist case are thus satisfied, although at the cost of retreating to a form of separatism much weaker than many extant varieties.

I have tried to show that a persuasive argument for separate schooling can sometimes be made in ways that concede the importance of common education. But the argument must be made against the background of a presumptive case for common schooling during the culminating years. This creates serious, though not necessarily insuperable difficulties for exponents of the radical separatist argument. Moderate separatism will tend to fare much better, once we acknowledge the contribution liberalized versions of separate schooling can make to the ends of political education during the early phase of the morality of association.

The question I now want to raise is whether the separatist case in either its radical or moderate incarnations can be derived from the parental right to educational choice discussed in Chapter 6. The question is deeply important because rights entail moral reasons of a notably powerful kind: they are the 'heavy artillery' in our moral arsenal (Lomasky 1987: 8). So if demands for separate schooling are rightly cast in the language of parental rights, as they very commonly are, whatever argument there is for policies that favour common schooling would amount to little or nothing of real consequence.

## 53. Separate Schools and the Right to Educational Choice

The concept of a right is intended to capture the special moral significance of certain interests whose importance is such that they warrant the assignment to others of duties regarding the protection or promotion of that interest (e.g. Raz 1986: 166; Waldron 1993c: 575–6; Ingram 1994: 11). The concept presupposes that some interests are not right-constituting. If all interests were on the same footing so far as moral significance goes, none could give rise to the stringent duties of forbearance or support through which we express respect for rights. I take it that those who are sceptical of claims about the relevance of parents' rights to debate about public support for separate schools assume that the desire many might have to receive support does not have the special importance of right-constituting interests. The sceptics will say that this is just one interest among others to be accommodated when it serves the public good and ignored when it does not. Those who have sided with the government of Newfoundland in recent attempts to wrest control of schooling from denominational boards have sometimes argued along these lines (e.g. Krueger 1995).

Morally responsible statecraft must for the most part assess interests according to a guiding sense of the common good that takes shape in democratic deliberation. We give tax shelters to entrepreneurs to stimulate investment and economic initiative, and then we eliminate the shelters when we can make better use of their taxes; we give subsidies to farmers and then take them away once we decide they have come to do more harm to the economy than good. New policies for new conditions is a banal fact of political life. Even when new policies hurt badly there is no necessary infringement, much less any violation, of the rights of those who are hurt. Why should state sponsorship of separate schooling be any different?

The beginning of an interesting answer might draw attention to the continuity between the interests threatened by the denial of sponsorship and the interests thwarted by practices that patently are a violation of parents' rights to educational choice, such as the banning of religious education in totalitarian states. Suppose I am a religiously devout parent within a society whose public culture is severely in conflict with my faith. The expressive interest I have in my child's upbringing means that I want badly to ensure an education that goes against the current of the culture. If my government flatly refuses to permit me to act on that interest, I am oppressed. But suppose the state is merely indifferent rather than hostile, and poverty leaves me with no option but to send my children to common schools permeated with an irreligious public culture. My situation is certainly better than it was under the first scenario. But the expressive interest that was directly frustrated in the first case is still seriously endangered here because I have no real choice but to send my child to a school that I sincerely regard as corrupting.

The logic of this argument can be clarified by looking more closely at the general relationship between interests and rights. Waldron has argued that if an interest is morally important enough to constitute a right, then given the complexity of human well-being and the variable circumstances in which it is realized, the interest will create much more than a single, easily interpreted duty across all possible moral relations with the right-holder. On the contrary, important and complex human interests will tend to generate what Waldron calls 'waves of duty':

For example, if an individual's interest in speaking freely is important enough to justify holding the government to be under an obligation not to impose a regime of political censorship, it is likely also to be sufficiently important to generate other duties: a duty to protect those who make speeches in public from the wrath of those who are disturbed by what they say; a duty to establish rules of order so that possibilities for public speech do not evaporate in the noise of several loud-speakers vying for the attention of the same audience; and so on. (Waldron 1989: 510)

Waldron's 'and so on' is worth dwelling on. For a little thought will add many additional duties to his list. If the interest in free speech is as much a matter of the speech we are able to hear and understand as the speech we utter, as many liberal philosophers have claimed, then it will support duties to forstall the development of media monopolies, duties to provide an education that will empower people to participate knowledgeably in public deliberation, and so on. As Waldron suggests, 'our conception of the interest will operate like a normative power base from which a whole array of moral requirements can be developed' (Waldron 1989: 511).

The case for extending the argument for a parental right to choice from its consensual core in the sphere of negative duties to more contested terrain in debates about state-sponsored schooling follows the same pattern that Waldron outlines. The expressive interest that parents have in rearing their children according to the values they cherish also operates like a normative power base from which an array of moral requirements are generated. The first and most obvious of these is the duty not to block the choices of parents when they attempt to instil their faith in a manner that does not violate their children's rights. But other positive duties may be generated by the same power base, given conditions in which the underlying expressive interest is imperilled by the denial of positive provision.

Suppose we accept the thesis that rights-constituting interests generate waves of duties. Even if the interests that qualify are confined to a very short list, we need to be worried about being morally drowned by the successive waves of duty that come crashing in upon us. If every right-constituting interest generates an open-ended array of requirements, each of which speaks with the peremptory voice of duty, not only do rights threaten to become self-defeating by leaving so little room for the claim to individual fulfilment; they may also leave us with a sense of paralysing conflict as different positive duties demand actions not all of which can be done.

Two important constraints on our interpretation of rights would seem to follow. First, we cannot be so prodigal in the ascription of duties on the basis of a given right that any action or omission on the part of others that would serve the underlying interest becomes a requirement of due respect for the right. Perhaps my own descent into impiety would have been arrested during adolescence had my parents taken me on a pilgrimage to the holy places of Europe and the Middle East. But I doubt that even the most zealous defender of Article 26 of the Universal Declaration of Human Rights would say that the failure of the Irish government to offer my parents the necessary funding constituted a failure to live up to the terms of that solemn international agreement.

A reasonable inference from a right-constituting interest to a duty will not only show that the action required by the putative duty bears in some direct and vital way on the underlying interest; it will also cohere with a lucid sense of what could reasonably be demanded of others, given the lives they are entitled to lead and the other duties that press upon them. Judgements about the duties a right imposes must be conducted with a keen eye to the larger fabric of rights talk, and the still wider context of human good and bad in general, if moral understanding is not to be vitiated by a perseverant focus on whichever right-constituting interest happens to rivet our attention at a given moment. That is a vague but important point, and it shows, by the way, that an Aristotelian sense of balance and proportion is as central to a sense of justice that focuses on rights as it is to any other virtue.

Second, even if we are suitably cautious in what we count as a 'wave of duty', once positive duties enter the picture on any substantial scale, we are compelled to think hard about which duties are central to respect for any right and which have a more peripheral status. The positive duty to provide protection to people who promulgate unpopular political views is central to our interest in free speech. But the duty to provide institutional settings in which such views can reach a wide audience is surely more peripheral, if it is a duty at all. Resources are finite. Our ability to perform one costly positive duty adversely affects our ability to carry out another, and so the responsible adjudication of conflict requires us to make comparative judgements about the weight of conflicting duties.[9] The waves of duties which flow from different rights will commonly create predicaments in which we cannot avoid infringing one right or another by not fulfilling some duty it imposes. However, we may yet avoid violating the right we infringe if the duty we choose to discharge occupies a more central role in the overall scheme of rights than the one we forgo.

I want now to consider how these two constraints on the interpretation of rights might apply to the argument for a parental right to state-sponsored religious schooling. I think the constraints are such that it is unlikely any such right-based argument could succeed. Imagine a religious group that seeks state funding for its schools. The New Age sect have long controlled schools that are irreproachable by common academic standards. On standardized tests, their students fare substantially better than students in common schools, and graduates of New Age academies are often paragons of civic-mindedness. The sect has strong ecumenical leanings, fosters an appreciation of the value to be found in other religious traditions and viewpoints, and encourages its members to show respect and extend fellowship to all infidels.

No doubt we have strong, perhaps compelling grounds for granting the plea for sponsorship. After all, New Age schools appear to be doing a better job of fulfilling the public mandate of common schools than the publicly funded alternatives. If the latter receive the benefits of state support when the former do not, we have discrimination that ill serves the common good. The problem of injustice will increase if a likely consequence of the denial of sponsorship is that some children and their parents will be left without access to good schools. However, none of this means that the parents in the New Age sect have a basic right to state-sponsored schooling that we have a duty to respect. Sponsorship might be something that justice requires of us only in the sense that morally defensible policies must aim at the common good using means that do not arbitrarily disadvantage any particular group or individual. But this is merely the sense in which tax breaks for business people or subsidies for farmers may be claimed on grounds of justice; it is not the sense in which freedom to worship may be claimed as a matter of justice.

The distinction between a morally persuasive demand for support which is expressed as a matter of parents' right to educational choice and one that is cogently framed in terms of the collective pursuit of the common good may seem needlessly subtle, if not downright spurious. But it matters a lot at a practical level. Suppose we had reason to worry that public support for New Age separate schools would not in the long run redound to the common good. Maybe any feasible policy that gave public support to New Age schools would have untoward consequences by accelerating the withdrawal of the more affluent and able students from common schools, at some cost to the education of those who remained. In that event, our efforts might be better directed to the improvement of common schools than to the strengthening of alternatives. Or we might decide, on the basis of the presumptive case for common schooling during its later stages and the possible benefits of separate schooling earlier on, to split the difference with the New Agers and give them sponsorship for their schools only during the elementary years. Now if all we had to worry about was effectively pursuing the common good in a manner that eschews arbitrary discrimination, then these reasons might lead us to reject the demands of the New Age sect or offer only a partial accommo-

dation with a good conscience. But we cannot get off so easily if we have
a duty to support their educational choice by virtue of their rights to educational choice. Moral requirements that derive from rights are far too
important to be brushed aside whenever we think the common good
might be advanced by so doing.

Yet once we accept the first of the two constraints I have stipulated on
the interpretation of rights, there can be little basis for saying that the parents have a right to sponsorship. The first constraint forbids us from
inferring a duty from a right-constituting interest merely because fulfilling the putative duty would serve the interest. To flout that constraint
invites an absurd proliferation of right-derived duties. But it is very hard
to see the difference between a world in which the New Age sect have
state-sponsored denominational schools and a world in which they do
not as anything of greater consequence than the difference between a
world in which their expressive interest in child-rearing is served well and
one in which it is served not quite so well. Therefore, the grounds for saying that a duty to sponsor their schools can be deduced from their rights
to educational choice must be weak. The apparent exception is when the
denial of sponsorship leaves New Age children without access to good
schools. But the appearance is deceptive. For if the moral problem is
access to acceptable schooling, the right our decision would infringe must
be the child's right to educationally adequate schooling—which might be
either common or separate—rather than the parental right to choose separate as opposed to common schooling, regardless of the educational
quality of the latter option.

Furthermore, even if the argument from parental rights worked, the
second constraint I stipulated suggests that the duty to sponsor New Age
schools would be relatively peripheral rather than central to respect for
their rights. That is so because reduced access to denominational schooling would pose no grave threat to parents' expressive interest in child-
rearing, given the broadly liberal content of that interest. Therefore, the
duty is one that we might have strong reason not to fulfil once more
morally weighty positive duties, derived from other rights, command our
attention.[10]

Now imagine a religious group very different from the New Age sect
who are also suing for state support. The True Believers abhor the ecumenical tendencies of other churches and insist that nothing of merit can be
found in religious creeds other than their own. Students in True Believer
schools are encouraged to be law-abiding and economically productive citizens, and that is how graduates almost always turn out. But they are also
taught that the world beyond their faith is thoroughly corrupt and those
who inhabit that world are to be treated with grudging tolerance at best.

At first glance, the argument from parental rights may seem strong at precisely the point it is weak in the case of the New Age sect. The True Believers sincerely want an education for their children that is drastically at variance with what they are liable to learn in common schools penetrated by the worldliness they despise. Since the adherents of the New Age creed have made their peace with pluralism, the common schools to which they might send their children can pose no such threat to their convictions. They may rationally prefer to send their children to New Age Schools. But nothing crucial to their expressive interest in child-rearing is at stake. The True Believers, on the other hand, have a profound conscientious objection to the common school. If economic hardship gave some members no alternative but to send their children to a common school, their expressive interest in child-rearing is gravely harmed.

Unfortunately, the same reasons that lead to that conclusion also support the claim that common school may be the best chance that children of True Believers have to receive an education that will countervail ethical servility. Worries about the educational rights of children of True Believers might not suffice to warrant closure of the separate schools they support out of their own pockets. That is a question about the limits of our tolerance towards unsponsored schools under pluralism, and I turn to that issue in the next section. Be that as it may, if the parental right to educational choice is limited by the moral parity of the child's educational rights, we can hardly have a duty to sponsor an educational option that parents want to take when that option is markedly less satisfactory, given the child's educational rights, than the option of common schooling that might otherwise be accepted by the parents.

My tale of the New Age sect and the True Believers is intended to disclose a dilemma for those who would adduce the parental right to choice in defence of state-sponsored separate schooling. The more parents' educational aspirations are in harmony with the public culture of a pluralistic society, the less plausible it is to say that these cannot be respected in good common schools; and therefore, arguments that appeal to the right to educational choice lack credibility. The demand for state-sponsored separate schooling may yet be decisive on grounds of the common good. But we should also expect the merits of the demand, all things considered, to vary greatly with different circumstances. On the other hand, the more parents' educational ends are at odds with the public culture of a pluralistic society, the less plausible it is to suppose that these can be accommodated in common schools. Yet to the extent that a form of schooling satisfies their culturally alienated aspirations, it must warrant strong doubts about how adequately the educational rights of children are being served, and therefore, we would have strong reason to deny sponsorship out of respect for children's rights. So whether the educational ends that parents pursue cohere with the public culture of a pluralistic society or diverge sharply from its values, the case for a parental right to state-sponsored separate schooling looks pretty weak.

## 54. Separate Schools and Tolerance

Whatever threshold we set for schools whose prospects of success in common education are good enough to justify state support, that threshold cannot do double duty as the standard for schools we should tolerate. I distinguished in Chapter 2 between the idea of reasonable pluralism, which marks the boundaries of the diversity whose source is the burdens of judgement, and the ampler scope of toleration, which is our selective forbearance to the persistence of unreasonable pluralism in any recognizably human world. To make our willingness to tolerate go no further than the range of reasonable pluralism would be tantamount to Jacobin liberalism, in which any lapse from the high demands of liberal virtue makes one fair game for political coercion. Morally defensible policy regarding state-sponsored schooling is constrained by the limits of reasonable pluralism. Good policy will seek to respect the many conceptions of separate education that endure under reasonable pluralism within institutional structures that effectively serve common educational ends. What I have said already about the assets and liabilities of separate and commmon schooling is an attempt to indicate something of what the relevant institutional structures might look like. But whatever structures are best, some people will still want schools for their children outside because they want no part of reasonable pluralism. The ideal of tolerance suggests that sometimes we should let them go their way. What are the moral reasons that justify letting them go their own way?

The argument of Chapter 6 provides the most important consideration in fixing the limits of tolerable schooling. Children have a right to an education whose content is given by their prospective interest in sovereignty. Most obviously, that means they need to be equipped with the capabilities to live more than the one way of life their parents would prescribe. Otherwise children will lack a meaningful right to exit should the prescribed path turn out to be unfulfilling (Galston 1995: 533–4). But this rules out very little. Negligible educational accomplishments will confer the bare abilities necessary to some different ways of life. The adolescent who has been taught no more than is necessary to work effectively on an Amish colony probably has the knowledge and skills to move away and work in a factory or a fast-food outlet.

The more substantial requirement I have defended is that the education children are entitled to receive must eschew ethical servility. Effective protection for the prospective interest in sovereignty necessitates a degree of autonomous development incompatible with servility. In many cases the only effective way of securing the necessary degree of autonomy will be through a form of schooling that provides not only exposure to ethical diversity but takes some active measures to enable independent critical reflection on that diversity. Other requirements of a tolerable common education might derive more directly from its political content: curricula that encourage hatred of particular racial, ethnic, or religious groups would be ruled out, for example. The necessary measures the state enforces should fall short of what we would want in the best common education. Teaching that addresses ethical diversity might occupy a less salient role in the curriculum than we would require of state-sponsored schools. Similarly, certification requirements for teachers in unsponsored schools might be less stringent, albeit stringent enough to ensure that those entitled to teach were able and willing to provide a minimally acceptable common education.

But the distinction between the tolerable and the intolerable in education cannot be seen just by looking at children's rights and common educational values in abstraction from the shifting circumstances in which they might be enforced. Suppose we agree that certain educational ends are a necessary part of any decent common education, and that socially established schools of some particular kind do not adequately teach to those ends. We have strong reason to prohibit such schools. But the reason might still not be conclusive. The blunt instrument of coercive law is not necessarily the best means of advancing even the more modest ends of common education against those who would oppose them. Coercion may intensify the political alienation of those who are on its receiving end, with still more unfortunate consequences for their children's education, and encourage the continuance of illiberal values that would gradually fade in a more indulgent environment. A self-defeating intransigence in the imposition of common educational ends is no virtue.

This instrumental moral argument for tolerance is grounded in scepticism about the universal efficacy of coercion in containing social practices repugnant to liberal democracy in educational as in other institutions. No doubt scepticism about the universal efficacy of non-interference is equally fitting. Thus the instrumental argument creates no powerful presumptive barrier against interference with parental choice (cf. Lomasky 1987: 186–7). To argue for that barrier only makes sense on the assumption that all the real moral risks lie on the side of interference, with little to be lost by letting parents choose whatever education they wish. That is just false. Large moral losses are incurred by permitting parents to rear children in disregard of the minima of political education and their children's right to an education that protects the prospective interest in sovereignty. But just as a prudent political response to the physical abuse of children in families can avoid the excesses of heavy-handed state paternalism and an equally damaging policy of laissez-faire, a similar via media can surely be found in the regulation of what is and is not educationally tolerable.[11]

A different argument would stress the intrinsic value of the ways of life to which toleration might be extended. One of the burdens of judgement that Rawls notes is the inevitable partiality of anyone's conception of the good, given the many values that are worthy of election (Rawls 1993: 57). In living a life that revolves around teaching, scholarship, and familial intimacy, I choose one way to live at the cost of many other worthwhile possibilities. Much of what I do not choose continues to endure within the wide borders of reasonable pluralism. Still, other good lives will lie beyond those borders. The thought that not all good lives can be led under the aegis of liberal pluralism often colours our half-envious or half-admiring response to some who partially withdraw from it, like certain religious groups, or whose ancient traditions may be threatened by it, like some aboriginal communities.

I think Rawls is right to say that one moral reason for forbearance in the face of diversity is our acknowledgement of the ethical selectivity and partiality that afflict all our lives. But the point can be pressed further. Our recognition that some conceptions of the good go against the grain of democratic culture might also support tolerance of ways of life that repudiate the political virtues and the educational practices that go with them. This must be a strictly limited tolerance if our commitment to common education is to mean anything at all. Nevertheless, the fact that the ends of common education may be resisted because of a fidelity to goods that free societies cannot fully accommodate may moderate the zeal with which we prosecute those ends in dealing with cultural enclaves who reject them.

Thoughts like these seem to be at the root of Joseph Raz's suggestive remarks about toleration towards the educational practices of groups who renounce autonomy. I think by a commitment to autonomy Raz means something like the transcendence of servility. For he is rightly averse to the exaltation of autonomy that mars some liberal accounts of the good, and so the conception he has in mind cannot be taxing (Raz 1986: 391). Raz suggests that those who deserve toleration among the enemies of autonomy are groups who can offer the young a 'viable' way of life outside the cultural mainstream. The limits of the tolerable are crossed by those who cling to some 'dwindling community' that lacks viability. Their children are imprisoned by a hopeless culture so long as they are denied the autonomy-promoting education necessary to survive outside the group. In their case, assimilative educational policies may be 'the only humane course' even if the necessary policies have to be coercive (Raz 1986: 424).

I assume that what Raz has in mind is something like this. If an aboriginal community wanted to restrict their children's education to the skills of hunting and trapping, and the community's certain future were such that its members simply could not survive on hunting and trapping alone, then their culture would not be viable, and the education they wanted for their children could not be tolerable. But this kind of example verges on science fiction. No one on the right side of sanity wants an education for their children that prepares them only for a world that is rapidly ceasing to be. What is much more likely is that culturally dissident communities will want an education for their children that combines a continuing aloofness from the surrounding society with selective appropriations from the lore and technology of that society. That will enable them to survive as a community in some altered, culturally hybrid form. The aspiration is very familiar and often feasible. In that event, the community passes Raz's test of viability, and the educational practices they want should be tolerated.

I think Raz is probably right here to the extent that the very notion of an education for cultural viability will tend to bring in a curriculum that militates to some substantial degree against servility. The group may strenuously insists on its disengagement from the wider world. But its viability depends on extensive educational borrowings from the cultural capital of the society they shun, and this necessarily opens the door somewhat to independent reflection on beliefs and values that the group repudiates. Nevertheless, some ways of ensuring the viability of the group through education might keep the door shut tightly for many. That would occur if gender, caste, or similar criteria were used to determime who would receive the sophisticated education necessitated by changing conditions of viability and who would learn no more than traditional folkways.

Here I would say that separatist educational practice is unlikely to be morally tolerable. *Ex hypothesi*, the community is viable in an altered form by virtue of an education that opens it to the cultural mainstream. Why should anyone believe that it cannot afford its members worthwhile lives once that education is distributed without regard to entrenched hierarchical relations? The argument for viability presupposes that the traditional culture is no brittle fossil but an adaptable body of social practices subject to intelligent revision. Intelligent revision might be expected to include the erosion of received hierarchies. If a viable future must be different from the traditional past so that a new, more complex education is required, the viability worth having is surely compatible with allocating the new education fairly. Some might complain that it is not compatible. But we should probably take the complaint with the grain of salt that properly accompanies the receipt of specious arguments for traditional patterns of domination.

The upshot of all this is that although we may have reason to acknowledge the intrinsic value of ways of life to which the culture of liberal societies is repugnant, that fact amounts to nothing in determining the limits of the tolerable in educational policy. It amounts to nothing because the requirement of cultural viability that any tolerable separatist community must satisfy will include an education that brings in much of an education for sovereignty and no tolerable separatist practice will deny that education to children who are capable of profiting from it.

## 55. Who Wants Common Schools?

The serpentine arguments I have traced in this chapter about desirable and tolerable separate schooling will arouse at least one powerful worry about their political relevance. In the well-ordered society, the cultural triumph of reasonable pluralism would make a common education for reasonable citizenship an essentially conservative undertaking that virtually all would commend. That is far from being true for us. Common education as I have interpreted it is a controversial, even a subversive undertaking, and common schooling wedded to that process will arouse much antipathy. This will be especially true of the dialogical task that education entails. Of course, minimalist common education is also a controversial, even a subversive undertaking, and what I said about its deficiencies shows that no morally credible agenda for common schooling can keep everyone happy. But I also said that common schooling of any kind will not succeed unless it can win a fair degree of trust across the cleavages that divide us politically. Because the vision I have sketched for that institution is so patently controversial, the sources of the trust it could win might appear elusive, to say the least.

One distracting issue needs to be set aside before the core of the problem can be directly confronted. There is every reason to think that good common schooling might do much to address many of the problems that have bedevilled its merely de jure versions without ceasing to be genuinely common in the sense I have specified. The large, culturally amorphous and impersonal supermarkets of learning that comprehensive secondary schools have sometimes been is not the necessary model for the common school. Such schools lack a distinctive identity that can mobilize the mutually reinforcing commitment of students, teachers, and parents (Grant 1986). A commonplace of recent research on effective schools is that their distinctiveness is critical to their effectiveness. Good schools are not all things to all people (Lee, Bryk, and Smith, 1993; Glenn 1994). Yet to accept my argument is not to deny that fact. The common schools that matter might differ in curricular emphasis, pedagogical styles, organizational traditions, or the like for the simple reason that not all such differences correspond to social cleavages. To adapt David Hargreaves's felicitous phrase, common schooling may be most effectively implemented 'through shared missions within diverse provisions' (Hargreaves 1996: 140). If the very diversity of provisions makes it more likely that parents, teachers, and children obtain the kind of schooling that will engage their effort and allegiance, it may also make them more receptive to the shared missions when these have become part of institutions they really care about. Nevertheless, if part of the shared mission is a political education that threatens many established sources of conviction and loyalty in the background culture, the problem of social acceptability has simply been recast rather than resolved. Too many people will turn away from schools that offer that education. Against this worry, I want to make the case for cautious optimism about the social viability of common schooling. The case is speculative but I hope not unreasonably so.[12]

According to Robert Westbrook, 'a general two-mindedness about democracy has been a feature of American political culture since the nation's founding.' On one side of that ambivalence has been attraction to a polity of self-governing citizens; on the other, the appeal of a kind of anti-democratic republic in which government is the business of elites and a shared civic culture withers or endures in some anaemic form at the edges of most people's lives. Westbrook argues trenchantly that the American common school has been the site of ongoing conflict between these contending political identities, with American anti-democratic elitism now securely ascendant (Westbrook 1996: 125–50). America is hardly exceptional in the inherent tensions of its public life. Ambivalence about political virtue, as well as disagreement about what it demands of us, is surely to be expected in all free societies, especially when unreasonable pluralism abounds, and the ambivalence and disagreement will be powerfully evidenced in conflict about the control and direction of shared educational institutions. Liberal politics need not be civil war conducted by other means. But those of us who inhabit societies where democratic values often seem a fragile and threatened cultural achievement may find ourselves combatants in such a war, like it or not, and education may be one of the bloodier battlefronts, figuratively speaking. Furthermore, victory is not always on the side of the angels, as Westbrook might say.

But ambivalence and disagreement about the basic character of the polity and our civic roles therein are not simply a matter of conflict between people; they are also a matter of conflict within them. We are apt to be two-minded, or more likely, many-minded about the political future that we construct, in part, through the education of our children. The matter would be simpler if we were only differently minded. But precisely because we are many-minded, common schooling of the sort I have advocated need not be a hopeless undertaking. After all, the Rawlsian ideal of reasonable citizenship is not some arbitrary philosophical invention: it refines and articulates values of moderation and public justification that are abroad in the political culture of any free society (cf. M. Holmes 1995; Callan 1995: 319–21). And the idea that love of one's country is honourable as a sentiment that binds us to a community in which justice must be done is no intellectual eccentricity; it is a central motif within the republican tradition that still has some purchase on our lives (Viroli 1995).

I suspect that many people, regardless of social cleavages, would be ready to send their children to common schools that vigorously pursued the dialogical task of common education if they were good schools by more humdrum standards as well. At least they might be ready when they can trust those who prosecute the task to know and teach the difference between reasonable moral disagreement and an indiscriminate tolerance or indifference. I suspect that many would also be willing to see their children taught to cast a morally critical eye on the past and the present of their country. Or at least they might be willing so long as they could be assured that such teaching proceeds in the service of a liberal patriotism and not merely as an exercise in academic self-righteousness or educated despair.

But if these claims can amount to a sober faith in the possibilities of common schooling rather than idle wish-fulfilment, we need to know much more about the dialogical task of common education. I want now to look more closely at that task.

# CHAPTER 8

## Virtue, Dialogue, and the Common School

### 56. Introduction

Moral education requires ongoing dialogue with children as they grow up, and the requirement holds in schools and not just in families. That is nearly a truism in contemporary academic discussion about moral education, part of the small common ground among many different and contradictory approaches that have been advocated in recent years. But for many outside academic discourse, who merely have unscholarly worries about the education of the young, the truism will seem troubling so far as it applies to schools.

Real moral dialogue is risky business for at least one very obvious reason: in its unpredictable twists and turns, dialogue can persuade people to give up the truth on some critical ethical question in favour of error. That risk will vary from one situation to another, according to participants' virtues and vices, knowledge and ignorance. But the excursions of teachers into the hazardous territory of moral dialogue are naturally viewed with suspicion in societies that distrust the ability of schools to do even the easy things well, and the hazards may seem especially great when the convictions that students bring to dialogue reflect the bewildering pluralism of the larger society. Movement towards agreement will then tend to seem corrupting to those who would reject the emergent consensus, and pluralism means there will be many such people. Yet dialogue that merely gives expression to divergent moral views might encourage among children or adolescents a sense of the futility of deliberation about the good and the right or engender a feckless scepticism or relativism in the face of apparently intractable differences. It is noteworthy that attempts to revive character education in American schools have often been framed as an alternative to dialogue that is open to pluralism, as if the latter were a threat to morality that had to be discarded before a real education for virtue could even begin (e.g. Bennett and Delattre 1979).

These worries apply to the dialogical task of political education I described in Section 51. That task is intended to cultivate the abilities and virtues that ensure competent engagement in public reason by practising and refining them in a setting that mirrors, to some degree, the pluralism that the public reason of citizens must subsume. But I claimed that a socially viable form of common schooling must win support across social cleavages if it is to be entrusted with the dialogical task, and that is why the doubts I just indicated about moral dialogue in schools are troubling. An important part of any response to that problem is being able to delineate the task in a way that is sensitive to its avoidable hazards. That is my primary purpose in this chapter. The role of the school as an instrument of civically edifying dialogue is not well understood, and much of the chapter will be devoted to exposing some influential misunderstandings.

I start by making and defending some claims about moral character. The point of this first stage of my argument is to bring to light certain fundamental conditions of virtue that will enable me to test the adequacy of two starkly opposed approaches to moral dialogue and its educational role in a free society. One of these is found in Nel Noddings's influential writings on education and the ethic of care; the other is championed in Mill's classic essay, *On Liberty*. The comparison is revealing because both offer radically different accounts of dialogue under pluralism that yet conceive it as an arena for the cultivation of virtue. Both accounts also founder on the fact of pluralism. They help to bring into relief what is distinctive and appealing about a conception of the dialogical task that is grounded in the values of reasonable citizenship.

## 57. Moral Commitment and Character

The idea of virtue includes not just our behavioural dispositions but also the distinctive motivational patterns and habits of perception and judgement that constitute one character rather than another. Honest and kind people care about truth in their dealings with others and the relief of others' suffering, and they will be alert to the ways in which these matters impinge on their choices. They are not just people who habitually behave in ways that we associate with honesty and kindness. That being so, an education that includes particular virtues among its aims will seek to establish those virtues' distinctive motivational and perceptual patterns.

The psychological patterns that constitute character are rooted in our general commitments to what we see as having value in the world and giving meaning to our lives. To be sure, some commitments have little directly to do with character. Some figure in my psychological make-up, for example, simply because I habitually desire certain things and see nothing bad in occasionally indulging the desire. My moderate taste for Irish whiskey falls into that category. But if my taste changed, that change alone could not make my life any worse. I do not think of this as a desire I should or should not have, and so I can see nothing good or bad in losing it. But all my desires cannot be plausibly interpreted in this way, as reducible to facts about what I just happen to want and deem innocent. For my overall commitments are determined in large part by thought regarding the desires I *should* have—that is, by my understanding of those wants that are worthy of affirmation, and conversely, by my recognition that others may need to be suppressed or held in check.

I cannot entertain the possibility of losing my desire for the love of my children in the way that I can contemplate losing my taste for Irish whiskey because in the first but not the second instance I must envisage a life that is worse, indeed much worse, because of the lost desire. So our commitments are often, as Ronald Dworkin suggests, *critical* in the sense that they entail beliefs about the desires we should have. These will be desires whose experience and fulfilment we think make our lives truly good, as well as desires we might regard as honouring some important source of value outside our own lives. Commitments that involve no such beliefs, like my taste for Irish whiskey, are merely *volitional*, in Dworkin's terms (R. Dworkin 1990: 42–7).

I make three interlocked claims about the relation between moral character, the self, and its commitments. First, the virtues that compose moral character, whatever they are, must be maintained by a self who has a critical commitment to maintaining them. Second, the relevant commitment must occupy a deep role in the structure of the self. Third, the structural role of moral commitment involves a range of emotional susceptibilities that includes, among other things, a propensity to what I call 'moral distress'.

Why should virtue require a critical commitment to maintaining virtue? Imagine someone—call him David—who has at many times evinced the kind of behaviour we associate with kindness. We also have good evidence to believe that on those occasions his conduct was to be explained by the desire to help others for their sake. Now we see David in circumstances where he must deal with someone who needs his help, and to whom help might be given at no real cost. Unexpectedly, David reacts with brusque indifference.

When we express puzzlement at his behaviour, David shrugs and says (sincerely), 'I just felt like being nice on those earlier occasions. I felt like being nasty today. That's all there is to it.' What all this would mean is that David's pattern of 'kind' behaviour was a merely volitional commitment, like my taste for Irish whiskey, and in that event, it would follow that he never had the virtue of kindness in the first place: it was never a part of his character. That inference would be forced on us because David's words indicate he does not value relieving the distress of others, save in the trivial sense that he sometimes desires to help them but all the while believing that a sufficient warrant for doing otherwise would be available if the desire to help were absent or eclipsed by stronger inclinations. In ascribing a moral virtue such as kindness, we properly look for a deeper evaluation than this. We expect kind people to regret and often to condemn their lapses and the lapses of others into indifference and malice, however strong the desire may be to behave indifferently or maliciously. They commend kindness even when it can only be achieved through a struggle with competing desires because they see malice and indifference as evil, and requiring the most strenuous resistance on that account. That is to say, we expect kind people to have a critical commitment to the maintenance of their own kindness (Callan 1994).

The necessity of critical commitment in moral character has do with the corrective function of virtue, its ability to keep us on the right track when temptation assails us (Foot 1978: 8–14). Critical commitment confers an authoritative status on certain desires in deliberation, putting the authority of the self behind them when motivational conflict occurs. After all, David is not a person whose help we would confidently depend on in the future, even if his pattern of kind-seeming behaviour were to re-emerge. By his own admission, his concern for others' well-being is entirely a matter of the whim of the moment; and though his whims may typically drift in the right direction, the vulnerability of his whimsical altruism to rival inclinations makes it at best a fragile proto-virtue, liable to shatter under even slight pressure from desires that would prompt unkind behaviour.

The corrective function of virtue does not presuppose the essential corruption of our desires; it can be explained by the heterogeneity of motivation in even the most exemplary lives. Among those whose virtue approaches the heights of saintliness or heroism, many commitments will still have aspects that cannot be compressed into an exclusive interest in rectitude. Moral monomania is no criterion of virtuous character (Wolf 1982). The commitments of people who have such character might include the love and affection they feel for particular others, and their desire that these emotions be reciprocated; the cultural and intellectual interests they pursue; as well as the relatively frivolous preferences that give colour to any life when more pressing requirements are met. The range and richness of this motivational economy inevitably generates internal frictions, and the deepest critical commitments, even when they ordinarily function in ways that incur no moral criticism, are not always so innocent. A basically unselfish love can harbour possessive tendencies or blind us to the claims that others we do not love make on our goodwill; an honourable patriotism can be hard at times to distinguish from a noxious tribalism.

The fact of persistent, morally relevant motivational conflict in our lives takes me to my second major claim. If such conflict commonly engages different critical commitments, then its satisfactory resolution requires more than a critical commitment to maintaining virtue. Moral commitment must rather occupy a notably deep and pervasive role in the motivational structure of the self or else the corrective role of virtue will not be adequately fulfilled. That is a vague conclusion. To make it more precise I would have to take sides in important and difficult controversies in moral philosophy, which in turn reflect fissures in our ordinary moral thought.[1] But the conclusion is precise enough to reveal the important relationship between moral character and moral distress.

By 'moral distress' I refer to a cluster of emotions that may attend our response to words or actions of others or our own that we see as morally repellent. Moral distress comes in two basic varieties: the other-regarding kind triggered by the perceived failings of others, and the self-regarding kind that entails some negative evaluation of what we have done or who we are.[2] These emotions must as a rule be experienced as painful and seriously disturbing: the mild annoyance that the rudeness of another might arouse, or the twinge of shame or embarrassment we might feel at some small oversight on our own part, will not suffice. The experience of moral distress will naturally be common in societies where people often strongly disagree about the good and the right; it will also be common in schools within such societies, at least when schools are not confined to morally homogeneous populations and do not evade the ethical differences that divide the communities they serve. Moral distress is an unwelcome experience, at least as a rule, and it may be a solvent of social cooperation. Yet a discriminating susceptibility to moral distress is a fundamental aspect of virtue, and therefore, that troubling cluster of emotions must be evoked, and suitably shaped, in the process of moral education.

A recent review of the selected letters of the great Australian novelist Patrick White ends with the following paradoxical but brilliantly apt description of White: he was 'cruelly disdainful and supremely compassionate' (Cumming 1995). At first glance, we might think these words could only describe an incoherent self, someone who oscillated from cruel disdain to its very opposite in supreme compassion. But that is naive. A man who is supremely compassionate cannot view with impassivity the many blameworthy ways in which people fail to be compassionate nor can he regard his own failures in that light. Because a great compassion is pivotal to the self, he will be disposed to view such failure with moral distress, and at least on the more drastic occasions of failure, the distress will properly take the form of a sharp disdain for those who fail.

So we might think of Patrick White's notorious propensity to disdain as an aspect of his compassion: 'cruelly disdainful and supremely compassionate' merely juxtaposes twin aspects of the one virtue. But that also is too simple a reading. Moral distress, like other subclasses of moral emotion, may lend itself to certain pathologies, and 'cruelly disdainful' refers to one of these. I said that moral distress is an unwelcome experience as a rule, but the rule does not always apply. We may learn to experience other-regarding moral distress as a confirmation of our own moral superiority, and this may give a cruel pleasure to criticism of all who do not meet our taxing moral standards. Even when that is not so, an insufficiently discriminating proneness to moral distress may blind us to the complex social and psychological context of moral failure in others' lives, a context that may itself warrant compassion. In both cases, our susceptibility to moral distress pulls us towards the vice of self-righteousness, and there is more than a little evidence that Patrick White's compassion, for all its intensity and capacious range, was disfigured by a certain self-righteousness.

White is a revealing case for my purposes because he shows both the necessity of a susceptibility to moral distress as an aspect of virtue as well as the moral dangers we incur in cultivating that susceptibility in ways that are insufficently discriminating. Sensitivity to such dangers makes it tempting to try to interpret moral education in a way that discards moral distress. But we should resist the temptation. The complexity of human motivation means that our moral capabilities will naturally hinge on fine and delicate evaluative discriminations, and a corollary of this is that we are never far from sliding into vice of one sort or another (Nussbaum 1985; Callan 1993). If moral distress lends itself to certain pathologies, so too does gratitude or any other morally relevant emotion or attitude one cares to imagine. That means there can be no risk-free morality, and no risk-free moral education.

This point is worth dwelling on for a moment because it undermines what is perhaps the most familiar complaint about moral dialogue in schools. The idea that schools should give no 'offence' to children and their parents is very often voiced in popular educational discussion, especially by those on the religious right in North America. Since real moral dialogue, as opposed to carefully policed conversations about the meaning of some moral orthodoxy, cannot occur without the risk of offence, an offence-free school would oblige us to eschew dialogue. But to avoid offence is to suppress all that might arouse other-regarding moral distress. That means a policy of suppression would destroy the school's role as a vehicle of moral education, given the centrality of an understanding of moral failure to the cognitive abilities that virtue requires. What the exponents of offence-free schooling overlook is the huge difference between the preservation of moral innocence and the cultivation of moral virtue on any sensible interpretation of what virtue is. The development of virtue may entail experiences of temptation and opportunities for culpable failure that the preservation of innocence does not. But the experiences and opportunities are a necessary part of the very practice of morality. A moral education cleansed of everything that might give offence is not a coherent possibility.

## 58. Care against Truth in Dialogue

I said that moral distress is an inevitable consequence of real moral dialogue under pluralism, and this will be true of the dialogical task of common education in common schools. The experience of such distress cannot be deplored in general as just so much disagreeable and avoidable emotion; it is instead a necessary part of the growth and exercise of virtue. Nevertheless, the morality of association reveals the importance of enlarging ties of mutual trust and attachment in increasingly complex and pluralistic schemes of cooperation as the role of citizen is approached. But distress-provoking dialogue in the common schools might seem a threat to the necessary affective ties. We cannot cope with the threat just by avoiding dialogue, given the argument of the preceding section, but we can reasonably ask how it might proceed in ways that keep faith with the values of community and mutual regard.

If we want an account of educational role of dialogue under pluralism that is attuned to the importance of forging strong interpersonal ties, the obvious place to look is the literature on the ethic of care. The argument of Chapter 4 discredits the claim that care can be conceived as an independent moral orientation that rivals justice. But to discredit that claim is not to show that care is morally and educationally unimportant. In fact, what I have argued about reasonable citizenship and its developmental antecedents strongly suggests otherwise. For several reasons, Noddings's views in particular might seem a promising focus. Her account of the psychological components of caring acknowledges their strong affective aspects; her most recent work stresses the ways in which pluralism can be understood within the ambit of care; and finally, she has written extensively about dialogue as a method for the teaching of virtue.

For Noddings the purpose of moral education is to develop virtues that make one both a caring person as well as someone who is ready appropriately to receive the care of others. Dialogue is said to be one of the essential processes by which care is developed (Noddings 1984: 182–5, 1992: 53–4). The kind of dialogue Noddings regards as having prime educational importance is what she calls 'ordinary conversation', and this is contrasted with the combative and individualistic varieties that have tended to dominate the patriarchal traditions of the West. The reasoning to which ordinary conversation is wedded is 'interpersonal' rather than 'analytic', and its main concern is the quality of relationship between interlocutors: 'Interpersonal reasoners build each others' confidence and self-esteem, and they direct their efforts to strengthening the relation' (Noddings 1991: 162). This overriding concern with the quality of relationship must not be compromised by our interests in victory or defeat, truth or falsehood in argument:

Perhaps most significantly of all, in ordinary conversation, we are aware that our partners in conversation are more important than the topic. Participants are not trying to win a debate; they are not in contest with an opponent. They are conversing because they like each other and want to be together. The moment is precious in itself. The content of the conversation, the topic, may or may not become important. Sometimes it does, and the conversation becomes overtly educational and memorable on that account. At other times, the only memory that lingers is one of warmth and laughter or sympathy and support. (Noddings 1994: 115)

This would be unassailable good sense if Noddings were merely emphasizing the need for teachers and students to form through conversation some basis of mutual goodwill and understanding before useful moral dialogue could be expected to occur. The point becomes badly misleading once we take Noddings's view that 'ordinary conversation' is the prime example of morally educational dialogue.[3] But before we can see just what has gone wrong, we might ask what gives this train of thought its appeal.

An essential aspect of learning to affirm one's dignity as a person is becoming capable of independent moral judgement and judiciously confident in the use of that ability. 'Independent' in this context does not signal a rejection of care with its emphasis on interdependence; it is intended rather to signify the importance of something without which the care worth having, or any other human good for that matter, would be indistinguishable from counterfeit versions. In the absence of some capacity for independent judgement, I cannot see when what is offered to me as a caring relationship, say, is really abusive. But the capacity and willingness

to exercise independent judgement are achieved slowly and with difficulty, and the combative model of dialogue is dangerous partly because its
hidden curriculum may suggest that independent moral judgement is not
for those who lack the courage or aggression for rhetorical combat.
Furthermore, the combative model may corrupt those who do not lack
either courage or aggression by teaching them to confound the dignity of
their autonomy with the glory of rhetorical victory. I return to this
important point in the next section.

Yet the need to conduct dialogue in ways that encourage among children a growing confidence and competence in moral judgement does not
mean we should teach them that our partners in conversation are more
important than the topic. If the conversation is about something of more
than slight moral consequence, then part of coming to appreciate the
gravity of what is at stake is learning to understand that one is *not* more
important than the topic of conversation. I am not more important than
the problems of racism, censorship and pornography, sexual responsibility and exploitation, women's reproductive rights and the moral status of
the fetus, the requirements of economic justice or any other matter of real
moral weight that might arise in thoughtful dialogue between teachers
and their students. Nor is anyone else more important than these things.
Indeed, we might wonder if the combative style of academic argument
that Noddings rightly dismisses is sometimes corrupt and corrupting not
because 'we usually find [there] a tremendous emphasis on the search for
truth' (Noddings 1994: 115). An alternative explanation is that narcissism
in the quest for status readily masquerades as heroism in the search for
truth, and the importance of what is discussed in the heat of dialectical
conflict is liable to be eclipsed by a preoccupation with how much pres-
tige we win or lose in battle. If the combative model of dialogue is deficient when it elevates status over moral truth, then it is not clear that we
make much progress by adopting an alternative model that elevates caring
attachments over moral truth.

In fact, the very idea that we might treat the other and our relationship
to the other as 'more important' than the topic of moral dialogue cannot
be right given my earlier argument that strong critical commitment to
virtue is constitutive of the virtuous self. Consider how serious moral
deliberation and dialogue look when we examine them from the perspective of a moral conception that takes the claims of virtue seriously. In solitary deliberation, I might ask what is required on their best interpretation
by the virtues I regard as basic to my very identity. I consider possible
options according to ideals of kindness, decency, and the like. There
might be no one correct answer to the questions I ask, and given any situation of real complexity, the answer I arrive at will properly be tempered

by a sense of my own fallibility. But the ideal of truth nonetheless operates as a regulative ideal, alerting me to deliberative distortions that are liable to pull me astray (Murdoch 1970: 17–23). These will include distortions that arise from the inevitable motivational conflict I noted earlier between my commitment to moral virtue and other critical or volitional commitments internal to my identity. I may be reluctant to see my options in ways that suggest the only morally responsible choice requires some sacrifice within the career I love, even when that is obviously true to an impartial onlooker. The truth has precisely the same authority when we move from solitary deliberation to moral dialogue. One of the great advantages of dialogue is that it may help us achieve better success in overcoming deliberative distortions than we can achieve alone. To ask with another human being what certain virtues require of us in particular circumstances is to seek the truth in answer to questions where a great many possible obstacles stand in the way of grasping the truth, but where collective effort is likely to be a lot more promising than our own unaided myopia. To invoke the ideal of truth here is not to affirm any extravagant metaphysical reading thereof; it is simply to say that serious moral thought only makes sense on the assumption that we share a practice of justification in which the aspiration to true or correct judgement is operative.

On this understanding of moral dialogue, the topic of conversation is inextricably tied to the identity of those who participate because the topic is engaged in a way that expresses a critical commitment to virtue that is part to their self-understanding. To treat a topic of serious moral dialogue as something to be subordinated to the value of our interlocutors and our relationship to them is to treat moral questions as if they were external to the constitution of one's own self and the self of the other, matters of mere volitional commitment that should not distract us from the real business of who we are and why we matter.

These difficulties in Noddings's conception of moral dialogue rise brightly to the surface of the text on one occasion. She concedes that interpersonal reasoning between two people may converge on a conclusion that affirms their mutual caring but is 'morally deplorable when the interests of others are considered' (Noddings 1991: 164). I assume Noddings means that the conclusion is morally deplorable by the standard of her ethic of care since that is the standard she thinks should determine judgements about what is morally deplorable. Now suppose that one of the participants in the conversation sees that the conclusion is indeed uncaring, all things considered, but nevertheless abides by what was concluded because affirming a caring relation with the other is more important to him than avoiding what is deplorable from a wider caring perspective. The importance of his interlocutor and their relationship has been established over any shared interest they might have in the moral truth. Paradoxically, that outcome must be condemned from the viewpoint of the same ethic that purports to exalt the value of relationship above that of truth.[4]

I have stressed the importance of truth as a regulative ideal in moral dialogue because it is necessary to underwrite the gravity of what is at stake in such dialogue and the centrality of critical commitment to the development of virtue. But I have argued for that conclusion on grounds that do not call into question Noddings's claim that the care she espouses is indeed an appropriate and sufficient basis for moral education. My argument has depended only on the generic analysis of virtue offered in the Section 57, an analysis that is silent on the question of whether Noddings's virtues of care are better or worse than any other catalogue of the virtues. Therefore, my criticism might be thought to require only some adjustments to Noddings's approach to dialogue, without any alteration to her conception of the aims that dialogue should serve. But that is not so. The claim that the virtues of care can suffice as the aims of moral dialogue becomes increasingly contestable the more we probe what it means to acknowledge the regulative ideal of truth in dialogue under pluralism.

## 59. *Moral Distress and the Limits of Care*

A genuinely common school mirrors the diversity of the society it serves. If students can speak their minds, the deep moral tensions of the society to which they belong will be manifest in their dialogue (Fine 1993, 1995). Often students may not speak their minds because, for example, they are either ashamed to talk about beliefs that put them at odds with their peers or intimidated by the unyielding orthodoxy of a teacher's views. Then we have no real dialogue, and therefore, none that could serve the ends of political education. But the turbulent diversity to which candid dialogue gives expression will also, necessarily, release powerful currents of other-regarding moral distress.

Consider one of the more notorious remarks of Robert Bork, George Bush's unsuccessful nominee to the Supreme Court. The remark was made about women who agreed to undergo sterilization to keep their jobs: 'I suppose they were glad to have the choice' (quoted in Wills 1995: 38) In moral dialogue with another adult, I doubt that I would be able to respond to that observation without indignation. But notice that what Bork appeals to here is an ideal that is an important part of our pluralism, although you will not see much of it in multicultural manifestos. It is an ideal of uncomplaining self-reliance in a world where people must make the most of opportunities under conditions that are harsh, even predatory. The ideal collides directly with other elements in our public culture: ideals of compassion and notions of a minimal decency to which all institutions, including the market, must defer. Real pluralism generates just this sort of emotionally fraught conflict because we believe the truth, not just personal preference, to be at stake, and we should not expect—indeed, we cannot expect—real pluralism in the classroom to be any different.

The literature on multicultural education often ignores this troubling conclusion because of a tendency to attend only to what are usually the more tractable aspects of diversity—the outward trappings of ethnicity, say, or divergent life-styles. This is misleading because ethnic differences or variety of life-style can thrive alongside an amicable moral unanimity, and ethnic commonality and convergent life-styles may coincide with profound and divisive moral conflict. Yet the existence of these other kinds of diversity make it tempting to try to recast real moral conflict, with all its attendant distress and estrangement, into some more comfortable mode of divergent valuation. My indignation at Robert Bork's remark would dissipate for example, if I came to think of our differences as matters of taste or life-style, so that the conflict between his moral values and mine were reduced to the level of mere volitional commitment. Then I might regard Bork with the friendly indulgence I extend to those who foolishly prefer scotch to Irish whiskey. But recasting conflicting moral judgements in this way comes at the price of suppressing the critical commitment on which real moral virtue depends; it is a strategy for coping with moral pluralism that can only work by destroying the morality in the pluralism.

Perhaps the most influential approach to moral dialogue in American schools in recent decades—so-called 'values clarification'—has been corrupting in just this way. It invites children to think of rival moral judgements as no more than so many different preferences to be tolerated as we tolerate the odd tastes of people who do not share our own. Values clarification has been subject to overwhelming criticism (e.g. Carter 1984: 49–54; Strike 1990: 493–502). But its influence lingers, and the more general point its failure exemplifies is that a standing temptation for any approach to moral dialogue under pluralism, given the appeal of conflict avoidance, will be to pretend that the moral truth does not matter or is less important than something else. But this in turn imposes a conception of dialogue that must be repugnant to the conscience of all who think the moral truth does matter, which is to say, all who have a strong critical commitment to moral virtue. Values clarification is a notably crude example of the strategy of evasion, but it also undermines Noddings's version of moral dialogue. (Indeed, Rawls's own observations on truth and public reason show a lot to be desired in this regard. I return to this point in Section 61.)

Could the ethic of care be recast in a way that better accommodates genuine moral pluralism? There is strong reason to doubt that it could. One criticism of Noddings is that the criteria of ethically admirable caring she gives us are negligible, or at least too scant to give us useful moral guidance (Blustein 1991: 40–1; Flanagan 1991: 423–7). Certainly a risk of the language of care is that it may drift towards uninformative vacuity. And if the language is extended to subsume caring for ideas and inanimate objects, as Noddings now suggests, it is unclear that it can mean anything more determinate than valuing something or other in a vaguely heartfelt way (Noddings 1992: 126–38). Yet in fairness to Noddings, there are elements within her thought which pull against the drift towards empty abstraction. In particular, caring relationships as Noddings conceives them gravitate towards intimacy in the sense that Jeffrey Reiman has specified: 'Necessary to an intimate relationship . . . is a reciprocal desire to share present and future intense and important experiences together' (Reiman 1984: 305). No plausible ethic can enjoin a universal intimacy, and Noddings is clear that it cannot (Noddings 1988: 219). But even in chance encounters with a stranger, care is supposed to prompt an engrossed and solicitous regard that approximates attitudes intrinsic to full-blown intimacy (Noddings 1992: 16). The pervasive emphasis in her writings on the reciprocal emotional fulfilments of care, and the need for social arrangements that will nurture ever closer and more enduring personal ties, point to a pivotal normative role for intimacy within her moral conception.

All this points to a dilemma for those who would champion an ethic of care such as Nodding's as a basis for moral dialogue under pluralism. So far as any conception of care drifts towards empty abstraction, it can give no useful direction to our efforts to talk together in morally profitable ways when we disagree strongly about the moral truth. On the other hand, if the conception is anchored in anything like the value of intimacy, it cannot give useful direction in the face of serious moral conflict, given the other-regarding moral distress that inheres in such conflict. Why not? Bruce Ackerman describes political dialogue in a liberal democratic state as conversation with strangers as well as soul-mates (Ackerman 1989: 22). I might be able to talk with Robert Bork about workers' or women's rights, and some good might come of it. But it would still be dialogue between strangers rather than soul-mates, and it would be dialogue that was animated with a certain moral enmity. It could not *become* a dialogue among soul-mates without one or the other of us undergoing a radical transformation of moral identity. An ideal of care that urges us to approximate intimacy in moral dialogue effectively asks us to turn strangers into soul-mates. But that is only possible by extirpating real moral diversity.

It is noteworthy that when Noddings considers how to address the problem of pluralism in education her thought-experiment assumes that it can be broached in the context of familial intimacy writ large:

We will pretend that we have a large heterogeneous family to raise and educate. Our children have different ethnic heritages, widely different intellectual capacities, different physical strengths, and different interests. We want to respect their legitimate differences. At the same time, we think there are some things they all should learn and some other things they should all be exposed to so that they can make well-informed choices. How shall we educate them? (Noddings 1992: p. xiii)

This obscures where it claims to enlighten. For the question Noddings asks us to consider here would be the one we faced only in a world where ethical differences had been reduced to the level of contrasting volitional commitments so that pluralism was indeed just a matter of varying talents, strengths, interests, and ethnic colour. But that is not our world. Our world is a place of real moral pluralism. We need an account of dialogue that does not pretend otherwise.

## 60. *Moral Belligerence and Dialogue*

At the beginning of Section 58 I raised the question of how the antipathies that open moral discussion under pluralism will generate can be reconciled with the construction of ties of fellowship and trust that common education requires. We cannot answer that question by suppressing the authority of truth as a dialogical norm. That is Noddings's error. A more promising answer might seem to be available in J. S. Mill's *On Liberty*, an essay that attempts to make a virtue of the emotional antagonisms that caring dialogue would suppress.

Millian moral dialogue takes place in the setting of what Waldron calls 'ethical confrontation': the conflict of different and earnestly held moral views in circumstances where no one has the right to silence dissent (Waldron 1993*d*: 102). Ethical confrontation is the engine of collective moral enlightenment. Only by its means do we enjoy the opportunity of giving up uncritically held error in favour of truth. Without ethical confrontation, even the most profound moral truths are liable to ossify in the minds of those who subscribe to them. The persistent challenge of dissent sustains our personal investment in the truths that really matter and reminds us of their full significance by showing us vividly what it means to speak and live against them. Furthermore, the views that clash in ethical confrontation are characteristically neither pristine truth nor pure error; they are instead tangled composites of truth and error, and the hard business of separating the one from the other is impossible without the pressures that ethical confrontation exert upon rival views (Mill 1976 edn.: 21–6). As Waldron notes, other-regarding moral distress is not for Mill an emotional distraction from the cognitive processes that ethical confrontation engages. On the contrary, distress is an integral part of those very processes:

That a man is morally distressed by another's homosexuality, for example, is a sign that he takes his own views on ethics seriously, second, that he recognises now the need to reassert vigorously his own convictions, being confronted so dramatically and disturbingly with a case of its denial, and third—if (as is probable) the moral truth about sexual relations is the monopoly neither of his opinion nor its rival—it is a sign that ideas are struggling and clashing with one another in the way that Mill thought most likely to lead to a more balanced and sober truth about human sexuality. (Waldron 1993*d*: 125)

Other-regarding moral distress is the emotional fuel of ethical confrontation, and therefore, its presence in dialogue should hearten us as a sign that public moral education is proceeding as it should rather than alarm us as a portent of social conflict or demoralization. That means dialogue must be characterized by a certain belligerence. But Mill could cheerfully celebrate dialogical belligerence as a virtue, and dismiss those who would prefer a more 'temperate' style of debate because 'in the great practical concerns of life . . . [truth] has to be made by the rough process of a struggle between combatants fighting under hostile banners' (Mill 1976 edn.: 58, 65–6).

Mill does not establish with much precision the general conditions under which ethical confrontation is most likely to reap the benefits that he associates with it. The conditions he does indicate, such as the avoidance of outright verbal abuse and the fair depiction of rivals' views by antagonists, are sparse (Mill 1976 edn.: 65–7). They suggest that if unbridled verbal belligerence does not suffice for productive confrontation, then all that needs to be added are some constraints against the most obvious kinds of rhetorical abuse. That might be plausible if we are considering moral dialogue among informed and highly autonomous adults.[5] But a fuller account of the conditions of fruitful ethical confrontation is surely needed if we are to implement it in a specific institutional setting, like the common school, where much less can be taken for granted. If we cannot assume that ethical confrontation, barring the gross abuses that Mill deprecated, must conduce to enlightenment on any and every occasion, then we need to ask what additional conditions have to be in place for it to be successful. As we investigate these conditions, the defensibility of Mill's endorsement of dialogical belligerence becomes increasingly questionable.

Consider again the three elements that Waldron differentiates in Mill's interpretation of edifying moral distress. First, other-regarding moral distress signifies the seriousness of the individual's ethical convictions. That is perhaps true. But ethical confrontation can arouse other and powerful kinds of distress that obstruct the variety that Mill wanted, and these may block the benefits of enlightenment that are supposed to accrue through the educationally privileged species of distress. The very fact that Mill's preferred style of dialogue makes it a kind of verbal warfare means that it must engage all the vast emotional energy that human beings, as social animals, invest in matters of status, including that especially painful self-regarding distress (shame) that we associate with losing face. Moreover, even if we could somehow eliminate that problem, the many emotions stirred in the rough and tumble of dialogue that affect what we say or how we interpret others would still likely have deep roots in values other than critical moral commitment. We do not have to take a reductively Marxist interpretation of morality to see that the passion of ethical confrontation commonly has much to do with whose economic interests are served by one view rather than another. Similarly, dialogue can be affectively coloured and cognitively distorted by disparities of power among interlocutors, and by the residual resentments and misunderstanding deposited by histories of oppression, real or imagined. These particular sources of distortion have received much attention in recent educational research (cf. Ellsworth 1989; Burbules and Rice 1991). At any rate, it should be clear that if we are to establish supportive conditions for edifying ethical confrontation, one general and very difficult task is to find ways of curbing the influence of the myriad and powerful morally distracting emotions that confrontation is liable to release, and the difficulty of the task is compounded when confrontation is conducted in a belligerent spirit.

Even when the distress aroused by confrontation has a truly moral source, it does not necessarily signify the seriousness of our own ethical convictions. Distress may also be a sign of disturbing (and not necessarily conscious) doubts about the correctness of our moral beliefs or about the importance of the differences between what we and others believe. It may betoken not a healthy ethical self-confidence, as Waldron suggests, but rather its very opposite—a desperate uncertainty in the face of alien values.

This possibility has an important bearing on the second and third elements in the Millian conception of ethical confrontation that Waldron identifies: the inspirational role of moral distress for the belligerent parties, and its contribution to dialectical progress once they take up arms against each other. Although the distress of moral uncertainty may well constitute a kind of progress, given that the convictions whose disturbance occasions the distress are false, the outcome of emotional turmoil may well be a humiliated silence or a fearful withdrawal from the dialogical fray. Here again we see general conditions that must be in place if we can expect ethical confrontation to bear the fruit that the Millian conception promises. Participants need a judicious confidence in their own powers of moral judgement if the experience of uncertainty is not to be disabling, and here again, the very belligerence of Millian dialogue may impede us in trying to satisfy the preconditons of dialogical success.

The dangers of belligerence become especially clear when we look at the ideal terminus of ethical confrontation. Recall that the ultimate point of combatants fighting under hostile banners is to permit the best in contending views to emerge gradually to view and win widespread acceptance. If that is to happen, combat must give way eventually to moments of ethical conciliation when the truth and error in rival positions has been made clear, and a fitting synthesis of factional viewpoints is achieved. Moments of conciliation require ethical abilities and habits that go beyond the skills of dialogical combat; they require an imaginative hospitality to what is now fashionably called difference, as well as a readiness to apply those lethal skills of critical combat to whatever is deficient in the view one initially defended against others under hostile banners. Yet the fierce partisanship of belligerents entails an emotional resistance to conciliation, and to that extent, is an obstacle to the enlightenment that gives ethical confrontation its educational rationale.

Three important conclusions follow from an understanding of the conditions under which we could rationally expect ethical confrontation to have the salutary consequences that Mill anticipated. First, even though the moral distress that inevitably attends ethical confrontation may give a flavour of hostility to dialogue, this is an immensely dangerous phenomenon that threatens to defeat the very point of dialogue. To learn to participate fruitfully in ethical confrontation is to learn to chasten the experience of distress, to forgo the temptations of an implacable belligerence, without at the same suppressing an emotion that is inseparable from a serious interest in moral truth. Second, the control of belligerent proclivities is merely one of a complex range of personal dispositions that includes, for example, the affective self-knowledge to differentiate moral from the other varieties of distress that conflict may trigger, and without which, dialogue can create far more darkness than light. Third, ethical confrontation may be conducted in ways that make it not merely unsuccessful; under familiar circumstances, it may actually militate against the virtues that would conduce to success in the future. When confrontation badly shakes a child's ethical confidence it may render the child less likely to profit from subsequent dialogue.

These three conclusions shed a somewhat unexpected light on the unscholarly worries about moral dialogue in common schools that I noted at the beginning of this chapter. The concern that through dialogue children might give up truth in favour of error or that they might be in some other way corrupted is sometimes waved aside with a few hackneyed phrases about the benefits of moral diversity, liberal tolerance, and a free market-place of ideas. The irony of the three conclusions I have defended about the conditions of edifying ethical confrontation is that in many cases they may support rather than allay worries about moral dialogue in common schools. The conditions of fruitful ethical confrontation are not easily achieved, they require much of participants in the way of emotional sophistication and cognitive ability, and when the relevant conditions are not met, dialogue may be worse than useless: it may be morally debilitating.

That being so, some will doubt that ethical confrontation can be responsibly practised in common schools, given that children and adolescents are unlikely already to have the virtues that make dialogue under conditions of diversity a promising undertaking; and since ethical confrontation comes with the territory in common schools, the improbability of confrontation being beneficial and the risk of its being corrupting give us reason to dispense with that institution. But this is much too quick. The virtues that make ethical confrontation worthwhile are not an all-or-nothing matter, and the process of developing them is not separable from the experience of moral conflict in social settings where the vices of confrontation can be gently corrected and the virtues encouraged. The common school is just such a setting, and contemporary liberal democracies hardly furnish an abundance of alternative institutions in which this kind of learning might occur. My argument so far has stressed the difficulties of creating the conditions of successful ethical confrontation in common schools or anywhere else; it does not entail the futility or undesirability of attempts to do so.

Yet a more radical objection to Mill might be pressed at this point, an objection that draws on the idea of reasonable pluralism. Despite its celebration of conflict and belligerence, Mill's conception of moral dialogue ultimately depends on the value of a reasoned and inclusive agreement about how we should live. The hope for a more balanced and sober truth that transcends the partial visions of dialogical combatants is the very purpose of ethical confrontation, and Mill was sanguine that in due course the hope would be realized. However, the moral epistemology that such hope presupposes is at best implausible in the context of late twentieth-century moral philosophy. An increasingly influential view is that the significance of moral disagreement goes much deeper than Mill supposed: the obstacles to convergent judgement in morality are far too recalcitrant for a shared and comprehensive vision of good and the right to be more than a utopian aspiration (e.g. Berlin 1969; Nagel 1979: 128–46; Taylor 1985: 230–47). This does not mean that no one can reasonably be an ethical monist, as Mill was; what it means is that no one can rightly condemn all alternatives to monism as untenable or reasonably suppose that moral dialogue is steady progress along a road to comprehensive ethical agreement. Pluralism seems an ineradicable aspect of the human condition, not a useful but temporary station on the road to a place where it will disappear.

   If the moral epistemology that undergirds Mill's conception of dialogue is now implausible, we cannot look to ethical confrontation with his optimistic expectations. Ethical confrontation will often not dissipate in shared endorsement of a more balanced and sober truth, even when the virtues that conduce to successful dialogue are securely in place; instead, dialogue may take us nowhere because there is no more balanced and sober truth to be had. Therefore, the sensible course for coexistence might often be ethical *avoidance* rather than confrontation. Institutions, like common schools perhaps, that conduce to confrontation are thus to be abandoned in favour of social arrangements that do not encourage a pointless dialogue in the face of irreconcilable difference. Within more morally homogeneous institutions, robust ties of care and community can be established, but without suppressing the interest in moral truth that is intrinsic to virtue. Perhaps scepticism about the project of constructing an overarching moral unity for diverse societies is rarely stated as baldly as this. But the argument I have indicated does make explicit a line of thought to which many now seem drawn who defend the value of particularistic identities against the claims of more inclusive ideals of moral community (e.g. MacIntyre 1981: 235; M. Holmes 1992; Stolzenberg 1993). Should we accept that argument?

## 61. Confrontation and Conciliation

At the root of Mill's notion of dialogue is epistemological hope: when dialogue proceeds as it should, the distress and belligerence of confrontation will naturally give way to conciliation as moral truth is pieced together from the fragmentary insights of conflicting viewpoints. That hope now looks recklessly speculative at best. One response to the loss of Mill's hope is ethical avoidance; another is to seek a different kind of conciliation. By a different kind of conciliation I mean this: the fitting response to ongoing moral conflict is sometimes not renewed effort to achieve dialogical victory over our adversaries but rather the attempt to find and enact terms of political coexistence that we and they can reasonably endorse as morally acceptable. That is the purpose of public reason as Rawls conceives it, and teaching future citizens what they need to participate competently in public reason is the dialogical task of common education.

Rawls vacillates between saying that public reason simply substitutes the end of reasonable agreement for moral truth in politics and saying that we rightly accept the ideal of reasonable agreement as the politically fundamental part of the moral truth (cf. Rawls 1993: p. xx, 116, 127, 129, 153). The first of these views tends to predominate in Rawls's recent work, and it has been justly criticized (Raz 1990; Hampton 1993; Bird 1996). The second view is the defensible one. Why should we suppose that seeking reasonable agreement matters unless we thought it was true that reasonableness is the virtue that rightly shapes the way we live together under pluralism? Neutrality on that point cannot be squared with commitment to the reasonable as the authoritative norm of political morality. That being so, the end of reasonable agreement is not an ideal of interpersonal solidarity that trumps truth, an ideal of the sort that grounds Noddings's conception of caring dialogue. The interest in moral truth is as important to public reason as it is to Millian ethical confrontation. The difference is that we modestly seek a circumscribed reasoned agreement on how to live with each other because we know that trying to find and enforce a more ambitious consensus exceeds the limits of our ability to reason together towards the truth and invites oppression.

But if we think of public reason as directed towards a kind of reasoned conciliation, what is learned in the dialogical task of common education cannot be that every enduring source of moral difference is something we should agree to disagree about.[6] The dialogical task is about learning to think wisely about the difference between reasonable and unreasonable pluralism, and so far as unreasonable pluralism is a part of our lives, there is much that we cannot agree to disagree about.

Part of the educational challenge here is cultivating the intellectual virtues that reasonableness entails and developing a discerning eye for the corresponding vices of unreason that threaten to contaminate public reason. These vices are dispositions that entail some culpable deficiency of ability or motivation in the exercise of reason, like a feeble commitment to evidence gathering, a weak propensity to alter beliefs in the light of evident inconsistencies or decisive counterevidence, a reluctance to respond to criticism with relevant replies, and the like.[7] A further source of moral pluralism that discredits what it explains is the desire to dominate. By 'domination' I mean the abuse of some inequality of power or influence to advance purportedly justified moral views that in fact merely serve individual or factional interests.

The fact that much extant pluralism is to be explained in ways that divest it of any title to respect is often dangerously overlooked in discourse on moral education under pluralism. In an otherwise very useful discussion of the educational problems of pluralistic moral dialogue, Melinda Fine speaks of the 'contradictory' experience of students in a classroom where the teacher is sometimes neutral between divergent moral views and sometimes not: 'On the one hand, they talk about valuing open-mindedness, a plurality of opinions, and the importance of free expression; on the other, at times they seek closure to controversies and rest easier in being told which opinions are "right" ' (Fine 1993: 430). Fine's meaning is not entirely obvious here. But she might be taken to imply that teachers who seek closure to a particular episode of dialogue by explicitly opposing certain views their students have voiced are thereby 'contradicting' the values of open-mindedness, free expression, and respect for a plurality of opinions. However, on no plausible interpretation are these values inconsistent with a forthright opposition to the vices of unreason and domination, and therefore, their practical requirements are not violated by a teacher who would evince that opposition or move towards closure in dialogue when resistance to closure is evidently motivated by the relevant vices.

There are certainly risks that the intellectual authority of the teacher will be abused here, and my quotation from Fine is immediately preceded by an example that seems perilously close to such abuse. But in their preoccupation to avoid the abuse of authority, teachers cannot responsibly embrace an 'anything goes' attitude to moral pluralism. Some years ago a colleague of mine witnessed a discussion of language rights in a social studies class in which a number of students claimed that linguistic uniformity is essential to social unity and that francophone Canadians should be 'sent back to France' if they think otherwise. The students' views plainly indicated much sheer ignorance about the French presence in Canada, as well as a morally puerile understanding of democracy as the domination of the majority. But the student teacher who presided over the discussion welcomed all that was said with scrupulous neutrality. When my colleague asked him afterwards why he behaved in this way, his answer was that he wanted to respect the plurality of moral opinions his students held, even though his own views were more tolerant than theirs. No doubt the vexing problem of language rights in a liberal democracy such as Canada admits more than one reasonable solution, and therefore teachers who imperiously affirm the unique moral authority of their own views on the matter may be guilty of a kind of domination. But the one who accepts all possible answers, no matter how palpably corrupted by the vices of unreason and domination, hardly does any better. The vices of unreason and domination are as commonplace in the classroom as they are anywhere else, and that means any serious attempt to teach reasonableness in the world as we know it cannot altogether escape ethical confrontation with its collateral impetus towards moral distress and estrangement, even if we try to mitigate the evils I noted in Section 60.

A crucial aspect to the virtue of reasonableness restrains any peremptory contempt for the views of our fellow citizens, and it will properly be salient in the dialogical task of common education. The distinction between moral disagreements correctly explained by the burdens of judgement and those that owe their existence to some more ignoble source is *itself* subject to those burdens, and therefore, making use of the distinction in dialogue requires a certain caution if we are to keep faith with the demands of reciprocity. Such caution will take the shape of an interpretive charity toward interlocutors: a determination to confront one's opponents' arguments in their strongest rather than their weakest forms and to reformulate those arguments, where necessary, to bring out their full latent force (Fullinwider 1993).[8] Moreover, active acceptance of the burdens of judgement will also require reflection on the many differences that divide us in our lives outside politics. (See Section 11.) Thus the dialogical task necessarily modulates into wider reflection on the background culture of public reason, as students learn to understand, with the same interpretive charity that holds inside public reason, something of the different ways of life that reasonable pluralism encompasses.

The educational importance of this point helps us to take the measure of one of the more interesting objections that has been levelled against Rawlsian public reason. Waldron takes issue with the view that political deliberation requires us to prescind from reasonable differences so that religious pluralism, for example, would rule out religious political argument.

I mean to draw attention to an experience we all have had at one time or another, of having argued with someone whose world view was quite at odds with our own, and of having come away thinking, 'I'm sure he's wrong, and I can't follow much of it, but, still, it makes you think . . .' The prospect of losing that sort of effect in public discourse is frankly, frightening—terrifying, even, if we are to imagine it being replaced by a form of 'deliberation' that, in the name of 'fairness' or 'reasonableness' (or worse still, balance) consists of blind appeals to harmless nostrums that are accepted without question on all sides. That is to imagine open-ended public debate reduced to the formal trivia of American television networks. (Waldron 1993*e*: 841–2)

To some extent Waldron is importantly right. The vigour of our own ethical identities depends in part on dialogical encounters in which we can engage imaginatively with religious and metaphysical views very different from our own. The prospect of never having that experience is as terrifying to me as it is to him, and part of what seems wrong with our public culture is that we create such little opportunity for that kind of encounter. Rawls does not seem sensitive enough to that point.[9] But notice that the implicit happy ending to the enounter Waldron describes—the interlocutors going their separate ways, each half baffled and half exalted by the strangeness of the other—depends on certain assumptions about what will not happen next. We are invited to think that they can indeed go their separate ways without penalty, and that political power will not be used to impose one set of contested religious or metaphysical views at the expense of another. The implicit happy ending disappears once we imagine that what is at stake between them is political victory or defeat rather than mutual edification.

So in another way, Rawls is right and Waldron wrong. We may indeed need an open-ended, unrestrained discourse about the good life and the good society. But we also need a more circumscribed and disciplined kind of deliberation that will respect the limits of reasonable disagreement when questions of political coercion are at stake. Indeed, the moral authority of the second kind of deliberation—public reason in the strict sense—is parasitic to some degree on the vitality of the open-ended, unrestrained kind of ethical discourse because it is only to the extent that we have thought seriously together about the nature of the good life and the good society that we can expect to find a common standpoint of justification that deserves our allegiance. Only then have we earned the confidence to assume that our pluralism is indeed reasonable. Unless our public standpoint of justification grows out of that wider ethical thought, it remains vulnerable to the objection that it is no more than the trite common ground that the wise and the foolish, the vicious and the virtuous, can all agree on. The appeal of the common school is precisely that it is one institution that might provide a setting in which the kind of encounter that Waldron celebrates might often occur and still students would learn to respect the differences that such encounters will never overcome.

Reasonableness is plainly a sophisticated virtue that demands subtle powers of moral discernment, and the fact that it does will naturally arouse some doubt about its feasibility as a educational goal for all future citizens. Macedo observes that 'The whole notion of the burdens of judgment . . . is extremely subtle and very likely beyond the sophistication of all but the most extraordinary high school seniors' (Macedo 1995*b*: 313). He is quick to add that this does not make the notion educationally irrelevant. But if he were right about its intellectual inaccessibility to all but adolescent prodigies, it is hard to see how it could have more than tenuous educational relevance. I think Macedo might be right if we equate understanding the burdens of judgement with a grasp of the philosophical rationale of pluralism. But an explicit understanding of that rationale is neither necessary nor sufficient for reasonableness as a political virtue.

An example we have already touched on will help to clarify this vital point. Consider the predicament of the teacher in an officially bilingual and multicultural liberal democracy who confronts a class of adolescents some of whom say their country should become unilingual, by force if necessary. Part of the responsible pedagogical response to this has already been indicated. Political beliefs that clearly reflect the vices of unreason and domination need to be confronted as such, albeit with all the tact and sensitivity that successful correction is likely to demand in dealing with children or adolescents. But successful correction is not the end of the matter because students, as future citizens, still face a wide spectrum of opinion regarding the political significance of linguistic and cultural diversity, even after the effects of crass prejudice and ignorance have been overcome. Surely a large part of the residual task is learning how differences that arise within that spectrum of reasonable opinion may reflect, for example, the difficulties of weighing and assessing empirical evidence about the relationship between cultural and linguistic diversity on the one hand and political stability on the other, the susceptibility of concepts like patriotism and national unity to hard cases, and the ways in which our use of such concepts are deeply affected by contingencies of personal and communal history that vary greatly from one individual and group to another. This is just the kind of learning that the burdens of judgement require as a practical matter. It does not necessarily issue in unanimity on matters of language rights or anything else, but it still infuses into political discussions that are so often venomous a spirit of accommodation and a concomitant restraint in the advocacy of coercive solutions to conflict.

To learn the specific ways in which the burdens of judgement may deeply affect our divergent prereflective responses to political questions is not the same as coming to understand Rawls's philosophical argument for mutual respect in the midst of pluralism. But then again, one might come to understand Rawls while remaining intransigently convinced of the exclusive rightness of one's own perspective on matters of practical politics. My general point is that acceptance of the burdens of judgement as an operative principle of our political thought is not the same as understanding its abstract intellectual grounding. And even if the latter may seem an appropriate educational goal only for prospective philosopher kings, the former seems a more realistic, though no less noble aim for the ordinary citizens of a free society.

I began this chapter by juxtaposing a vague but complacent academic orthodoxy about the value of moral dialogue in schools with the worries of many people outside the academy that such dialogue, given the context of diversity, is liable to be corrupting. The argument I have traced bears a complex relation to these contrasting attitudes. Clearly, some prominent grounds for doubt about moral dialogue in our schools are untenable. The assumption that we can substitute the preservation of innocence for the cultivation of virtue, and then dignify the substitution with the name of 'moral education', is utter foolishness. Hardly less destructive is the idea that deep pluralism may warrant a policy of ethical avoidance rather than confrontation in educational institutions. Ethical avoidance is a blindly regressive social tendency that pulls us away from the dialogical conditions that would enable us collectively to distinguish the pluralism that deserves our respect from the pluralism that does not. Nevertheless, my argument has also shown that pluralistic moral dialogue is a difficult and delicate endeavour, and that influential conceptions of such dialogue may indeed be corrupting by either suppressing the gravity of moral conflict for the sake of a specious conviviality or by taking a rashly optimistic view of the educational benefits of belligerent confrontation. More generally, the reality of our existing schools, with many teachers who do not understand the character of pluralistic moral dialogue or have little latitude to act on that understanding should they have it, may make doubts about excursions into the hazardous territory of moral dialogue more than justified so long as current conditions persist. But this gives us no reason to dispense with the ideal of the common school. What we need instead are common schools worthy of the ends of common education.

# CHAPTER 9

## Conclusion

The pluralism of free societies makes urgent the task of creating citizens who share a sufficiently cohesive political identity. At the same time, the sheer range and power of pluralism make it hard to see how reasoned agreement on the content of that identity and the educational practices that would make it safe for the future could be more than an idle wish: 'The very state of affairs that makes common citizenship so important to us seems at the same time to expose it as a pipe-dream' (Miller 1995*a*: 433).

In the preceding chapters I outlined a conception of political education that befits a democratic society, honours the sources of diversity that thrive within the boundaries of a strong common citizenship, and yet supports a judicious tolerance to ways of life that conflict with some of its demands. To the extent that the conception builds on values that are already woven into the political culture of liberal democracies, it is no pipe-dream. But if the political education I have described is more than academic wish-fulfilment, neither is it a task we could ever undertake with any certainty of success; it is rather an object of rational moral faith, even at the best of times, to say nothing of our times. By calling the relevant attitude 'rational' I mean that commitment to the education I have in mind is one we have strong reason to make. Yet the commitment is one whose ultimate efficacy we also have strong reason to doubt, and therefore it is one we can only sustain, barring self-deception or ignorance, as a matter of moral faith (Adams 1995).

The most obvious ground for doubt is the durability of unreasonable pluralism in communities of free and equal citizens, and its unpredictable tendency to escalate in the mass politics of ethnic hatred or religious intolerance. There is also the tendency for the rational and the reasonable to come apart, so to speak, in more humdrum ways once individual and group interest inclines us to favour political arrangements that dominate others. The imperatives of unregulated capitalism, and especially global capitalism, do much to feed that tendency. At the very least, we are compelled to agree with Jurgen Habermas: 'there is no linear connection between the emergence of democratic regimes and capitalist moderniza- tion' (Habermas 1992: 8). In fact, the seeming disconnection between the two in many cases should make us worry that a real democratic education might do no more than prepare children for a citizenship that will not be theirs to practice when they become adults (Westbrook 1996: 141). To be sure, much of what I have said here is about the way in which common citizenship could work to reconcile the rational and the reasonable under favourable conditions. Since widespread diffusion of the right kind of political education is one such favourable condition, we have reason to put our faith in it. But even under the best conditions we might realist- ically hope for, centrifugal tendencies inhere in the very values that con- stitute liberal politics, and hence these tendencies cannot be extirpated without distorting the ends that political education must serve.

There can be no guarantee that a common reasonableness will yield terms of cooperation that all reasonably endorse in good faith (Nagel 1991: 169–79). Interests can diverge so sharply that any proposed set of social rules will be reasonably rejected by many. This is but one example of the the general point that differences due to the burdens of judgement will vary in severity from one context to another, and may be so great sometimes that our shared capacity for moral reason cannot create enough common ground, even if we did not have to worry about the cor- rupting influence of unreasonable pluralism.

Public deliberation that honours the distinction between reasonable and unreasonable pluralism will not be the sedate and harmonious endeavour we might sometimes want it to be. The many different con- ceptions of value that we bring to deliberation will generate moral friction and distress, and if the virtues of reasonable citizenship can often contain the friction and distress, the latter may also work to block the develop- ment of those virtues or erode them when they are already in place. No necessary concord holds between the diverse ethical ideals to which we might rationally cleave and the demands of reasonableness. So even when a shared reasonableness could give us the common ground we need, we will be rationally motivated to resist its appeal by virtue of the many values that must give way if that common ground is to prevail.

That is one reason why the dialogical task of common education is always a risky undertaking that many of us will regard with ambivalence at best. The unavoidable risk is that our children might be shaken in their commitment to values we cherish and have good reason to cherish, and the depth of our expressive interest in child-rearing makes us recoil from that possible outcome. But if that is so, our ambivalence is not directed towards some inessential educational process that we might prudently discard to keep everyone happy; its object is rather the unpredictable and disturbing variety of conclusions and choices that human reason will reach under conditions of freedom. Acceptance of that variety is central to civic virtue, even if the best we can manage is an ambivalent acceptance.

The tension between the rational and the reasonable is also ineradicable in the design of policy regarding common and separate schooling. We rightly insist on the necessity of common education. But we must also accommodate many kinds of separate education that people will rationally choose under pluralism. No feasible set of policies will give us maximal feasible success in both the common education all need and the many kinds of separate education that different people will permissibly choose. Trade-offs will be the order of the day here as elsewhere in the politics of education, and we will disagree, sometimes bitterly, in ways that pull against the norms of reasonable discourse.

It might seem strange to end a book that argues for a certain kind of political education by canvassing reasons that should make us doubt the efficacy of commitment to that education. Of course, political commitments in general are more likely to be resilient the more keenly aware we are of the pitfalls that will beset our efforts to enact them. The deeper point at issue here is that some of the risks we incur in political education for a free people are inherent in the kind of public culture which that education seeks to perpetuate, and so we do not even understand the task we are committed to unless we grasp the vulnerability to failure it necessarily contains.

But faith in any moral undertaking is not fuelled by doubt about its likely success, however well-taken the doubt may be. On the contrary, the necessary faith has to be sustained despite the corrosive power of rational doubt. The real though very imperfect and fragile accomplishments of our liberal democracies offer much that would nourish that faith if we can look at them with the right cast of mind. That is a mind informed by the same virtues that would give direction to the political education we should want for our children. For it is a hard truth that we must work hard to find those virtues in ourselves if we ever hope to see them in our children.

# NOTES

## CHAPTER 1

1. For an excellent acount of some political virtues I overlook, see P. White 1996. Although I do not pretend to offer an exhaustive catalogue of the political virtues, I assume that whatever might be added to create a complete account would not require radical revision to the partial conception I defend here.

2. The quotation captures one of the best contemporary political philosophers in a careless moment. Elsewhere he flatly contradicts what he says here (cf. Feinberg 1990: 111).

3. This argument bears a more complicated relation than might appear to the vexing question of whether liberal politics is rightly constrained by some notion of 'procedural neutrality'. The most plausible doctrine of neutrality says that the justification of state action under a liberal constitution eschews 'perfectionist' premises. That is to say, the intrinsic superiority of some ways of life over others is not rightly claimed in political justification; instead, we rely on principles of right that are neutral between rival conceptions of the good. But even if the doctrine were coherent and true, it is still the case that citizens would need whatever virtues will ensure that they discharge their civic obligations in a way that keeps faith with the relevant principles of right. Some defenders of liberal neutrality explicitly acknowledge that necessity, and argue for educational practices that would shape the character of citizens in substantial ways (e.g. Kymlicka 1995a) If there were a defensible version of the doctrine of neutrality, it would be consistent with the need for a politics of virtue in the sense I have specified. My target here is versions of the doctrine that pretend otherwise. The recent literature on liberal neutrality is vast. Among the most important contributions are Larmore 1987: 42–68; Kymlicka 1989a; Mason 1990; Hurka 1995; Bird 1996.

4. Jackson's ideal of 'the free mind' is not *contrasted* with the demands of patriotism at all. His point is rather that an honourable patriotism is one that is congenial to 'the free mind': 'To believe that patriotism will not flourish if patriotic ceremonies are voluntary and spontaneous instead of a compulsory routine is to make an unflattering estimate of the appeal of our institutions to free minds' (*West Virginia Board of Education* v. *Barnette*: 641). But the reasonable worry here is not just that compulsory rituals may be unnecessary but that they might install a counterfeit patriotism instead of the genuine article. That worry was expressed forcefully in the concurring opinion of Justices Black and Douglas: 'Words uttered under coercion are proof of loyalty to nothing but self-interest' (ibid. 644).

5. Other liberals may construe the liberty proper to a free society not in relation of a specific ideal of character, as Mill did, but as securing the widest possible

freedom to enact diverse projects and ideals, some of which might be utterly at odds with individuality. An important contemporary example is Lomasky 1987. What unites these strands of liberalism is an aversion to policies that would constrain education in the name of some robust conception of democratic virtue.

## CHAPTER 2

1. The passage is really an aberration in Galston's article. His avowed preference for simple as opposed to reasonable pluralism is not consistent with the substantial moral principles that regulate pluralism in his ideal 'Diversity State'. He argues for the protection of individual rights of exit from groups that some members come to find unacceptable. These rights have important educational implications by virtue of the 'psychological' and 'fitness' conditions that Galston assigns to them. The psychological aspect of the right rules out brainwashing, and fitness requires that individuals be equipped with the ability to function adequately in society beyond the boundaries of their group (Galston 1995: 533–4). The conditions are pretty vague. But even if they are given the most cautious interpretation, they amount to a criterion of reasonable rather than simple pluralism. Moreover, if the state 'zealously safeguards' these rights, as Galston recommends (ibid. 533), then in some forseeable circumstances its zeal might well provoke civil strife.

2. My distinction between the wide scope of the tolerable and the narrower range of liberal virtues such as moderation owes much to Stephen Macedo's illuminating discussion of these matters (Macedo 1990: 69–73).

3. Anne Phillips takes Rawls to task for translating all questions about pluralism into 'yet another version of the politics of competing ideas' and thereby failing to recognize the moral weight of political differences that have to do with disparities in identity and experience (Phillips 1995: 18–20). Rawls's exclusive focus on doctrinal differences certainly gives credence to that criticism. But the idea of the burdens of judgement is a cogent way of explaining the relevance of the differences that Phillips wants political theory to take seriously. For example, the under-representation of women or minority cultures in democratic assemblies is rightly condemned as unfair, given the burdens of judgement, insofar as this excludes from public reason voices that tend to be different but no less reasonable than the voices that are over-represented.

4. Elsewhere he does suggest that the conditions are not so minimal as to be devoid of content. Reasonable doctrines cannot 'reject the essentials of a democratic regime' (Rawls 1993: pp. xvi–xvii). For example, forms of fundamentalism which deny that faith must be freely given are not reasonable doctrines (ibid. 170).

5. The idea of a free-standing political conception, as I have explored it here, is based on the initial account that Rawls gives near the beginning of *Political*

*Liberalism* (12–13). But that account bears a puzzling connection to his view that the development of political liberalism must proceed in two stages. At the first stage, a conception of justice is supposed to be defended as a free-standing view by working out principles of justice and norms for their application, using ideas basic to the political culture of liberal democracy, such as the notion of free and equal citizenship. At the second stage, we ask if the conception developed at the first could win an overlapping consensus among the many reasonable comprehensive doctrines that might thrive across generations in a society whose basic structure was regulated by that conception (e.g. Rawls 1989; Rawls 1993: 140–1; Cohen 1993). The trouble is that if argument at the first stage requires us to show that the political conception can function appropriately as a module within the comprehensive doctrines of those to whom the argument is addressed, the question of coherence with their comprehensive doctrines has to be answered at the first stage. That being so, the second stage seems to collapse into the first.

To avoid the collapse, one might say that Rawls's initial characterization of a free-standing conception is a mistake. His considered view ought to be that argument at the first stage simply ignores the relation of justice to our comprehensive doctrines. Whether the conclusions of the argument can function as a module within those doctrines is postponed to the next stage. But I would argue that the two-stage view distorts the most central and interesting features of Rawlsian political liberalism. The guiding idea is that we might devise a conception of public reason that is adjusted at the outset to the full scope of reasonable pluralism. This idea is expressed through the political conception of the person at the very foundation of the so-called first stage. That conception contains within itself the idea of an overlapping consensus among reasonable comprehensive doctrines because it necessarily coheres with all doctrines that are consistent with reciprocity and acceptance of the burdens of judgement. Despite Rawls's emphasis on the importance of the argument's two-stage structure, I am inclined to think it is really a distraction from the deepest currents in his own thought.

I do not deny that there are important aspects of stability that cannot be resolved by adjusting our conception of justice to the fact of reasonable pluralism, and I think Rawls is wrong to rely on the idea of an overlapping consensus as the linch-pin of stability. I return to these matters in Chapter 4. But so far as stability is advanced by an overlapping consensus, the project of achieving such consensus is built into the so-called first stage of Rawls's theory.

6. The interest in dodging controversy may sometimes seem stronger than it actually is because Rawls is never clear enough about how large or small the gap is between his ideal well-ordered society and the liberal democracies we actually inhabit. Consider the following passage: 'Citizens in a well-ordered society roughly agree on these beliefs [about human nature and society] because they can be supported by . . . publicly shared methods of inquiry and forms of reasoning . . . I assume these methods to be familiar to common

sense and to include the procedures of science and social thought when these are well established and not controversial' (Rawls 1993: 66–7). Some of Rawls's most perceptive critics have pointed out that this would seem to rule out the appeal to any radical social theory, such as feminist critiques of the family, inside public reason (Exdell 1994: 456–60; McCarthy 1994: 53). But whether that implication follows or not depends upon whether we are *already* the inhabitants of the well-ordered society that Rawls is talking about. Suppose we agree that our society is far from being well-ordered. Much of its pluralism is to be explained not by the burdens of judgement but by inordinate self- and group interest and other lapses from the ideal of reasonableness. The persistence of patriarchy in contemporary liberal democracies is plausibly explained in that way. Therefore, public reason in our far less than well-ordered societies should—indeed must—engage controversial social theories and values in the attempt to render political deliberation more fully reasonable in the long term. The entrenched commonsense of a society that is less than well-ordered cannot be relied on to disclose the difference between what is relevant and irrelevant to a morally adequate public reason.

7. I assume here that we have ruled out the kind of integrity-destroying compartmentalization that I discussed earlier as a way of preserving doctrines learned in the non-public sphere from doubts provoked by the burdens of judgement.

8. The subversive impetus of the educational task to which Rawls is implicitly committed is easy to underestimate if we think of the autonomy that is relevant merely as a particular capacity. The claim that autonomy is a capacity (or repertoire of capacities) is familiar in contemporary philosophical literature (e.g. G. Dworkin 1988; Meyers 1989). By itself, the acquisition of new capacities does not necessarily affect the learner's basic values at all, however complex the capacities might be. People acquire the ability to do calculus or speak a foreign language, and what they learn has not the slightest effect on their prior ethical loyalties. But the accession of autonomy in the sense that matters here is an alteration of character rather than a mere expansion to a repertoire of capacities. 'Autonomy' signifies not merely the ability to subject received ideas to critical scrutiny; it also refers to the motivational and affective propensities that guide the exercise of the ability in securing a self-directed life. Rawls's argument compels us to construe its latent commitment to autonomy as a matter of character rather than bare capacity because we fall short of active acceptance of the burdens of judgement in the absence of the motivational and affective propensities that would support the exercise of the capacity for criticism. The difference between capacity and character is educationally as well as politically important. For it suggests that an education directed towards autonomy in the sense that sustains civic virtue will attempt to elicit the desire to think autonomously, nourish a proper pride in independent judgement and a disdain for both thoughtless conformity and nonconformity, all the while refining the deliberative capacities that desire

and emotion will inform. All this makes the educational task a lot more controversial than it might otherwise be.

## CHAPTER 3

1. The difference between the formation of a liberal theory on some broad matter of principle, like political education, and the imposition of that theory on others is well drawn in Will Kymlicka 1992: 144–5; see also Raz 1986: 427–9.
2. The superiority of a constitutional consensus over an overlapping consensus has been defended by some of Rawls's recent critics. See K. Baier 1989 and Adams 1993.
3. Johnston's vocabulary is a bit different than mine. He distinguishes three concepts of autonomy that he says are often confused. Autonomy in the sense relevant to my argument corresponds to what he labels 'personal autonomy', and he calls the sense of justice 'moral autonomy' (Johnston 1994: 71–7). But the different vocabularies do not affect the substance of our disagreement. Johnston also equates the modest conception of agency and moral autonomy he regards as foundational to a liberal polity with Rawls's political conception of the person (Johnston 1994: 75). Here again the differences are more apparent than real. Johnston's equation is defensible if we are interpreting Rawls's conception in its minimalist sense as the normative qualification for the status of citizen. My interest is in what the conception says about the political virtue proper to those who have that status, even if many who rightly possess citizenship lack the virtues appropriate to their station.
4. The moral inadequacy of a political education limited by a constitutional consensus is also discernible in Shelley Burtt's forceful argument for a 'privately' oriented conception of civic virtue (and hence civic education) (Burtt 1993). Burtt is sceptical of the 'publicly' oriented conceptions espoused by republican theorists because she thinks their moral demands are unrealistically onerous. The extent of political participation prescribed by republicans is one we cannot reasonably expect to be widely attainable in societies where people find their primary sources of fulfilment in extra-political pursuits. A better course would be to construe civic virtue more modestly, as dispositions to participate politically when one's own private interests are threatened by injustice. I think Burtt is probably right that conceptions of civic virtue that require heroic levels of political participation are utopian in an invidious sense. But as I argue in Section 32, we have good reason to affirm substantially the same political virtues, regardless of whether we favour democratic regimes which stress participation or representation. Once the issue of participation is set aside, Burtt's argument becomes vulnerable to much the same objection that is decisive against the idea of a constitutional consensus. We can only commend 'privately' oriented civic virtue as morally sufficient on the rashly optimistic assumption that the basic structure of society is already substantially just so that there are not groups who will continue to be

exploited (or come to be exploited) if political conduct is as closely circumscribed by self-interest as Burtt suggests it can permissibly be.

5. The conflict between liberal and communitarian conceptions of political
morality has produced a voluminous literature since the publication of
Macintyre 1981 and Sandel 1982. Among the other important contributions
are Bellah, Tipton, Swidler, and Sullivan 1985; Gutmann 1985; Sher 1989;
Taylor 1989; Kymlicka 1989*b*: 47–73, 1990: 199–337; Macedo 1990; Mulhall
and Swift 1992; Ryan 1993; D. Bell 1993. A curious feature of the literature is
that those whom liberal theorists classify as communitarians are rarely comfortable with that label. For my purposes, a political theory qualifies as 'communitarian' if it rejects liberal understandings of autonomy and justice on the
basis of their supposed inability to accommodate the moral importance of
ascribed roles and communal attachments. Sandel and MacIntyre qualify as
communitarians on this account.

6. If I say this or that is a matter of conscience for me, I am saying something
about what I believe (for example, that this or that action would be morally
wrong) and how I am disposed to feel under certain conditions (for example,
guilty if I do what my conscience condemns). What gives conscience its peculiar force in deliberation is the overarching conviction that what it requires or
forbids is right or wrong, good or bad, in a sense that is not explicable in
terms of what we just happen to desire. If it were explicable in such terms, the
familiar conflict between conscience and desire could not occur.

7. The reflection on alternatives that is relevant here need not issue in choosing.
If Michael asks seriously about whether the career in which he finds himself
is really worthy of his continued commitment, he need not reassign that
career to a choice-set of eligible options, rank all members in terms of their
comparative desirability, and then ask if his current line of work comes out
on top. This might even seem silly because although he must believe some
careers are worthless—otherwise the question about the value of his choice
would be senseless—he might also feel that many worthwhile kinds of work
are strictly incommensurable, including some that he might realistically pursue if he left his present job. Indeed, willing commits us to the idea of incommensurable values unless we assume that only one thing merits categorical
valuation. [Alternatives are incommensurable when it is neither true that one
is better than the other nor true that they are of equal value (Raz 1986:
321–66).] Nevertheless, if Michael's choice of career is responsible, in the
sense I have stipulated, he must still be ready to ask seriously if his career
really is worth the commitment he has given it. That question might naturally
be pursued by juxtaposing and comparing what could be accomplished or
enjoyed in other feasible pursuits with what is possible in his current choice.

8. Another confusion common among critics of autonomy is the assumption
that attachments whose beginnings were in something other than choice must
therefore be regarded as outer limits on the sphere of autonomy. Since such
attachments are often essential to our good, the value of autonomy must be
more circumscribed than its liberal exponents suppose. Thus Sandel seems to

think that autonomous religious affiliation has to do with its 'mode of acquisition' (Sandel 1996: 66). Similarly, Annette Baier decries the supposed failure of mainstream liberal political theory to recognize the significance of unchosen relations of the sort that obtain between family members or compatriots (A. Baier 1994: 29–30). But the fact that someone's religious, familial, or patriotic commitments might have unchosen beginnings does not reveal the importance of something alien to her autonomy. The connection between such commitments and autonomy depends on why one continues to be committed, not on the origins of commitment. To maintain a close relationship with aged parents out of love and gratitude is not to experience a good beyond autonomy just because the love and gratitude began before one was capable of autonomy.

9. The aspiration towards objectivity or truth that is relevant here might be expressed through the kind of ethical cognitivism that P. F. Strawson has expounded: 'One cannot read Pascal or Flaubert, Nietzsche or Goethe, Shakespeare or Tolstoy, without encountering these profound truths. It is certainly possible, in a cooly analytic frame of mind, to mock the whole idea of the profound truth; but we are guilty of mildly bad faith if we do. For in most of us the ethical imagination succumbs again and again to *these* pictures of man, and it is precisely as truth that we wish to characterize them while they hold us captive' (Strawson 1974: 28–9). Notice that it is crucial to the kind of experience Strawson here describes that 'the profound truth' is encountered not as a mere object of desire. Finding such 'truth' in Tolstoy, say, is not like discovering a new flavour of ice-cream one likes. The 'truth' is rather something that holds us captive, that elicits an assent at least phenomenologically the same as we experience in the shock of insight in less epistemologically controversial areas of our lives. What is intimated in such experiences is an understanding of value quite different from crass subjectivism. But since 'the profound truth' may point in directions at odds with the roles we currently occupy and the shared values of our community, it is an understanding of value which does not lend itself to a comfortably communitarian reading either.

# CHAPTER 4

1. The argument that follows pursues a line of thought suggested by Kymlicka: 'the key concepts Gilligan uses to distinguish the two ethics do not define genuine contrasts' (Kymlicka 1990: 276).
2. Kohlberg took Rawls's device of the original position as a version of the all-purpose procedure of moral choice that supposedly operates at the pinnacle of moral development—so-called 'Stage Six' moral reasoning (e.g. Kohlberg 1986: 527). The original position is an imaginative construction that asks us to choose distributive principles to regulate the basic structure of society without knowing what particular roles each of us will have in that society,

and hence without knowing how well or badly we would fare as a consequence of the principles we choose. But this is nothing like an all-purpose moral decision procedure; it is the basis of an argument with the limited purpose of identifying the most fundamental principles of justice, given that society is to be a fair scheme of cooperation between rational and reasonable citizens (Rawls 1971: 11–22; 1993: 22–8). At the highest stage of moral development as Rawls interprets it, agents do not take up residence in the original position whenever moral judgement has to be exercised. On the contrary, role obligations and special ties of affection continue to be relevant, and there is ample room for many virtues alongside justice (Rawls 1971: 485–90). That is precisely what we should expect since the moral life is far from being co-extensive with the special task of designing principles of justice for the basic structure. Attempting to reason and choose as an occupant of the original position would nearly always be to discard most of what is relevant to Rawlsian principled morality. Yet it should also be said that Rawls failed to indicate in *A Theory of Justice* how very different his own view of moral development was from Kohlberg's (Rawls 1971: 461 n). (Rawls's conception of moral development is discussed more fully in Section 26 below.)

3. Kohlberg did concede that the perspectives of different roles needed to be rendered 'rational' in moral musical-chairs so as to neutralize the effects of egoism and the like. But he seemed to think this was possible by dissolving role-reversal into some variation of choice in the original position (Kohlberg 1986: 527). For reasons given in note 2 above, that is preposterous.

4. A similar convergence between the values of justice and care is reached by Joan Tronto from a somewhat different route. Tronto worries about how an ethic of care may be extended beyond the limits of face to face relationships so as to address wider political issues: 'How are we to guarantee that people who are enmeshed in their daily rounds of care-giving and care-receiving, will be able to disengage themselves from their own local concerns and to embrace broader needs and concerns for care?' The answer that comes a bit later is this: 'care needs to be connected to a theory of justice and to be relentlessly democratic in its disposition' (Tronto 1993: 142, 171). The insights Tronto says accrue through making 'care a tool for political analysis' are sensible claims about inequality in America and the exclusion from power of traditionally subordinate groups (ibid. 172–80). But making rights a tool for political analysis will support claims that are much the same as these: rights to political equality for all—including the traditionally disempowered—are as familiar as any others on the agenda of liberal justice. If what Tronto offers is the beginnings of an ethic of care for politics, is only so in a sense that makes it equally an ethic of justice.

5. The process of moral development outlined in *A Theory of Justice* depends critically on the family being just, and therefore, the justice and stability of the well-ordered society is founded on the justice of the family (Rawls 1971: 490). But Rawls has been notably silent on the issue of what a just family would look like. His current project of constructing a liberalism of minimal

scope and generality might seem to rule out political criticism of family patterns so long as they cohere with the content of an overlapping consensus
(Exdell 1994). On the other hand, justice as reasonableness provides a telling
critical perspective on families in which domination corrupts the division of
domestic labour and gender identity is moulded so as to entrench the subordination of women. Susan Moller Okin has written trenchantly on both
Rawls's myopia regarding injustice in the family and the potency of his
theory as a basis for political criticism of the same institution (Okin 1987;
1989: 89–109; 1994).

6. The virtual invisibility of rights in Dewey's social philosophy is no doubt less
   sinister than it might seem to many contemporary Americans, whose image
   of progressive politics has been fixed by the civil rights movement of the
   1960s. That said, I think Alan Ryan lets Dewey off the hook too easily when
   he suggests that it is 'not indefensible' to recast rights in terms of Dewey's
   ideal notion of the common good (Ryan 1993: 95–6). That manoeuvre might
   work when the conception of the common good selected as the basis for
   rights is hospitable to dissent, eccentricity, and selective withdrawal from
   public life, as it is, for example, in J. S. Mill's liberal utopia. But Dewey's
   vision of democratic progress, with its emphasis on the sharing of interests,
   the overcoming of conflict in cooperative problem-solving, and its impatience with the values of privacy, is a far less plausible basis for a consequen-
   tialist theory of rights.

7. This point might seem to be corroborated by Bernard Williams's influential
   argument about the putative limits of impartiality. The argument hinges on a
   case in which a man saves his drowning wife rather than a stranger just
   because she is his wife. The man's action is presented as the reflex of a loyal
   and loving husband rather than the upshot of deliberation in which reasons
   of duty play a determining role (Williams 1981: 1–19). But the example cannot begin to establish any general conflict between the claims of impartial
   justice and loving attachment. The difficulty is that Williams describes a crisis so urgent that if love did not spontaneously motivate the man's decision,
   without any dithering about duty, his unfortunate wife might reasonably
   wonder afterwards whether he really loved her at all. However, if he were to
   save her the bother of taking the dog for a walk by doing it himself, and was
   motivated by something other than his undying love for her, she would not
   have reason to complain. Being motivated by something other than spontaneous love is in some situations evidence of the absence or weakness of love.
   But they are pretty odd situations. I discuss Williams's argument in Callan
   1994.

8. The importance of appreciating moral conduct that exceeds the requirements
   of duty against the background of our commitment to justice has been brilliantly explored in Tomasi 1991.

9. A revealing example is found in the preface to Thomas Nagel's *Mortal
   Questions*: 'Some of these essays were written while the United States was
   engaged in a criminal war, criminally conducted. . . . Citizenship is a surpris-

ingly strong bond, even for those of us whose patriotic feelings are weak. We read the newspapers every day with rage and horror, and it was different than reading about the crimes of another country' (Nagel 1979: p. xii). The abuse of the language of patriotism to rationalize 'a criminal war, criminally conducted' may explain why Nagel wants to account for his righteous rage and horror during the Vietnam war in terms of 'citizenship' rather than 'patriotic feeling'. Yet the citizenship he appeals to has to be more than mere legal status. Only emotional identification with the American polity—that is, patriotism—could plausibly explain why his country's participation in an unjust war would trigger an outrage more intense than the crimes of other nations.

Nagel's example is revealing for another reason. A common libel against patriotism is that it must come at the price of a diminished concern for the rights of those who are not compatriots. But what Nagel's patriotism explains is precisely the intensity of his indignation regarding injustices done to Vietnamese, Laotians, and Cambodians by his fellow Americans. The example is not eccentric. Nagel's reaction is precisely what we should expect when the political community that elicits patriotic love is a community one wants deeply to be just. Since grave moral crimes against outsiders is as much a betrayal of justice as comparable crimes against insiders, both should be expected to evoke patriotic rage and horror.

10. Webber's position bears obvious affinities to arguments advanced by Taylor 1993: 155–86; and Kymlicka 1995*a*: 187–91.

11. One assumption that is very likely wrong is that moral understanding among children is confined to the dictates of authority and then, somewhat later, to conventionally defined roles. The ability to grasp moral reasons as irreducible to authority and convention is thought to come only much later. That assumption reflected the orthodoxy in developmental psychology at the time *A Theory of Justice* was written. The evidence now appears to suggest that even young children are capable of distinguishing between what is morally wrong on the one hand and what merely defies authority or breaches convention on the other. See Turiel, Killen, and Helwig 1987; and Nucci 1989*a*.

12. I prefer to focus on the idea of patriotism rather than nationality or nationalism for two reasons. I want to underscore the possibility of an overarching patriotic loyalty in multinational states. (That is a common preoccupation among desperate Canadian federalists!) The language of patriotism also has the advantage of stressing a shared civic life as the focus of particularistic attachment rather than common ethnicity, religion, or the like. My thoughts on that issue have been influenced by Maurizio Viroli's recent attempt to disentangle the ideal of patriotism from the history of nationalism (Viroli 1995). But nothing much rides on these points. Liberal-minded exponents of nationalism or nationality espouse conceptions of political community that are no great distance from mine (Tamir 1993; Miller 1995*b*). My argument about the way patriotic attachment can and should be melded with the virtue of justice certainly applies to civic virtue in nation states, and the argument

would still hold good if stable multinational states proved to be very rare exceptions.

13. I do not rule out the possibility that at the most fundamental level of moral justification special obligations to compatriots might hold. That could be true given what David Miller calls 'ethical particularism', according to which 'agents are . . . encumbered with a variety of ties and commitments to other agents, or to groups or collectivities, and they [rightly] begin their ethical reasoning from those commitments' (Miller 1995*b*: 50). If particularism were true, and compatriots constituted one of the relevant 'groups or collectivities', Weinstock's distinction between genuine moral reasons and phoney incentives could not be used to discredit the appeal to patriotic attachment because that attachment would be a source of moral reasons as basic as any other. But Weinstock's argument fails even if we accept the universalist assumptions that might seem more supportive of his position. On the universalist picture of morality, relational facts—the fact, say, that my life is linked to particular others by virtue of common Canadian citizenship—carry no weight at the most abstract level of moral justification (Miller 1995*b*: 50). Although Rawls's recent work leans toward particularism, his conception of morality in *A Theory of Justice* is clearly universalist. The basic moral consideration that binds the individual citizen to the institutional structures of the well-ordered society is the natural duty to support just institutions (Rawls 1971: 115). Jeremy Waldron has argued, successfully in my view, that this duty can explain why citizens of just societies have special obligations with regard to their own societies that they do not have to others. He concedes that 'there may be other elements of patriotic affect and allegiance that this account does not capture' (Waldron 1993*a*: 19). True enough. But a universalist account of political obligation need not capture everything that rightly motivates our political conduct. If elements of 'patriotic affect and allegiance' are needed to ensure that justice is done, these become morally relevant motives and their inculcation becomes a necessary part of political education, even if they do not figure in the basic justification of our special obligations.

## CHAPTER 5

1. I do not suggest that Yeats's attitude to the insurrection in particular and Irish nationalism in general was a model of moral acuity. His attitude contained a large element of self-serving illusion. See Foster 1993: 262-80.

2. There is a chilling example of this in Milan Kundera's great novel, *The Book of Laughter and Forgetting*. Kundera describes a scene in which young Czechs living under Communist rule dance in the streets of Prague the day after the execution of a politician and an artist on trumped up charges: 'And knowing full well that the day before in their fair city one woman and one surrealist had been hanged by the neck, the young Czechs went on dancing

and dancing, and they danced all the more frantically because their dance was the manifestation of their innocence, the purity that shone forth so brilliantly against the black villainy of the two public enemies who had betrayed the people and its hopes' (Kundera 1981: 66).

3. For example, Spike Lee's recent movie, *Malcolm X* is as crass a specimen of political sentimentality as any mawkish evocation of John Kennedy's Camelot, notwithstanding the film's chic radicalism. Lee's leftish conservatism is strikingly evident at the end of the film when a sequence of children, at the instigation of their teacher, announce 'I am Malcolm X', as if their destiny were to make themselves replicas of the film's protagonist. (Imagine how risible a movie would be that ended with children proclaiming 'I am Barry Goldwater'. In some cultural settings the sentimentality of the left is easier to get away with than that of the right.)

4. One way of understanding Galston is that he is sceptical not about the ability or desire of ordinary people to think deeply about politics but only about their ability or desire to think philosophically about politics. Indeed, his juxtaposition of philosopical and civic education might appear strongly to support that reading. But if philosophical political thought is all that is at issue, its alleged unsuitability for most people does not begin to warrant sentimental civic education. The fact that most people are likely to find the outer reaches of social contract theory uninteresting or incomprehensible—a fact I am very willing to grant—is not even relevant to the justification of a civic education that instils a sense of political obligation through reverence for a pantheon of political heroes. So whether we read Galston's worries about the limited appeal of reason in either a technically philosophical or in some broader sense, this does not affect the objections I have levelled against his argument.

5. The possibility of a sense of the past that combines receptiveness to value with a judicious critical distance is pursued in a rather different context by Margret Buchmann (1993). I am happy to acknowledge a debt to Buchmann's argument.

6. Notice I do not say that historical distance means we cannot pass moral judgement on others. The point is that the judgement must be constrained by an understanding of the cultural horizon within which their choices and actions took place. To ignore that horizon and insist on the ahistorical authority of our own, is about as arrogant and idiotic as criticizing Velázquez for failing to anticipate the stylistic innovations of Picasso.

7. Afrocentrism of this variety should be distinguished from its educational use as what Benjamin Barber calls a 'developmental strategy' (Barber 1992: 134–6). As a developmental strategy, Afrocentric education would be intended to give African-American children the cultural self-confidence to participate effectively in the public life of a liberal democracy. Furthermore, the Afrocentrism I criticize must also be contrasted with the sensible thesis that the African-American story in North America should be presented in schools to all students, regardless of race, in ways that give it due salience and

accurately depict 'the interdependence of experience among people' (Olneck 1993: 250).

8. The root of the trouble here is MacIntyre's assumption that liberal political values cannot be integral to communities and traditions with which people profoundly identify. For criticism of MacIntyre on that point, see Barry 1989; Slattery 1991.

## CHAPTER 6

1. Burtt argues that exposure to diversity is an inevitable fact of life in modern society, even for religious groups who seek to protect themselves from much of its influence. 'Our high-tech, consumer-oriented society provides plenty of opportunity for exposure to competing lifestyles, especially for those who are attempting to construct lives that depart significantly from the mainstream. Apostolic Lutherans can forbid their children to watch television, but they cannot shutter the windows of the local toy store with its tempting display of electronic games. Christian fundamentalists can send their children to schools that forbid dates and dancing but they cannot keep them from hearing about the high school prom from the girl next door' (Burtt 1996: 426). Yet the relevant question is not whether children will inevitably endure some exposure to 'competing lifestyles' but whether, without schooling as the great sphere, they are likely to arrive at a satisfactory understanding of the alternatives to the way of life their parents would choose for them. I do not suppose that anyone thinks children who grow up in a thoroughly secular way of life achieve a sufficient understanding of the religious alternatives simply because the family car occasionally speeds by buildings with crosses on top or they sometimes hear from the children next door about worship in their family.

2. The problems of what morally entitles one to become a parent in the first place and what conditions justify depriving people of that role are not my main interest here. Recent attempts by gays and lesbians to adopt children, conflict in the courts between biological and adoptive parents, as well as efforts by some children legally to dissolve their relationship with feckless parents, all attest to the importance of questions about the allocation and withdrawal of primary responsibilities in child-rearing. For valuable discussions of some of the relevant questions see Schrag 1973; Kymlicka 1991; Simmons 1992: 180–4; Matthews 1994: 68–80.

3. A society in which the role of parent does not exist at all is conceivable, as Plato demonstrated in one of the more infamous passages of the *Republic* (Plato 1955 edn: 212–24). Whether or not there ever has been such a society and whether child-rearing practices without parents could adequately serve the interests of both adults and children is another matter. Cross-cultural studies of the family have shown that the role of parent is far more susceptible to cultural variation than we might sometimes suppose. But they do not show that it is merely another disposable convention of human societies. For

an interesting account of the cultural variability of parents' roles, see Collier, Rosaldo, and Yanagisako 1992.

4. By appealing to equality here I do not take sides in contemporary controversies about the relationship between equality and justice. The appeal is rather to a purely negative egalitarian idea that divides the moral universe of modernity from the world it succeeded: the idea that no one legitimately rules over others for his own ends (Galston 1991*b*: 242–3). Our problem is to interpret the rights of parents in education in a way that remains consistent with the abstract egalitarian basis of rights discourse.

5. The tendency to confound patriarchal with divine authority is a very common theme in the historiography of evangelical child-rearing. See Sangster 1963: 78–81; Greven 1977: 21–61.

6. The point can be expressed in Rawlsian terms, which is not to say that they are the terms Rawls would himself use: In a well-ordered society, children are entitled to an education that includes the great sphere because anything less risks denying them essential conditions for the adequate development of the moral powers over a complete life.

7. My argument here converges with one Jeremy Waldron has advanced about the foundational role of liberty in rights discourse: 'What I have taken as the underlying idea of rights—an individual leading her life on her own terms—is not simply the idea of an individual's *being alive*. It is of a life's being led, and that connotes agency, choice and a sense of individual responsibility' (Waldron 1993*c*: 582–3). Ethical servility is a drastic dilution of individual responsibility for the life one leads, even if individuals might often be faulted to some degree for failing to overcome the effects of child-rearing that instilled the vice in them. Therefore, ethical servility would seem to be amenable to the generic analysis of servility that Hill offers because the ethically servile individual cannot fully appreciate or even exercise the kind of liberty which, given Waldron's claim, the very idea of rights engages at its deepest level.

8. Burtt is critical of liberal philosophers who have condemned conservative religious upbringing on the assumption that 'to reason from the basis of God's word as reflected in Scripture is somehow to abandon the exercise of critical rationality' (Burtt 1996: 416). That is fair comment. But even if we concede that a vigorous critical rationality is compatible with acceptance of Scriptural authority, that concession does not suffice to justify an education that would seek to expunge, so far as possible, all influences that conflict with what parents specify as the one correct interpretation of Scripture. Critical thought must always proceed within a context of some taken-for-granted assumptions. But that does not entitle us to infer that the context can never be so severely circumscribed in child-rearing that real criticism is effectively and more or less permanently pre-empted on many matters that children should be encouraged to think critically about. The strongest reason to reject the parents' demands in *Mozert* is precisely that they argued as if that preemption were what they wanted and were entitled to receive.

9. The kind of minimal tolerance required under a constitutional consensus, for example, would depend at least on some rudimentary understanding of ways of life different from one's own because to appreciate the legitimacy of the claims to forbearance that others might make, one must to some degree be able to reappraise one's own basic values in the light of theirs. This is the sort of connection between tolerance and autonomy that David Johnston seems to have in mind (Johnston 1994: 97). See my discussion in Section 16.

10. The main difficulty is that charges of educational bias can rarely be vindicated simply by looking at texts in isolation from the context within which they are taught. For example, a required history text that systematically slighted the role of religious belief in shaping European or American history will justly be regarded as biased. But a good teacher might correct the bias in the way the text is used in the classroom. Compensating for the omissions and par-tialities of texts is a routine aspect of good teaching everywhere. The available facts do not show that the controversial reading programme in *Mozert* was or was not taught in a manner systematically biased against Protestant Christianity. If students were permitted and encouraged to draw on their own beliefs in interpreting the reading material, and the religious views they expressed were treated with due respect, then the charge of bias would be weak.

11. Vitz argues that 'every organization must have a particular philosophy, a set of values, a common vision, in order to function'. This means that whatever the common vision that a system of schooling is based on, it will be biased against those who reject the vision (Vitz 1986: 91). This is confused. Bias pre-supposes a departure from some standard of judgement that should be impar-tially applied. Presumably even Vitz would agree that some such standards are properly applicable in the rearing of children. If the state chose to act against parents who sexually abused their children, it would not be 'biased' against the parents, given any minimally acceptable standard of competence in child-rearing. I suspect that Vitz's underlying assumption is that there are no specif-ically educational standards to which anyone could rightly appeal against the wishes of parents. But that is a substantive, and outlandish moral claim that cannot be justified by playing fast and loose with the meaning of 'bias'.

# CHAPTER 7

1. Artistic and scientific interests do not ordinarily count as cleavages. A sec-ondary school with an outstanding programme in the fine arts but not in the sciences and another that excelled in the sciences but not in the fine arts might equally be common schools in my sense even though neither would be equally accommodating to all students, irrespective of artistic or scientific aptitude. The possibility of common schools that might vary greatly in their distinctive curricula, pedagogical philosophy, or the like is important. See Section 55 below.

2. The empirical research on school choice grows apace. But responsible scholars emphasize how little we yet know that can be confidently generalized about voucher schemes and other ways of bolstering diversity of educational provision: 'Unfortunately, given the importance of the topic, the evidence in the US, UK and Australia is scanty . . . often based on small samples over short periods of time, and especially times of change when the effects of reform may be far from stable; and it is often highly contextualised, with little justification for transposing either the evidence or the policy implications from the context of origin to other situations' (Hargreaves 1996: 132; see also Fuller, Elmore and Orfield 1996*a*: 18). There is troubling evidence that increasing the scope for choice might accelerate the separation of students by race, class, and culture (Elmore and Fuller 1996: 189–93). But it is much too early to say with assurance that all feasible measures for enlarging choice will have that consequence. A heartening feature of some recent scholarship has been the development of arguments about how policies to provide school choice might be constructed to serve democratic and egalitarian rather than merely libertarian ends (Brighouse 1994; Gintis 1995). Too often the opposition to school choice has been an intransigent defence of public schools that are simply appalling, given the ideal of common schooling. Francis Schrag's animadversions on that topic are required reading (Schrag 1995: 97).

3. A common and fallacious objection to state-sponsored schooling that adopts any transformative educational aim is pressed by Brenda Almond. She says that the state should not be in the business of funding the myriad educational practices that parents are morally entitled to choose as alternatives to a common, secular system of education. That is so because state funding for alternatives would require 'the levying of money from the general tax-payer to support beliefs which may conflict with that person's own beliefs, values or ideological commitments' (Almond 1991: 201). But if taxation is unjust whenever it is used to support educational purposes to which the taxpayer has religious or anti-religious objections, then state support for secular common schools is also unjust, given the objections that religious believers will naturally have to educational practices cut adrift from faith. A consistent application of the principle underlying Almond's argument would seem to undermine public support for *any* schools under pluralism because none could command the conscientious approval of all who are taxed. That is not an outcome Almond would welcome nor would it be acceptable to any but the most militant libertarians. Perhaps Almond's considered view is that state sponsorship for common schools is uniquely justified because only these are confined to educational aims that (almost?) all citizens would accept. But this is arbitrary because an objection to a particular kind of school on the basis of educational aims it excludes is not inherently less worthy of consideration than an objection based on educational aims it includes.

4. A variation on Heaney's dictum might be 'Say a little about everyone, and make sure it's nice'. Versions of multicultural education that throw together insipid bits and pieces of many cultures are a case in point. See David

Cooper's swingeing critique of this kind of multicultural education (Cooper 1986).

5. If the minimalist conception were the only or the best one, the case against common schooling would be overwhelming. Much of the current argument against common schooling and for a radical diversification of educational provision is based on the assumption that the minimalist conception is the only one (e.g. McConnell 1991; M. Holmes 1992, 1993).

6. Since no dramatic developmental shifts in cognition distinguish the thought of adolescents and adults, no obvious psychological grounds are available for the view that the dialogical task is rightly deferred until adulthood: 'Stage theorists generally view the last major stage transitions as beginning no later than age 11 or 12 and see no general, qualitative difference between the typical adolescent and the typical adult. . . . Theorists dubious of developmental stages question whether even younger children are qualitatively different from adults. . . . Theorists postulating development beyond adolescence generally focus on relatively abstruse abilities that remain largely beyond the normal functioning of most adults' (Moshman 1989: 89–90).

7. To say this is not to endorse a Rousseauean faith in the natural goodness of children but only to affirm what sober empirical research has shown: 'During infancy, children discover by chance that other infants share an interest in toys and that joint play with the same toy is more fun and interesting than solitary play. . . . In early childhood, acts of sharing are irregular, erratic, and usually more bound to the needs of the self than those of others. Still, such acts are performed, and often voluntarily because they are themselves a source of fun for the child' (Damon 1988: 32–3). Damon goes on to point out that the satisfaction of sharing for young children can be genuinely altruistic to the extent that it derives from the empathic pleasures of relationsip with another.

8. My argument here converges with Terry McLaughlin's subtle defence of separate schooling within a liberal democratic framework, although he does not make use of my distinction between radical and moderate separatist arguments (McLaughlin 1992*b*).

9. We also need to ask if what appears to be a conflict of rights might really stem from a misinterpretation of the scope of one or other of the apparently conflicting rights. What some might interpret as a conflict between parents' rights to educational choice and the child's rights to an education for sovereignty is a bogus moral conflict, given the argument of Chapter 6. The conflict is bogus because the parental option of vetoing an education that countervails servility is not within the scope of anyone's rights to begin with. This is an example of what Waldron calls an 'internalist' reading of a putative moral conflict in that it offers a resolution by showing how certain moral considerations are internally related to each other—say, as reasons within a discourse that presupposes the evil of both patriarchy and its child-centred inversion—in such a way that apparent moral conflict dissolves on reflection. But Waldron is correct to insist that not all apparent conflicts of rights can be

tidily disposed of through internalist readings. In many instances we will have no alternative but to make comparative judgements about the weight or importance of different interests or harms (Waldron 1989: 516–19).

10. My schematic tale of the New Agers makes explicit what is centrally relevant to the argument for state support for Catholic schools in the USA. The case that Bryk, Lee, and Holland make for support wisely relies on considerations of the common good rather than parental rights (Bryk, Lee, and Holland 1993: 341–3). But part of the political difficulty here is that it may not be constitutionally possible to offer sponsorship save though a voucher scheme of some sort (McConnell 1991). This in turn might lead to a proliferation of private schools which would be less than impressive by the criteria of common education. The striking effectiveness of Catholic schools for disadvantaged youth are not characteristic of American private schools in general (Coleman and Hoffer 1987: 147–8). 'In our view, it is not simply a matter of private versus public, political-bureaucractic versus market mechanisms, or school-based accountability versus centralized control. Rather, it is critical also to consider the actual values operative in each school context, how these values are manifest in the school's organizational structure and functions and the consequences that emerge as a result' (Lee, Bryk, and J. B. Smith 1993: 230–1). More schools that are effective from *that* perspective might or might not be the long-term consequence of what is probably the only constitutionally feasible way of extending sponsorship to American Catholic schools.

11. A notable case in point is the conflict about compulsory schooling that intermittently flared between the government of British Columbia and the Doukhobors, a separatist Christian community, earlier this century. In 1932 and again in 1955 the conflict resulted in the imprisonment of parents who refused to send their children to school. Their children were sent to orphanages and industrial schools. Some of those who were taken from their parents in the 1930s reappeared among the more violence-prone members of the sect in the following decade. So much for the benefits of coercive enlightenment. There is good reason to believe almost all the Doukhobors would have accepted public schooling if some modest accommodation to their beliefs had been made in the public schools. For an excellent account, see Janzen 1990: 116–41.

12. There is also ample room for cautious pessimism about the educational viability of common schools. Cogent arguments in support of that attitude are offered by Strike (1991) and McLaughlin (1995).

## CHAPTER 8

1. The relevant controversies revolve around the relationship between moral and other considerations in practical reason (e.g. cf. Scheffler 1992; Brink 1994).

2. I borrow the term 'moral distress' from Jeremy Waldron (Waldron 1993*d*).

The only difference between Waldron's usage and mine is that I use 'moral distress' more expansively to refer to self-regarding as well as other-regarding emotion.

3. Noddings does not say that ordinary conversation is the only kind of morally educational dialogue. She acknowledges that the 'argumentative style' has some legitimate place in our lives, and that 'public debate' may require a combination of analytic and interpersonal reasoning (Noddings 1991: 163–4). But the concession to other kinds of dialogue here is insufficient in the light of the critique I offer. If what I say is correct, then ordinary conversation is not the prime vehicle of moral dialogue to be supplemented with something else in order to become sufficient for the purposes of moral education and public reason. The point is rather that morally educational dialogue must take a different form than the one Noddings specifies.

4. One way around this impasse would be to construe our relationship to the other in caring dialogue more widely than I have considered so far. On a wider interpretation, it is not the interlocutor who should be the exclusive focus of our attention and solicitude but rather all to whom we have a responsibility to care and whose interests might be affected by the conclusion we reach. Yet once this more inclusive view is taken, the proposal that we subordinate moral truth to the value of caring relationship(s) becomes explicitly incoherent. The purpose of dialogue is now to help us discern the truth about how we should live, given our responsibility to care for many who have no voice within the charmed circle of interlocutors with whom we converse. And in seeking that truth, we must acknowledge the obvious fact that giving due regard to the interests of outsiders will not necessarily be something that we and our interlocutors can agree on at all, much less agree on with warmth and laughter or sympathy and support.

5. The argument of *On Liberty* is explicitly framed to apply only to individuals in 'the maturity of their faculties' (Mill 1976 edn.: 13). But if it were right to construe public deliberation as Mill did, then it would also be right to ensure that such deliberation is anticipated within at least the latter stages of the educational process, when the virtues and abilities that govern competent participation in public deliberation are properly instilled and practised. For that reason, *On Liberty* can be reasonably understood as offering an implicit theory of the dialogical task of common education.

6. The emphasis on forbearance and moderation within the virtue of reasonableness might suggest to some a conception of politico-moral dialogue that is smugly conservative, emotionally sanitized, and hostile to the possible insight of the iconoclast. Some liberal conceptions of dialogue, including Rawls's, have been criticized on these grounds, with varying degrees of cogency (cf. Benhabib 1989; Burbules 1993: 29–30; Mouffe 1994). But the criticism would be wide of the mark if directed at the conception I am advocating. Serious critical commitment to the virtue of reasonableness may in some circumstances make the forceful expression of moral distress the only fitting response to moral conflict, even in the case of a teacher. Moreover,

although reasonableness as an ideal implies an aspiration towards political consensus, that must be a consensus we could reasonably affirm; and therefore, the relevant aspiration is inconsistent with acquiescence in any consensus that could only be unreasonably endorsed.

7. An account of the 'vices of unreason' is parasitic on a theory of intellectual or 'epistemic' virtue. I rely here on Gerald Gaus (1994: 338–9). For other valuable accounts, see Montmarquet 1987; Burbules 1991; N. Cooper 1994. I should stress that the vices of unreason are to be deplored in the specific context of collective deliberation about political morality. It does not follow that all lives which manifest the vices to some degree in other spheres are to be dismissed as 'irrational' (Callan 1995: 322–4). Moreover, even in the context of public reason, the corresponding virtues must be interpreted so as to contrast with what Aristotle called vices of 'excess' as well as deficiency. For example, an open-ended and obsessive desire to gather evidence would paralyse the decision-making that gives deliberation its point since additional evidence can always be sought. I focus on the vices of deficiency only because their subversive influence in collective deliberation is far more familiar.

8. The requirement of interpretive charity does not take us back to Noddings's interpersonal reasoning, even though it takes the rough edges off Millian ethical confrontation: 'Intellectual charity should not be confused with tactfulness, politeness, or mildness. Charity requires giving our opponent the benefit of the doubt; it does not mean downplaying his real and specific errors. Intellectual charity does not foreclose sharp and pointed dissent. It does not block vigorous and robust argument. We do not have to be nice to one another' (Fullinwider 1993: 109) I would add that *teaching* intellectual charity will often require more than a little tact, politeness, and even a good deal of niceness. But Fullinwider is right that intellectual charity itself does not strictly require these and that confusing interpretive charity with an intellectually evasive niceness is a bad mistake.

9. Rawls does recognize the many forms of 'non-public' reason in the background culture of liberal politics in so far as these support public reason. But he seems to assume that the many forms of practical reason might function as more or less discrete spheres of engagement without damage to our integrity (Rawls 1993: 212–54). The argument of Chapter 2 is in part an attempt to undermine that assumption.

# BIBLIOGRAPHY

ACKERMAN, B. A. (1980), *Social Justice in the Liberal State* (New Haven).

—— (1989), 'Why Dialogue?', *Journal of Philosophy*, 86: 5–22.

ADAMS, R. M. (1986), 'The Problem of Total Devotion', in Audi and Wainwright (1986), 169–94.

—— (1987), *The Virtue of Faith and Other Essays in Philosophical Theology* (New York).

—— (1993), 'Religious Ethics in a Pluralistic Society', in Outka and Reeder (1993), 93–113.

—— (1995), 'Moral Faith', *Journal of Philosophy*, 92: 75–95.

AIKEN, W., and LAFOLLETTE, H. (1980) (eds.), *Whose Child? Children's Rights, Parental Authority and State Power* (Totowa, NJ).

ALMOND, B. (1991), 'Education and Liberty: Public Provision and Private Choice', *Journal of Philosophy of Education,* 25: 193–202.

ARISTOTLE (1980 edn.), *The Nicomachean Ethics*, trans. with introd. by D. Ross, revised by J. L. Ackrill and J. O. Urmson (Oxford).

ASANTE, M. K. (1980), *Afrocentricity: The Theory of Social Change* (Buffalo, NY).

—— (1991), 'The Afrocentric Idea of Education', *Journal of Negro Education*, 60: 170–80.

AUDI, R., and WAINWRIGHT, W. J. (1986) (eds.), *Rationality, Religious Belief, and Moral Commitment* (Ithaca, NY).

BAIER, A. C. (1994), *Moral Prejudices: Essays on Ethics* (Cambridge, Mass.).

BAIER, K. (1989), 'Justice and the Aims of Political Philosophy', *Ethics*, 99: 771–90.

BARBER, B. R. (1992), *An Aristocracy of Everyone: The Politics of Education and the Future of America* (New York).

—— (1995), *Jihad vs. McWorld* (New York).

BARRY, B. (1989), 'The Light That Failed', *Ethics*, 100: 160–9.

—— (1990), 'Social Criticism and Political Philosophy', *Philosophy and Public Affairs*, 19: 360–73.

—— (1995), *Justice as Impartiality* (Oxford).

BECKER, L. C. (1992), 'Good Lives: Prolegomena', *Social Philosophy and Policy*, 9: 15–37.

BEINER, R. (1995) (ed.), *Theorizing Citizenship* (Albany, NY).

BELL, D. (1993), *Communitarianism and its Critics* (Oxford).

BELL, V., and LERNER, L. (1988) (eds.), *On Modern Poetry: Essays Presented to Donald Davie* (Nashville).

BELLAH, R., TIPTON, S., SWIDLER, A., and SULLIVAN, W. (1985), *Habits of the Heart: Individualism and Commitment in American Life* (New York).

BENHABIB, S. (1987), 'The Generalized and the Concrete Other: The

Kohlberg–Gilligan Controversy and Moral Theory', in Kittay and Meyers (1987), 154–77.

—— (1989), 'Liberal Dialogue Versus a Critical Theory of Discursive Legitimation', in Rosenblum (1989), 143–56.

BENNETT, W. J., and DELATTRE, E. J. (1979), 'A Moral Education: Some Thought on How Best to Achieve It', *American Educator*, 3: 6–9.

BERLIN, I. (1969), *Four Essays on Liberty* (Oxford).

BILGRAMI, A. (1992), 'What is a Muslim? Fundamental Commitment and Cultural Identity', *Critical Inquiry*, 18: 821–42.

BIRD, C. (1996), 'Mutual Respect and Neutral Justification', *Ethics*, 107: 62–96.

BLUSTEIN, J. (1991), *Care and Commitment: Taking the Personal Point of View* (New York).

BODNAR, J. E. (1992), *Remaking America: Public Memory, Commemoration and Patriotism in Twentieth Century America* (Princeton).

BORRIS, R., with JILES, PAULETTE (1989), 'At a Loss for Words', in Fetherling (1989), 131–42.

BRIGHOUSE, H. (1994), 'The Egalitarian Virtues of Educational Vouchers', *Journal of Philosophy of Education*, 28: 211–19.

BRINK, D. O. (1994), 'A Reasonable Morality', *Ethics*, 104: 593–619.

BROOK, R. (1987), 'Justice and the Golden Rule: A Commentary on Some Recent Work of Lawrence Kohlberg', *Ethics*, 97: 363–73.

BROWN, P. (1967), *Augustine of Hippo* (London).

BRYK, D., LEE, V. E., and HOLLAND, P. B. (1993), *Catholic Schools and the Common Good* (Cambridge, Mass.).

BUCHMANN, M. (1993), 'Figuring in the Past: Thinking about Teacher Memories', in Buchmann and Floden (1993), 174–92.

—— and FLODEN, R. (1991) (eds.), *Philosophy of Education 1991* (Normal, Ill.).

—— and —— (1993), *Detachment and Concern* (New York).

BURBULES, N. (1991), 'Two Perspectives on Reason as an Educational Aim: The Virtues of Reasonableness', in Buchmann and Floden (1991), 215–24.

—— (1993), *Dialogue in Teaching* (New York).

—— and RICE, S. (1991), 'Dialogue across Differences', *Harvard Educational Review*, 61: 393–416.

BURTT, S. (1993), 'The Politics of Virtue Today', *American Political Science Review*, 87: 360–8.

—— (1994), 'Religious Parents, Secular Schools: A Liberal Defense of an Illiberal Education', *Review of Politics*, 56: 51–70.

—— (1996), 'In Defense of *Yoder*: Parental Authority and the Public Schools', in Shapiro and Hardin (1996), 412–37.

CALHOUN, C. (1988), 'Justice, Care, Gender Bias', *Journal of Philosophy*, 85: 451–63.

—— (1995), 'Standing for Something', *Journal of Philosophy*, 92: 235–60.

CALLAN, E. (1988), 'The Moral Status of Pity', *Canadian Journal of Philosophy*, 18: 1–12.

—— (1993), 'Patience and Courage', *Philosophy*, 68: 523–39.

CALLAN, E. (1994), 'Impartiality and Virtue', *Journal of Value Inquiry*, 28: 401–14.
—— (1995), 'Rejoinder: Pluralism and Moral Polarization', *Canadian Journal of Education*, 20: 315–32.
CARENS, J. H. (1995) (ed.), *Is Quebec Nationalism Just? Perspectives from Anglophone Canada* (Montreal).
CARTER, R. E. (1984), *Dimensions of Moral Education* (Toronto).
CHAPMAN, J. W., and SHAPIRO, I. (1993) (eds.), *Nomos XXV: Democratic Community* (New York).
COHEN, J. (1993), 'Moral Pluralism and Political Consensus', in Copp, Hampton, and Roemer (1993), 270–91.
COLEMAN, J. (1991), 'Changes in the Family and Implications for the Common School', *University of Chicago Legal Forum*, 1991: 153–70.
—— and HOFFER, T. (1987), *Public and Private High Schools: The Impact of Communities* (New York).
COLLIER, J., ROSALDO, M. Z., YANAGISAKO, S.(1992), 'Is there a Family? New Anthropological Perspectives', in Thorn and Yalom (1992), 31–48.
COLLINS, R. E. (1973 edn.) (ed.), *Theodore Parker: A Critical Essay and a Collection of His Writings* (Metuchen, NJ).
COOPER, D. E. (1986) (ed.), *Education, Values and Mind: Essays for R. S. Peters* (London).
—— (1987), 'Multicultural Education', in North (1987), 135–51.
COOPER, N. (1994), 'The Intellectual Virtues', *Philosophy*, 69: 459–69.
COPP, D., HAMPTON, J., and ROEMER, J. E. (1993) (eds.), *The Idea of Democracy* (Cambridge).
CRITTENDEN, B. (1988), *Parents, the State and the Right to Educate* (Melbourne).
CUBBERLEY, E. (1909), *Changing Conceptions of Education* (Boston).
CUMMING, L. (1995), 'With a Lick and a Stamp', *Manchester Guardian Weekly*, 152 (5): 28.
DAMON, W. (1988), *The Moral Child: Nurturing Children's Natural Moral Growth* (New York).
DAN-COHEN, M. (1992), 'Conceptions of Choice and Conceptions of Autonomy', *Ethics*, 102: 221–43.
DARLING-HAMMOND, L. (1993) (ed.), *Review of Research in Education 1993* (Washington, DC).
—— and ANCESS, J. (1996), 'Democracy and Access to Education', in Soder (1996), 151–81.
DENT, G. W. (1988), 'Religious Children, Secular Schools', *Southern California Law Review*, 61: 864–941.
DEWEY, J. (1897/1972), 'My Pedagogic Creed', in Dewey (1972), 84–95.
—— (1916), *Democracy and Education: An Introduction to the Philosophy of Education* (New York).
—— (1932), *A Common Faith* (New Haven).
—— (1972), *The Early Works of John Dewey*, v. *Early Essays*, ed. J. Boydston (Carbondale, Ill.).
DILLON, R. S. (1995) (ed.), *Dignity, Character, and Self-Respect* (New York).

DOPPELT, G. (1989), 'Is Rawls's Kantian Liberalism Coherent and Defensible?', *Ethics*, 99: 815–51.

DWORKIN, G. (1988), *The Theory and Practice of Autonomy* (Cambridge).

DWORKIN, R. (1977), *Taking Rights Seriously* (Cambridge, Mass.).

—— (1989), 'Liberal Community', *California Law Review*, 77: 479–504.

—— (1990), 'Foundations of Liberal Equality', in Petersen (1990), 3–119.

ELLSWORTH, E. (1989), 'Why Doesn't This Feel Empowering?', *Harvard Educational Review*, 59: 291–324.

ELMORE, R. F., and FULLER, B. (1996), 'Empirical Research on Educational Choice: What Are the Implications for Policy-Makers?', in Fuller, Elmore, and Orfield (1996*b*), 187–201.

EXDELL, J. (1994), 'Feminism, Fundamentalism, and Liberal Legitimacy', *Canadian Journal of Philosophy*, 24: 441–64.

FEINBERG, J. (1980), 'The Child's Right to an Open Future', in Aiken and LaFollette (1980), 124–53.

—— (1986), *Harm to Self* (New York).

—— (1990), *Harmless Wrongdoing* (New York).

FETHERLING, D. (1989) (ed.), *Best Canadian Essays 1989* (Saskatoon, Sask.).

FINE, M. (1993), ' "You can't just say that the only ones who can speak are those who agree with your position": Political Discourse in the Classroom', *Harvard Educational Review*, 63: 412–33.

—— (1995), *Habits of Mind: Struggling over Values in America's Classrooms* (San Francisco).

FISHKIN, J. (1992), *The Dialogue of Justice: Toward a Self-Reflective Society* (New Haven).

FLANAGAN, O. (1991), *Varieties of Moral Personality: Ethics and Psychological Realism* (Cambridge, Mass.).

FLATHMAN, R. E. (1996), 'Liberal Versus Civic, Republican, Democratic, and Other Vocational Educations: Liberalism and Institutionalised Education', *Political Theory*, 24: 4–32.

FOOT, P. (1978), *Virtues and Vices* (Berkeley).

FOSTER, R. F. (1993), *Paddy & Mr Punch: Connections in Irish and English History* (London).

FOUCAULT, M. (1965), *Madness and Civilization*, trans. by Richard Howard (New York).

FRANKFURT, H. (1988), *The Importance of What We Care About: Philosophical Essays* (Cambridge).

FRANKLIN, J. H. (1993), *The Color Line: Legacy for the Twenty-First Century* (Columbia, Mo.).

FROTHINGHAM, O. B. (1874), *Theodore Parker: A Biography* (Boston).

FULLER, B., ELMORE, R. F., with ORFIELD, G. (1996*a*), 'Policy-Making in the Dark: Illuminating the School Choice Debate', in Fuller, Elmore, and Orfield (1996*b*), 1–21.

—— —— —— (1996*b*) (eds.), *Who Chooses? Who Loses? Culture, Institutions, and the Unequal Effects of School Choice?* (New York).

FULLINWIDER, R. K. (1993), ' "With Malice Toward None": Some Reflections on the Ethics of Argument', *Journal of Education*, 175: 99–113.

GALSTON, WILLIAM (1989), 'Civic Education in the Liberal State', in Rosenblum (1989), 89–101.

—— (1991*a*), *Liberal Purposes: Goods, Virtues, and Diversity in the Liberal State* (Cambridge).

—— (1991*b*), 'Practical Philosophy and the Bill of Rights', in Lacey and Haakonsen (1991), 215–65.

—— (1995), 'Two Concepts of Liberalism', *Ethics*, 105: 516–34.

GAUS, G. (1994), 'Public Reason and the Rule of Law', in Shapiro (1994), 328–63.

GILLIGAN, C. (1982), *In a Different Voice: Psychological Theory and Women's Development* (Cambridge, Mass.).

—— (1987), 'Moral Orientation and Moral Development', in Kittay and Meyers (1987), 19–33.

—— (1995), 'Hearing the Difference: Theorizing Connection', *Hypatia*, 10: 120–7.

—— and WIGGINS, G. (1987), 'The Origins of Morality in Early Childhood Relationships', in Kagan and Lamb (1987), 277–305.

GINTIS, H. (1995), 'The Political Economy of School Choice', *Teachers College Record*, 96: 492–511.

GLENN, C. L. (1988), *The Myth of the Common School* (Amherst, Mass.).

—— (1994), 'School Distinctiveness', *Journal of Education*, 176: 73–103.

GOLDSTEIN, S., FREUD, A., and SOLNIT, A. J. (1973), *Beyond the Best Interests of the Child* (New York).

GOODIN, R. E., and PETTIT, P. (1993), *A Companion to Contemporary Political Philosophy* (Oxford).

GOSSE, EDMUND (1979 edn.), *Father and Son* (Harmondsworth, UK).

GRAHAM, P. A. (1993), 'What America has Expected of its Schools over the Past Century', *American Journal of Education*, 101: 83–98.

GRANT, G. (1986), *The World We Created at Hamilton High* (Cambridge, Mass.).

—— (1991) (ed.), *Review of Research in Education 17* (Washington, DC).

GREENSPAN, P. (1988), *Emotions and Reasons: An Inquiry into Emotional Justification* (London).

GREVEN, P. (1977), *The Protestant Temperament: Patterns of Child-rearing, Religious Experience, and Self in Early America* (New York).

GROOME, T. H. (1996), 'What Makes a School Catholic?', in McLaughlin, O'Keefe, and O'Keefe (1996), 107–25.

GUTMANN, A. (1985), 'Communitarian Critics of Liberalism', *Philosophy and Public Affairs*, 14: 308–22.

—— (1986), *Democratic Education* (Princeton).

—— (1989), 'Undemocratic Education', in Rosenblum (1989), 71–88.

—— (1993), 'The Disharmony of Democracy', in Chapman and Shapiro (1993), 126–60.

—— (1995), 'Civic Education and Social Diversity', *Ethics*, 105: 557–79.

—— and THOMPSON, D. (1996), *Democracy and Disagreement* (Cambridge, Mass.).

HABERMAS, J. (1992), 'Citizenship and National Identity: Some Reflections on the Future of Europe', *Praxis International*, 12: 1–19.

HALDANE, J. (1996*a*), 'The Individual, the State, and the Common Good', *Social Philosophy and Policy*, 13 (1): 59–79.

—— (1996*b*), 'Catholic Education and Catholic Identity', in McLaughlin, O'Keefe, and O'Keefe (1996), 126–35.

HALSTEAD, M., and McLAUGHLIN, T. H. (forthcoming), *Education in Morality* (London).

HAMPSHIRE, S. (1989), *Innocence and Experience* (Cambridge, Mass.).

—— (1993), 'Liberalism: The New Twist', *New York Times Review of Books*, 40/14: 43–7.

HAMPTON, J. (1993), 'The Moral Commitments of Liberalism', in Copp, Hampton, and Roemer (1993), 292–313.

HARGREAVES, D. H. (1996), 'Diversity and Choice in School Education: A Modified Libertarian Approach', *Oxford Review of Education*, 22: 131–41.

HEANEY, S. (1975), *North* (London).

HERZOG, D. (1985), *Without Foundations: Justification in Political Theory*, (Ithaca, NY).

HILL, T. (1995), 'Servility and Self-Respect', in Dillon (1995), 76–92.

HOLMES, M. (1992), 'The Revival of School Administration: Alasdair MacIntyre in the Aftermath of the Common School', *Canadian Journal of Education*, 17: 422–36.

—— (1993), 'The Place of Religion in Public Education', *Interchange*, 24: 205–23.

—— (1995), 'Common Schools for a Secularist Society', *Canadian Journal of Education*, 20: 284–96.

HOLMES, S. (1995), *Passions and Constraint: On the Theory of Liberal Democracy* (Chicago).

HOULGATE, L. D. (1988), *Family and State: The Philosophy of Family Law* (Totowa, NJ).

HUME, D. (1983 edn.), *An Enquiry Concerning the Principles of Morals*, ed. J. P. Schneewind (Indianapolis, Ind.).

HUNTER, J. D., and GUINNESS, O. (1990) (eds.), *Articles of Faith, Articles of Peace: The Religious Liberty Clauses and the American Public Philosophy* (Washington, DC).

HURKA, T. (1995), 'Indirect Perfectionism: Kymlicka on Liberal Neutrality', *Journal of Political Philosophy*, 3: 36–57.

INGRAM, A. (1994), *A Political Theory of Rights* (Oxford).

JANOWITZ, M. (1983), *The Reconstruction of Patriotism: Education for Civic Consciousness* (Chicago).

JANZEN, W. (1990), *Limits on Liberty: The Experience of Mennonite, Huterite and Doukhobor Communities in Canada* (Toronto).

JEFFERSON, M. (1983), 'What Is Wrong with Sentimentality?', *Mind*, 92: 519–29.

JOHNSTON, D. (1994), *The Idea of a Liberal Theory: A Critique and Reconstruction* (Princeton).

KAGAN, J., and LAMB, S. (1987) (eds.), *The Emergence of Morality in Young Children* (Chicago).

KAMMEN, M. (1991), *Mystic Chords of Memory: The Transformation of Tradition in American Culture* (New York).

KANT, I. (1964 edn.), *The Doctrine of Virtue: Part II of The Metaphysic of Morals*, trans. Mary J. Gregor (Philadelphia).

—— (1970 edn.), *Kant's Political Writings*, ed. Hans Reiss, trans. H. B. Nisbet (Cambridge).

KEKES, J. (1990), 'Moral Depth', *Philosophy*, 65: 439–53.

KITTAY, E. F., and MEYERS, D. T. (1987) (eds.), *Women and Moral Theory* (Totowa, NJ).

KOHLBERG, L. (1981), *The Philosophy of Moral Development* (San Francisco).

—— (1986), 'A Current Statement on Some Theoretical Issues', in Modgil and Modgil (1986), 485–546.

KOLAKOWSKI, L. (1982), *Religion* (New York).

KRUEGER, L. (1995), 'School and Religion Don't Mix in Modern Times', *Toronto Globe and Mail*, Sept. 8: A20.

KUKATHAS, C., and PETTIT, P. (1993) (eds.), *A Companion to Political Philosophy* (Oxford).

KUNDERA, M. (1981), *The Book of Laughter and Forgetting*, trans. M. H. Haim (New York).

KYMLICKA, W. (1989*a*), 'Liberal Individualism and Liberal Neutrality', *Ethics*, 99: 883–905.

—— (1989*b*), *Liberalism, Community, and Culture* (Oxford).

—— (1990), *Contemporary Political Philosophy: An Introduction* (Oxford).

—— (1991), 'Rethinking the Family', *Philosophy and Public Affairs*, 20: 77–97.

—— (1992), 'The Rights of Minority Cultures: Reply to Kukathas', *Political Theory*, 20: 140–6.

—— (1995*a*), *Multicultural Citizenship* (Oxford).

—— (1995*b*), 'Education for Citizenship', in Halstead and McLaughlin (forthcoming).

LACEY, M. J., and HAAKONSEN, K. (1991) (eds.), *A Culture of Rights: The Bill of Rights in Philosophy, Politics and Law—1791 and 1991* (Cambridge).

LARMORE, C. (1987), *Patterns of Moral Complexity* (Cambridge).

LEE, V. E., BRYK, A. S., and SMITH, J. B. (1993), 'The Organization of Effective Secondary Schools', in Darling-Hammond (1993), 171–267.

LEICESTER, M., and TAYLOR, M. (1992) (eds.), *Ethics, Ethnicity and Education* (London).

LOMASKY, L. (1987), *Persons, Rights, and the Moral Community* (New York).

McCARTHY, T. (1994), 'Kantian Constructivism and Reconstructivism', *Ethics*, 105: 44–63.

McCONNELL, M. W. (1991), 'Multiculturalism, Majoritarianism, and Educational Choice: What Does Our Constitutional Tradition Have to Say?', *University of Chicago Legal Forum*, 1991: 123–51.

MACEDO, S. (1990), *Liberal Virtues: Citizenship, Virtue and Community in Liberal Constitutionalism* (Oxford).

—— (1995a), 'Liberal Civic Education and Religious Fundamentalism: The Case of God v. John Rawls?', *Ethics*, 105: 468–96.

—— (1995b), 'Liberal Civic Education and its Limits', *Canadian Journal of Education*, 20: 297–314.

—— (1996), 'Community, Diversity, and Civic Education: Toward a Liberal Political Science of Group Life', *Social Philosophy & Policy*, 13 (1): 240–68.

MACINTYRE, A. (1981), *After Virtue* (Notre Dame, Ind.).

—— (1988), 'Poetry as Political Philosophy: Notes on Burke and Yeats', in Bell and Lerner (1988), 145–57.

—— (1995), 'Is Patriotism a Virtue?', in Beiner (1995), 209–28.

MCLAUGHLIN, T. H. (1984), 'Parental Rights and the Religious Upbringing of Children', *Journal of Philosophy of Education*, 18: 75–83.

—— (1992a), 'Citizenship, Diversity and Education: A Philosophical Perspective', *Journal of Moral Education*, 21: 235–50.

—— (1992b), 'The Ethics of Separate Schools', in Leicester and Taylor (1992), 114–36.

—— (1995), 'Liberalism, Education, and the Common School', *Journal of Philosophy of Education*, 29: 239–55.

—— O'KEEFE, J., and O'KEEFE, B. (1996), *The Contemporary Catholic School: Context, Identity and Diversity* (London).

MARTIN, J. R. (1976), 'What Should We Do with a Hidden Curriculum When We Find One?', *Curriculum Inquiry*, 2: 135–51.

MARTIN, R., and NICKEL, J. (1980), 'Recent Work on the Concept of Rights', *American Philosophical Quarterly*, 17: 165–90.

MARTY, M. E., and APPLEBY, R. S. (1993) (eds.), *Fundamentalism and Society* (Chicago).

MASON, A. (1990), 'Autonomy, Liberalism and State Neutrality', *Philosophical Quarterly*, 40: 433–52.

MATTHEWS, G. B. (1994), *The Philosophy of Childhood* (Cambridge, Mass.).

MEYERS, D. T. (1989), *Self, Society, and Personal Choice* (New York).

MILL, J. S. (1976 edn.), *On Liberty* (Indianapolis).

MILLER, D. (1995a), 'Citizenship and Pluralism', *Political Studies*, 43: 432–50.

—— (1995b), *On Nationality* (Oxford).

MILLETT, KATE (1970), *Sexual Politics* (Garden City, NY).

*Minersville School District* v. *Gobitis*, 310 US 586 (1940).

MODGIL, S., and MODGIL, C. (1986) (eds.), *Lawrence Kohlberg: Consensus and Controversy* (Philadelphia).

MONROE, K. R., BARTON, M. C., and KLINGEMANN, U. (1990), 'Altruism and the Theory of Rational Choice: Rescuers of Jews in Nazi Europe', *Ethics*, 101: 103–22.

MONTMARQUET, J. A. (1987), 'Epistemic Virtue', *Mind*, 96: 482–97.

MOSHMAN, D. (1989), *Children, Education, and the First Amendment: A Psycholegal Analysis* (Lincoln, Nebr.).

MOUFFE, C. (1994), 'Political Liberalism: Neutrality and the Political', *Ratio Juris*, 7: 314-24.

*Mozert v. Hawkins County Bd. of Education*, 827 F.2d 1058 (6th Cir. 1987).

MULHALL, S., and SWIFT, A. (1992), *Liberals and Communitarians* (Oxford).

MURDOCH, I. (1970), *The Sovereignty of Good* (London).

NAGEL, T. (1979), *Mortal Questions* (Cambridge).

—— (1986), *The View from Nowhere* (New York).

—— (1991), *Equality and Partiality* (New York).

NEDELSKY, J. (1989), 'Reconceiving Autonomy: Sources, Thoughts and Possibilities', *Yale Journal of Law and Feminism*, 1: 7–36.

NICKEL, J. (1987), *Making Sense of Human Rights* (Berkeley).

—— (1990), 'Rawls on Political Community and Principles of Justice', *Law and Philosophy*, 9: 205–16.

NODDINGS, N. (1984), *Caring: A Feminine Approach to Ethics and Moral Education*. (Berkeley).

—— (1988), 'An Ethic of Caring and Its Implications for Instructional Arrangements', *American Journal of Education*, 96: 215–30.

—— (1991), 'Stories in Dialogue: Caring and Interpersonal Reasoning', in Witherell and Noddings (1991), 157–70.

—— (1992), *The Challenge to Care in Schools* (New York).

—— (1994), 'Conversation as Moral Education', *Journal of Moral Education*, 23: 107–18.

NORMAN, W. (1995), 'The Ideology of Shared Vales: A Myopic Vision of Unity in the Multi-nation State', in Carens (1995), 137–59.

NORTH, J. (1987) (ed.), *The GCSE: An Examination* (London).

NOZICK, R. (1989), *The Examined Life* (New York).

NUCCI, L. (1989*a*), 'Challenging Conventional Wisdom about Morality: The Domain Approach to Moral Education', in Nucci (1989*b*), 183–203.

—— (1989*b*) (ed.), *Moral Development and Character Education: A Dialogue* (Berkeley).

NUSSBAUM, M. (1985), 'Finely Aware and Richly Responsive', *Journal of Philosophy*, 82: 516–29.

—— with respondents (1996), *For Love of Country: Debating the Limits of Patriotism*, ed. J. Cohen (Boston).

OAKESHOTT, M. (1989), *The Voice of Liberal Learning: Michael Oakeshott on Education*, ed. T. Fuller (New Haven).

OKIN, S. (1987), 'Justice and Gender', *Philosophy and Public Affairs*, 16: 42–72.

—— (1989), *Justice, Gender, and the Family* (New York).

—— (1994), 'Political Liberalism, Justice, and Gender', *Ethics*, 105: 23–43.

OLNECK, M. R. (1993), 'Terms of Inclusion: Has Multiculturalism Redefined Equality in American Education?', *American Journal of Education*, 101: 234–60.

O'NEILL, O., and RUDDICK, W. (1979), *Having Children: Philosophical and Legal Reflections on Parenthood* (New York).

OUTKA, G., and REEDER, Jr., J. P. (1993) (eds.), *Prospects for a Common Morality* (Princeton).

PARKER, T. (1856), *Parker's Critical and Miscellaneous Writings* (Boston).

—— (1973 edn.), 'The Political Destination of America and the Signs of the Times', in Collins (1973 edn.), 139–69.

PAUKTUUTIT (1990), *The Inuit Way: A Guide to Inuit Culture* (Ottawa).

PEARSE, P. (1966 edn.), *Political Writings and Speeches* (Dublin).

PESHKIN, A. (1988), *God's Choice: The Total World of a Fundamentalist Christian School* (Chicago).

PETERSEN, G. B. (1990) (ed.), *The Tanner Lectures on Human Values XI* (Salt Lake City).

PHILLIPS, A. (1995), *The Politics of Presence* (Oxford).

PLATO (1955 edn.), *The Republic*, trans. with introd. by H. D. P. Lee (Harmondsworth, UK).

RAWLS, J. (1971), *A Theory of Justice* (Cambridge, Mass.).

—— (1980), 'Kantian Constructivism in Moral Theory', *Journal of Philosophy*, 77: 515–72.

—— (1985), 'Justice as Fairness: Political, not Metaphysical', *Philosophy and Public Affairs*, 14: 223–51.

—— (1989), 'The Domain of the Political and Overlapping Consensus', *New York University Law Review*, 64: 233–55.

—— (1993), *Political Liberalism* (New York).

RAZ, J. (1986), *The Morality of Freedom* (Oxford).

—— (1990), 'Facing Diversity: The Case of Epistemic Abstinence', *Philosophy and Public Affairs*, 19: 3–46.

REIMAN, J. H. (1984), 'Privacy, Intimacy, and Personhood', in Schoeman (1984), 300–16.

RICHARDS, D. A. J. (1981), 'Rights and Autonomy', *Ethics*, 92: 3–20.

—— (1986), *Toleration and the Constitution* (New York).

RICHTER, M. (1980) (ed.), *Political Theory and Political Education* (Princeton).

RORTY, A. O. (1980) (ed.), *Explaining Emotions* (Berkeley).

RORTY, R. (1989), *Contingency, Irony, and Solidarity* (Cambridge).

ROSE, S. (1993), 'Christian Fundamentalism and Education in the United States', in Marty and Appleby (1993), 452–89.

ROSENBLUM, N. (1989) (ed.), *Liberalism and the Moral Life* (Cambridge, Mass.).

RUDDICK, S. (1987), 'Remarks on the Sexual Politics of Reason', in Kittay and Meyers (1987), 237–60.

RUDDICK, W. (1979), 'Parents and Life Prospects', in O'Neill and Ruddick (1979), 123–37.

RUSHDIE, S. (1991), *Imaginary Homelands: Essays and Criticism 1981–1991* (London).

RYAN, A. (1993), 'The Liberal Community', in Chapman and Shapiro (1993), 91–114.

—— (1995), *John Dewey and the High Tide of American Liberalism* (New York).

SANDEL, M. (1982), *Liberalism and the Limits of Justice* (Cambridge).

—— (1990), 'Freedom of Conscience or Freedom of Choice?' in Hunter and Guinness (1990), 74–92.

SANDEL, M. (1996), *Democracy's Discontent: America in Search of a Public Philosophy* (Cambridge, Mass.).

SANGSTER, P. (1963), *Pity My Simplicity* (London).

SCANLON, T. M. (1982), 'Contractualism and Utilitarianism', in Sen and Williams (1982), 103–28.

SCARRY, E. (1996), 'The Difficulty of Imagining Other People', in Nussbaum with respondents (1996), 98–110.

SCHAMA, S. (1989), *Citizens: A Chronicle of the French Revolution* (New York).

SCHEFFLER, S. (1992), *Human Morality* (New York).

SCHOEMAN, F. (1980), 'Rights of Children, Rights of Parents, and the Moral Basis of the Family', *Ethics*, 91: 6–19.

—— (1984), *Philosophical Dimensions of Privacy* (Cambridge).

SCHRAG, F. (1973), 'Rights over Children', *Journal of Value Inquiry*, 7: 96–106.

—— (1976), 'Justice and the Family', *Inquiry*, 19: 193–208.

—— (1980), 'Children: Their Rights and Needs', in Aiken and LaFollette (1980), 237–53.

—— (1995), *Back to Basics: Fundamental Educational Questions Reexamined* (San Francisco).

SCRUTON, R. (1980), 'Emotion, Practical Knowledge and Common Culture', in A. O. Rorty (1980), 519–36.

SEN, A., and WILLIAMS, B. (1982) (eds.), *Utilitarianism and Beyond* (Cambridge).

SHAPIRO, I. (1994) (ed.), *Nomos XXXVI* (New York).

—— and HARDIN, R. (1996) (eds.), *Political Order: Nomos XXXVIII* (New York).

SHER, G. (1989), 'Three Grades of Social Involvement', *Philosophy and Public Affairs*, 18: 133–57.

SHERMAN, N. (1993), 'Virtues of Common Pursuit', *Philosophy and Phenomenological Research*, 53: 277–99.

SHESTOV, L. (1966 edn.), *Athens and Jerusalem*, trans. B. Martin (Athens, Oh.).

SIMMONS, A. J. (1992), *The Lockean Theory of Rights: Studies in Moral, Political and Legal Philosophy* (Princeton).

SIMPSON, E. (1989), *Good Lives and Moral Education* (New York).

SINGER, I. B. (1980*a*), *The Slave* (New York).

—— (1980*b*), 'The Blasphemer', in *A Friend of Kafka and Other Stories* (New York).

—— (1984), *Love and Exile* (New York).

SLATTERY, B. (1991), 'Rights, Communities, and Tradition', *University of Toronto Law Journal*, 41: 447–67.

SMITH, R. M. (1993), 'Beyond Tocqueville, Myrdal, and Hartz: The Multiple Traditions in America', *American Political Science Review*, 87: 549–66.

SODER, R. (1996) (ed.), *Democracy, Education, and the Schools* (San Francisco).

SOHN, B., and BUERGENTHAL, T. (1973) (eds.), *Basic Documents on International Protection of Human Rights* (Indianapolis).

STOLZENBERG, NOMI (1993), 'He Drew a Circle That Shut Me Out: Assimilation, Indoctrination and the Paradox of Liberal Education', *Harvard Law Review*, 106: 581–667.

STRAWSON, P. F. (1974), *Freedom and Resentment and Other Essays* (London).

STRIKE, K. (1990), 'Are Secular Languages Religiously Neutral?', *Journal of Law and Politics*, 6: 469–502.

—— (1991), 'The Moral Role of Schooling in a Liberal Democratic Society', in Grant (1991), 413–83.

—— (1994), 'On the Construction of Public Speech: Pluralism and Public Reason', *Educational Theory*, 44: 1–26.

—— (1996), 'Must Liberal Citizens be Reasonable?', *Review of Politics*, 58: 41–8.

TAMIR, Y (1993), *Liberal Nationalism* (Princeton).

TANNER, M. (1977), 'Sentimentality', *Proceedings of the Aristotelian Society*, 72: 127–47.

TAYLOR, C. (1985), *Philosophy and the Human Sciences: Philosophical Papers 2* (Cambridge).

—— (1989), 'Cross-Purposes: The Liberal–Communitarian Debate', in Rosenblum (1989), 159–82.

—— (1993), *Reconciling the Solitudes: Essays on Canadian Federalism and Nationalism* (Montreal).

THOMAS, L. (1989), *Living Morally* (Philadelphia).

THOMSON, J. J. (1990), *The Realm of Rights* (Cambridge, Mass.).

THORN, B., and YALOM, M. (1992) (eds.), *Rethinking the Family: Some Feminist Questions*, rev. edn. (Boston).

DE TOCQUEVILLE, A. (1840/1945), *Democracy in America*, ii, trans. Henry Reeve (New York).

TOMASI, J. (1991), 'Individual Rights and Community Virtues', *Ethics*, 101: 521–36.

TRONTO, J. (1993), *Moral Boundaries: A Political Argument for an Ethic of Care* (London).

TURIEL, E., KILLEN, M., and HELWIG, C. C. (1987), 'Morality: Its Structures, Functions and Vagaries', in Kagan and Lamb (1987), 155–243.

TYACK, D., and JAMES, T. (1985), 'Moral Majorities and the School Curriculum: Historical Perspectives on the Legalization of Virtue', *Teachers College Record*, 86: 513–37.

VAN GUNSTEREN, H. (1996), 'Neo-Republican Citizenship and Education', *Government and Opposition*, 31: 77–99.

VIROLI, M. (1995), *For Love of Country: An Essay on Patriotism and Nationalism* (Oxford).

VITZ, P. C. (1986), *Censorship: Evidence of Bias in Our Children's Textbooks* (Ann Arbor).

WALDRON, J. (1989), 'Rights in Conflict', *Ethics*, 99: 503–19.

—— (1990), 'When Justice Replaces Affection: The Need for Rights', *Harvard Journal of Law & Public Policy*, 11: 623–47.

—— (1993*a*), 'Special Ties and Natural Duties', *Philosophy and Public Affairs*, 22: 3–30.

—— (1993*b*), 'America's Uncivil Wars', *Times Literary Supplement*, no. 4686: 11–12.

WALDRON, J. (1993c), 'Rights', in Goodin and Pettit (1993), 575–85.

—— (1993d), *Liberal Rights: Collected Papers 1981–1991* (Cambridge).

—— (1993e), 'Religious Considerations in Public Deliberation', *San Diego Law Review*, 30: 817–48.

WALZER, M. (1980), 'Political Decision-Making and Political Education', in Richter (1980), 159–76.

WEBBER, J. (1994), *Reimagining Canada: Language, Culture, Community, and the Canadian Constitution* (Montreal).

WEINSTOCK, D. M. (1996), 'Is there a Moral Case for Nationalism?', *Journal of Applied Philosophy*, 13: 87–100.

WELTY, E. (1980), *The Collected Stories of Eudora Welty* (New York).

WENAR, L. (1995), 'Political Liberalism: An Internal Critique', *Ethics*, 106: 32–62.

*West Virginia Board of Education* v. *Barnette*, 319 US 624 (1943).

WESTBROOK, R. B. (1991), *John Dewey and American Democracy* (Ithaca, NY).

—— (1996), 'Public Schooling and American Democracy', in Soder (1996), 125–50.

WHITE, P. (1983), *Beyond Domination* (London).

—— (1996), *Civic Virtues and Public Schooling: Educating Citizens for a Democratic Society* (New York).

—— and WHITE, J. (1986), 'Education, Liberalism and the Human Good', in Cooper (1986), 149–71.

WILDE, O. (1962 edn.), *The Letters of Oscar Wilde*, ed. by R. Hart-Davis (New York).

WILL, G. (1983), *Statecraft as Soulcraft: What Government Does* (New York).

WILLIAMS, B. (1981), *Moral Luck* (Cambridge).

—— (1985), *Ethics and the Limits of Philosophy* (Cambridge, Mass.).

WILLS, G. (1992), *Lincoln at Gettysburg* (New York).

—— (1995), 'Thomas's Confirmation: The True Story', *New York Review of Books*, 42 (2): 36–43.

*Wisconsin* v. *Yoder*, 406 US 205 (1972).

WITHERELL, C., and NODDINGS, N. (1991) (eds.), *Stories Lives Tell: Narrative and Dialogue in Education* (New York).

WOLF, S. (1982), 'Moral Saints', *Journal of Philosophy*, 79: 419–39.

—— (1987), 'The Deflation of Moral Philosophy', *Ethics*, 97: 821–33.

WUTHNOW, R. (1991), *Acts of Compassion: Caring for Ourselves and Helping Others* (Princeton).

Yeats, W. B. (1937), *Collected Poems of W. B. Yeats* (London).

# INDEX